RASCALS AT LARGE,
OR,
THE CLUE IN THE OLD NOSTALGIA

ARTHUR PRAGER

Rascals at Large, or, The Clue in the Old Nostalgia

Doubleday & Company, Inc.
Garden City, New York, 1971

Library of Congress Catalog Card No. 70–158350
Copyright © 1971 by Arthur Prager
All Rights Reserved
Printed in the United States of America
First Edition

TO E.P.

FOREWORD

It is not remarkable that a downstart on the threshold of middle age should try to recapture the joys (or what he thought were the joys) of his youth by supervising and participating in the joys of his children insofar as he is allowed to do so. Thus it was not in the least remarkable that after I had shepherded my daughter through the perils of babyhood I should be delighted to see her begin to read of her own volition. This was the goal I had aimed at through the weary years of bedtime reading aloud, repeating over and over again the imbecilic adventures of saccharine kittens and puppies, and darling little mice.

As a child I had taken much pleasure in reading, and I wanted her to know it too. When I saw her absorbed in a Nancy Drew adventure at the age of ten it was like a fulfillment. I had never read Nancy Drew, but I remembered the happiness I had experienced with Tarzan and Bomba the Jungle Boy, and with the Hardy Boys, Tom Swift, Garry Grayson, and many others. Out of curiosity, I read one of her Nancy Drews to see if I could find out the secret of its lasting power. The experiment led to an article in the *Saturday Review*, and the article led to this book.

Before I finished the book, I had reread hundreds of the books of my childhood. If the rereading did not give me the same pleasure as the original exposure, at least I was able to greet them with a nostalgic fondness. Some of them, like people, had aged badly—had become seedy, decrepit bores. How could I ever have enjoyed the Boy Allies? Others retained a spry, youthful quality, full of good humor and excitement. Good old no-nonsense Tom Swift was his optimistic, never-say-die self, and so was his eccentric pal Mr. Wakefield Damon. The Hardys still solved their mysteries in the nick of time with the help of their splendid parent, Fenton Hardy, the first great private eye in children's literature. Dr. Petrie and Nayland Smith still dealt out thrills as they circumvented the Yellow Peril in the low-rent districts of East London. Jerry Todd and Poppy Ott played their practical jokes and Ted Scott gathered medals and honors for his flying exploits.

I was a member of the generation that fell between the sharp pincers of the Depression on one side and World War II on the other. There was no money, very little leisure, and no television. Society was definitely not permissive, sexually or otherwise. Youthful activities were strictly supervised and controlled. Pleasure was rare and hard to find. This toughened us. We learned to find happiness in small, inexpensive things. Whole families would gather on Sunday evenings to listen to a half-hour radio program. Sandlot baseball and football were a way of life. As I grew older the anticipation of a kiss after a movie date could be a kind of delirium. A dollar book, or better still a free one from the library, meant hours of pleasurable excitement. A Saturday afternoon movie was Heaven. Why did the inexorable THE END ever have to cross the screen? Why couldn't it last forever?

In my ten to fourteen period, few children were allowed out after dark. Home for supper meant home for good, until school the next morning. There was homework to do, and supper itself was something of a ceremonial in those days.

Evenings to us meant snow outside and tasseled orange lamps and radio music playing softly while my mother sang along in the kitchen, "Lover, Come Back to Me," or "Three O'Clock in the Morning" as she shelled peas or strung beans. Delicious odors of cooking filled the air, odors that don't seem to exist any more. In years to come I would be scandalized to see commercial products advertised that promised to neutralize cooking odors. And evenings meant reading. Supper over, homework finished, I would twist myself into one of those impossible semireclining postures affected by pre-teens through the ages, adjust a lamp to an angle that would certainly "ruin my eyes," and plunge into whatever literary masterpiece represented my latest frenzy.

The attitude in our house was that reading was good for the mind and that a lot of reading was the mark of a bright boy. Although my parents deplored many of my choices and considered them rubbish, an overabundance of love and pride (I was an only child) forced them to overcome their reluctance and fork over the necessary money to feed my habit. I was deluged with classics (a classic was anything published by Scribner's and illustrated by N. C. Wyeth) and I devoured them eagerly. But a steady diet of classics can pall. I wanted coarser, simpler fare. My classmates had introduced me to the wonderful adventure series and for the greater part of my boyhood I was never without a battered, grimy copy of one of them. They were ultraconservative, cheaply bound, badly printed and festooned with substandard art. Their literary value was practically nil. They were repetitive and windy, but they all had one thing in common. They went right to the heart of a boy's fantasy world. A boy's imagination has no limits, no budget, and certainly no casting restrictions. My Tarzan really swung through trees. He didn't hang on stunt-man tested ropes, or shadow box with toothless old circus lions. My Dr. Fu Manchu was capable of villainies no special effects man could ever devise.

When I was picking my way through the treacherous minefields of the ten to fourteen year old no-man's land, Edgar Rice Burroughs and Sax Rohmer were still alive and living in luxury, turning out lurid prose in massive quantities. They were my heroes. How could they think up such things? At the time I had never heard of Edward Stratemeyer, and if anybody had told me about him I would not have believed it. What an effect he had on generations of American kids!

Edward Stratemeyer, born 1862, died 1930, Newark shopkeeper with imagination and sixty-five pseudonyms from Victor Appleton (*Tom Swift, Don Sturdy*) to Lester Chadwick (*Baseball Joe*); from Roy Rockwood (*Bomba the Jungle Boy*) to Laura Lee Hope (*The Bobbsey Twins*). In all, he wrote more than 800 books, conceiving all the plots and doing all the editing himself, and leaving his syndicate of assistants to do the menial work of gap-filling. But Stratemeyer is discussed more fully in later chapters. Suffice it to say that he had as much of an effect on American kids, male and female, as the invention of television. And a more salutary effect at that. Nobody ever called *him* a wasteland.

When I took my place as a titular grown-up, after undergoing many trials as painful if not as flamboyant as the maturity rites of the Ogallala Sioux, I became a parent in my own right. I was taken aback when my first and only offspring turned out to be, of all things, a girl. No sandlot baseball for her. And no Tarzan either. No Bomba, no Jerry Todd or Don Sturdy. The X Bar X Boys would pass her by, unnoticed. I had never read a girl's book in my life. All my carefully laid plans for introducing my kid into my own beloved reading world were shattered. I watched her nervously as she sat mesmerized in front of the flickering blue television screen, absorbing the wisdom of Howdy Doody and Rootie Kazootie. She collapsed in helpless giggles at *I Love Lucy* and the *Beverly Hillbillies*. I was browbeaten into taking her to every extant Jerry Lewis movie. What kind of creature had I spawned?

But all is not lost, as Jules Verne wrote, as long as there is a man with a dream. One morning I found her as usual, in front of the tube, but chuckling over an Our Gang comedy I had loved when I was ten. Then she shed a tear or two at Katharine Hepburn in *Little Women*. She took to watching Laurel and Hardy every afternoon instead of *The Flintstones*. Maybe there was hope for her after all! And then one day, the kid was *reading!* Nancy Drew, the Dana Girls, Kay Tracey, all the Enid Blytons, and comic books, *Little Lulu, Archie,* love stories, *Hair-Do* magazine, *Ingenue*.

I made no attempt to censor or select. She could handle that part of it herself, later on. The important thing was that the *set was turned off and she was reading!* One evening I peeped into her room and saw her sitting up in bed absorbed in *The Little Minister*. A new phase was beginning. The worst was over. I closed her door softly. Maybe everything was going to be all right after all.

So, on with the book, and we'll worry about the grandchildren when they come along. In the meantime, let's have a look at the heroes and villains and the pretty girls and bullies that gave us such a time of it back then. If the thrills aren't as thrilling and the shocks aren't as shocking, after all, what is? They are well worth a reappraisal in the light of current taste, and like most items hand-crafted in those days, they wear like iron and last for years. We may outgrow them, but we can still hand them down to a new generation for another tour of duty.

CONTENTS

RASCALS AT LARGE,
OR,
THE CLUE IN THE OLD NOSTALGIA

CHAPTER ONE

THE VICTORY CRY OF THE BULL APE

"FINGERPRINTS PROVE YOU GREYSTOKE. CONGRATULATIONS."
D'ARNOT

(*Tarzan of the Apes*)

In the Kew Gardens of my boyhood, strolling suburbanites enjoying a summer evening were often petrified by a dreadful, piercing falsetto whoop emanating from one empty lot or another. Those who had boys in the twelve to fourteen year old bracket were able to identify the sound at once. It was I or one of my contemporaries, wrestling somebody's nondescript dog to the earth, placing a sneakered foot on the creature's thin ribs, and uttering the Victory Cry of the Bull Ape.

The cry, at once a paean of conquest and a challenge to any savage predators in the neighborhood, was described by Edgar Rice Burroughs, its creator, as a "horrid blood-curdling scream—inhuman—something part beast and part man." This procedure, he assured his young readers, was invariably followed by Tarzan of the Apes and his simian foster brothers every time they made a kill. It was guaranteed to stop a hunting lion in full charge, or make a superstitious cannibal finger his fetish. Issuing from my twelve-year-old larynx it bore little resemblance to the strident *heldentenor* yodel later lip-synched to the stolid pantomime of Johnny Weismuller in the Tarzan films. It was unique.

My dog, accustomed to subteen eccentricities and hamming it up in the role of Numa, the lion, only winced slightly, but the Victory Cry never failed to bring my mother to her kitchen window, fearful that I had been run over (her perpetual nightmare) and muttering her traditional "Oh, my God!"

It was on a family trip to Washington, D.C., that I first ran across Tarzan of the Apes, called the *tarmangani* or "white ape" in the language of the great jungle anthropoids. On arrival at Union Station I was promptly taken in charge by a wise uncle and propelled to the nearest People's Drug Store, where I was invited to buy a book, any book, to "keep me quiet." There he was, the Lord of the Jungle himself, complete with leopard skin breechclout, hunting knife and page boy hairdo, hanging from a vine and maiming a mixed bag of slavering carnivores. Checking a dust cover to determine the first of the series, I bought *Tarzan of the Apes*. It kept me quiet all right. I was speechless for days.

In the next few years I would buy the whole series, one by one, and read, reread and devour each of them. My mother bore little resemblance to Kala, the kindly she-ape who suckled the little foundling Tarzan and raised him as her own, but I too became a *tarmangani*, and stayed one for a number of lifetimes until one day in Womrath's I discovered *The Three Musketeers* and turned in my leopard skin to become the Finest Swordsman in All France. I may have been guilty of temporary infidelity, but I never forgot the Lord of the Jungle and the thrills and perils of his leafy habitat. I was a beginner in those days, and there was room in my heart for a whole Valhalla of heroes.

Tarzan was the brainchild of the late Edgar Rice Burroughs, with an assist from Kipling's *Jungle Book* and the Romulus and Remus legend. After a long series of unsuccessful attempts to establish himself in a lucrative career, Burroughs found himself at thirty-six a total failure with absolutely nowhere left to go. One day he was thumbing idly through a pulp magazine, muttering "Anyone could write this stuff," when lightning struck. He would become a writer! In 1912 he ground out *Under the Moon of Mars*, using the pseudonym "Normal Bean" ("the average mind in search of average readers"). He sold it to a publisher for $400, and that day, as they say, a Star Was Born.

A success at last, he reassumed his own name and wrote the first Tarzan story for Munsey Publications. In 1914 A. C. McClurg and Company of Chicago published the novel *Tarzan of the Apes*.

The book was hardly an unqualified critical success. *The New York Times Book Review* allowed it a tiny synopsis in an unsigned article entitled "One Hundred Books for Summer Reading," and gave it a one-line review ("The author has evidently tried to see how far he could go without exceeding the limits of possibility"). Literary critic Alva Johnston discerned "a certain galloping commonplaceness" as one of Burroughs's qualities. *Commonweal* placed *Tarzan of the Apes* "somewhat below Rider Haggard and above Trader Horn," but in spite of the critics Burroughs had hit the jackpot. In the next two decades the Ape Man would sell 35,000,000 copies in fifty-six languages, plus the rights for toys, radio programs, and games. He would appear in ten movies, each of which would sell 140,000,000 tickets. Two hundred newspapers would syndicate him as a comic strip. Two generations later, twenty years after his author's death, he would still be going strong as a television series.

Burroughs became a multimillionaire, wisely avoiding the stock market and investing in San Fernando Valley real estate; developing enormous tracts of land. He lived to see Tarzan become a generic term, and to have two towns named after his jungle hero, Tarzana, California, and Tarzan, Texas. When he died in 1950, Burroughs was holding fifteen unpublished Tarzan books and signed contracts for fifteen additional movies. "My writing," he said in his familiar laconic prose style, "helped me escape being broke."

Tarzan's hypnotic effect on his slavish young readers is one of the literary mysteries. Notwithstanding the lure and enchantment of the Dark Continent, and the high content of beloved zoo animals, the books contain some of the most dreadful prose of the century. They are unbelievably repetitive, and borrow heavily from most of the more successful adventure stories of the period. Browsing through the series at random, one can identify startling similarities to *Gulliver's Travels* (*Tarzan and the Ant Men*), *King Solomon's Mines* (*Tarzan and the Jewels of Opar*), *The Lost World* (*Tarzan the Terrible*), *A Connecticut Yankee* (*Tarzan, Lord of the Jungle*), *A Journey to the Center of the Earth* (*Tarzan at the Earth's Core*) and many more.

Burroughs never saw Africa in his lifetime. His research was perfunctory at best, and he had the tinnest of tin ears. His humor was heavy and obvious, and his dialogue, especially in love scenes, rivaled the flowery captions that punctuated the silent films. On one occasion, when Tarzan has rescued his Jane from the importunities of a libidinous ape, she recovers from a swoon to find him gazing down at her.

"My man!" she murmured. "No, it is the delirium which precedes death."

She must have spoken aloud, for the eyes that bent to hers lighted with a smile.

"Yes, your man, Jane Porter; your savage primeval man come out of the jungle to claim his mate—the woman who ran away from him," he added almost fiercely.

"John," she murmured, "tell me, is it really you?"

In reply he drew her closer to him. "It is I," he replied. "But there is something in my throat" he said haltingly, "that makes it hard for me to speak."

(Tarzan of the Apes, p. 382)

Not much "Me Tarzan, you Jane" there. A few tender moments later the Lord of the Jungle would borrow a leaf from the book of P. G. Wodehouse's lady novelettist, Rosie M. Banks, and "rain kisses on her upturned face."

With time Burroughs's style crystallized, and by 1930 he had achieved the hard-boiled simplicity of a Republic scriptwriter drafting a Lloyd Nolan film. When young Jason Gridley, Tarzan's traveling companion on a dirigible jaunt to the Earth's core, sees that Zora, the Red Flower of Zoram, is facing molestation at the hands of a hirsute Neanderthal masher with a tail and big toes at right angles to his feet, he leaps to the rescue:

. . . raising his revolver, he levelled it at the leading Phelian. "Beat it!" he said. "Your face frightens the young lady."

"I am Gluf," said the Phelian. "I kill."

"If I could understand you, I might agree with you," replied Jason, "but your exuberant whiskers and your diminutive forehead suggest that you are all wet."

(Tarzan the Terrible, p. 122)

In the resultant melee, Jason wipes out not only Gluf but his wing man and a number of unpleasant local fauna as well.

"Well," said Gridley, looking about him at the bodies of the two men and the corpses of the four hyaenodons. "This is a great little country, but I'll be gosh-darned if I can see how anyone grows up to enjoy it."

(*op. cit.*)

When he had warmed to a subject, Burroughs was a leading contender for the all-time open non-stop long sentence championship. He could baste together participles, stray adjectives, appositive clauses, and a gallimaufry of loose grammar, and string the resultant structure over half a page.

Behind him followed the four who owed to his humanity more than they could ever know, nor had they known could have guessed that his great tolerance, courage, and resourcefulness and the protective instinct that had often safeguarded them sprang not from his human progenitors but from his life-long association with the natural beasts of the forest and the jungle who have these instinctive qualities far more strongly developed than do the unnatural beasts of civilization, in whom the greed and lust of competition have dimmed the luster of these noble qualities where they have not eradicated them entirely.

(*Tarzan the Invincible, p. 317*)

When there was something Burroughs didn't know, it never occurred to him to look it up. He simply invented. Villainous Arab slave traders course through most of the books, and Burroughs created a whole new Berlitz-inspired Arabic patois for them, more melodious than the known dialects.

"*Billah!* thou missed," exclaimed Fejjuan.
"*Gluck!*" ejaculated Fahd, "Sheytan guided the bullet . . ."

"I will finish him," said Fahd, drawing his *khusa*.

"By Ullah no! Put back thy knife, Fahd," said Motlog. "Thou art always too eager for blood."

"It is but a *Nasrany*," insisted Fahd. Think thou to carry him back to the *menzil?*"

(Tarzan, Lord of the Jungle, p. 5–6)

The shiek Ibn Jad of the *fendy* of el-Guad squatted in the men's compartment of his *beyt es-sh'ar*, and beside him in the *mukaad* of his house of hair sat Tollog, his brother . . . As the men talked, the women were busy within at their housewifely duties. In a great brazen *jidda* Hirfa was placing mutton to be boiled, while Ateja fashioned sandals from an old bag of camel leather impregnated with the juice of the dates it had borne on many a *rahla* . . .

(op. cit., p. 8)

Never a man to break up a winning combination, Burroughs saw to it that the plot of each book was an exact duplicate of the last one. To keep his readers interested, he varied his locale from book to book, creating fantastic settings and weird, exotic peoples in the as yet unexplored wilds of Africa, but the stories followed an inflexible pattern.

At first Tarzan and Jane were the protagonists, but Burroughs had made the mistake of pairing them off too soon, and (in the third book) presenting them with a grown son. This dampened the romantic flavor somewhat, and he was forced to introduce other leading characters to provide love interest. The later books included a new juvenile and ingenue for each story; usually a wise-cracking, tousle-haired young WASP and "the most beautiful girl he had ever seen," invariably an exotic high priestess, princess, or other ranking member of some strange, lost jungle cult. In one book (could it have been a private Burroughs joke?) his principals were a vain and idiotic female movie star on location in Africa to film a jungle nature boy epic with a doltish Olympic athlete.

The plot pattern of the Tarzan books can be easily outlined. First, the leading characters are marooned in unexplored African jungle country, either by the mutinous crew of a coastal steamer, or by native bearers in mid-safari. They must find their way to civilization through lion-infested territory alone, helpless, and wearing the absolute minimum of clothing (Burroughs loved to undress his characters).

En route they are harassed by villainous Arabs, cannibals, Belgians, Germans, Russians, or whatever group he happened to dislike at the moment. The young protagonists fall in love at first sight but are prevented from doing anything about it by the classic boy-loses-girl misunderstanding in which each is fooled into believing the other has fallen in love with someone else. Disappointment and frustration make them wander into the jungle in opposite directions, away from the rest of the marooned party.

Enter Tarzan, swinging through the trees, shuttling back and forth from one to the other at terrific speed, dropping out of the foliage to save them from Numa the lion or Sheeta (who is sometimes a leopard and sometimes a panther) by wrestling bare-handed with the animals. These encounters are noisy and violent, and Tarzan always wins after a touch and go roughhouse of fang and claw against trusty hunting knife. The kill, of course, is followed by the Victory Cry of the Bull Ape.

While the Ape Man is rescuing the male member of the duo, the girl is carried off by a giant ape to become his She (and you know what that means) losing even more of her clothing if possible. The Lord of the Jungle doubles back and saves her before it is Too Late. Sometimes the ape is replaced by Arab slave traders, but the girl's virginity is always threatened, either by her captors or her prospective purchaser ("some black Sultan"). She is trussed up and thrown into a filthy tent to await the tender mercies of her ravisher, only to be rescued—again just in time—by Tarzan, who drops out of a tree and carries her off in a hail of musket balls, assegais, and poisoned arrows.

Male characters are always captured by cannibals and threatened with nameless tortures (after having first been stripped naked by the women of the tribe). At least once in every book, Tarzan himself is captured, but he escapes using one of three sure-fire methods.

(1) He bursts his bonds by flexing his steely biceps, and heads for the trees

(2) He calls out in the language of the Great Apes and gets Manu the monkey or one of his larger cousins to untie him

(3) He summons his crony, Tantor the elephant, to flatten the whole encampment or village and carry him away.

The lovers are reunited in the end, and the villains paid off in their own coin. In addition to finding bliss in each other's arms, the happy young couple also discover a hidden treasure, which ensures them financial security forever after.

These ingredients are interlarded with numerous Burroughs *obiter dicta*, inveighing against the corrupting influence of mankind and civilization, and explaining how only nature is truly pure. Put them all together and you have a Tarzan book.

Repetitive or not we loved it and would not have had it any other way. If a single ingredient was omitted or bent out of shape, we were cruelly disappointed, and Burroughs felt the weight of it at the box office.

The character of Tarzan was a bizarre, schizoid amalgam of all the better adventure heroes of the period. He was, on the one hand, a superbly muscled jungle demigod who could travel through the foliage at the speed of an express train, and, on the other, the incumbent of an ancient British peerage, with numerous quarterings and memberships in "the most select and exclusive clubs." Brought up in the jungle by a doting female ape, he spent his young manhood in Paris, where he became something of a boulevardier, sipping absinthe in street cafes, smoking cigarettes, and sampling the night life which, according to Burroughs, consisted almost entirely of music halls.

He could break a gorilla's neck from behind with a full nelson, shoot arrows like old Robin Hood himself, and whip any known carnivore armed only with a hunting knife. In his jungle habitat he subsisted on raw flesh, torn from the steaming, fresh-killed carcass of Bara the deer or Horta the boar. Failing that he was known to dine happily, ape-like, on grubs and caterpillars. Outside the green belt his manners were flawless and he had all the trappings of his class, even including engraved calling cards bearing the simple legend

M. JEAN C. TARZAN

His appearance, confused by a long succession of inept and muscle-bound movie actors, deserves a reappraisal. He was tall, with black hair and gray eyes. His face was

> one of extraordinary beauty. A perfect type of the strongly masculine, unmarred by dissipation, or brutal or degrading passions. For though Tarzan of the Apes was a killer of men and beasts, he killed as the hunter kills, dispassionately except on those rare occasions when he had killed for hate—though not the brooding, malevolent

hate which marks the features of its own with hideous lines.

When Tarzan killed he more often smiled than scowled, and smiles are the foundation of beauty.

(*Tarzan of the Apes, p. 266*)

Apparently the Paris night life had left no mark. The Ape Man's physical appearance was such as to reduce all female characters to so many quivering jellies, beginning with his own Jane Porter and continuing through the fierce, exotic La, High Priestess of Opar (an outpost of the lost continent of Atlantis) who was so overcome that she refused to sacrifice him to the Sun God, forfeiting her tenure of office to the extent that she was forced to escape into the jungle, pursued by an angry posse of her former parishioners. Poor La got little satisfaction from her brave act of devotion. She was too late. Tarzan was already mooning over Jane and had no eyes for the High Priestess of Opar.

In spite of Jane, Tarzan was no wooden stick like so many of the fictional and screen heroes of the day. He was susceptible to female attractions, a trait which endeared him to those of us in the twelve to fourteen-year-old group who had begun to produce secondary sex characteristics and take a scientific interest in girls. His first love was Teeka, a delectable little she-ape who had been his playfellow, but assumed a different role as he slid into his teens. Suddenly he saw her true beauty, the sleek pelt, the great yellow teeth, the flat nose and tiny bloodshot eyes. He worshipped her from a distance until one day he found her contentedly scratching the back of Taug, another old playmate, now grown into a splendid young bull.

In Teeka he had seen someone . . . to fight for and to

hunt for—someone to caress; but now his dream was shattered. Something hurt within his breast. He placed his hand over his heart and wondered what had happened to him. The more he thought of Teeka, as he had last seen her caressing Taug, the more the thing within his breast hurt him.

Tarzan shook his head and growled; then on and on through the jungle he swung, and the farther he travelled and the more he thought upon his wrongs, the nearer he approached becoming an irresolute misogynist.

(*Jungle Tales of Tarzan, p. 18*)

He stayed a misogynist, although he eventually forgave Taug and Teeka, resuming their former palship and protecting them from Hista, the snake, and the hunters of the tribe of Mbonga. At eighteen his misogyny came to an abrupt halt when he set eyes on Jane Porter, the first she-*tarmangani* he had ever seen, after she had been marooned by mutineers with her father and other castaways. Rescuing the swooning Jane from Sabor the lioness, and Terkoz, oversexed chief executive of his own tribe of Great Apes, Tarzan

. . . did what no red-blooded man needs lessons in doing. He smothered her upturned panting lips with kisses.

(*Tarzan of the Apes, p. 258*)

But Jane, a nice girl, "an outraged conscience suffusing her face with its scarlet mantle," shoved him away and buried her face in her hands. Tarzan had intended to return her to her companions, but everything was different now.

Tarzan of the Apes had felt a warm lithe form close pressed to him. Hot sweet breath against his cheek and mouth had fanned a new flame to life within his breast, and perfect lips had clung to his in burning kisses that had seared a deep brand into his soul—a brand that marked a new Tarzan.

(loc. cit.)

The new Tarzan swung her into the trees and off to his lair to make her his She, but of course he changed his mind and brought her home before it was Too Late. Once an English gentleman always an English gentleman. He not only brought her back to her father, but gave her up forever so she could marry his cousin, John Clayton, who had been to the right schools, and was, after Tarzan, the heir to the Greystoke title and fortunes. What nice girl would want a jungle roughneck who consorted with apes and ate grubs and caterpillars? Could you announce Kala as a mother-in-law in *The New York Times?* In the following book true love conquered, and Tarzan finally won his mate.

In the interim, misogyny again, and Tarzan headed for Paris, to forget. Aboard ship he caught the eye of the lovely Countess de Coude, twenty and very much married, who took one look at the Ape Man's trendy cruise costume and murmured *"Magnifique!"* The acquaintance ripened, and in Paris the Countess fired off a *pneumatique* to Tarzan stating simply

TOMORROW I SHALL BE AT HOME TO
MONSIEUR TARZAN AT FIVE

A few rendezvous later (all of them innocently friendly) a scoundrel tricked Tarzan into invading the Countess's boudoir by sending him a forged note asking for help. The Ape Man rushed into the room (brought there by a bribed servant) and found her in a wispy nightie that barely covered her rounded charms. Of course she swooned at once and Tarzan was forced to catch her in his arms.

> The result was electrical. Never before had he been so close to her. In startled guilt they looked suddenly into each other's eyes, and where Olga de Coude should have been strong she was weak, for she crept closer into the man's arms and clasped her own about his neck. And Tarzan of the Apes? He took the panting figure into his mighty arms, and covered the hot lips with kisses.
>
> *(The Return of Tarzan, p. 56)*

This was the obvious moment for the husband to enter and throw a roundhouse punch at the violator of his home. If he expected an apology, he reckoned without the reflexes of a man brought up by the Great Apes. With a snarl, Tarzan hurled the Count against the brocaded wall, placed his foot on the astounded Frenchman's body, and sent the Victory Cry of the Bull Ape reverberating out into the *faubourgs*. When the Count recovered his composure, and his eardrums stopped ringing, he challenged Tarzan, and in the resulting duel the Ape Man took two flesh wounds, refused to fire back. He left town the next day for Africa.

Olga de Coude in her nightie wasn't the only one who was panting after that bedroom scene. My contemporaries and I still had some years to go before we would read *The Tropic of Capricorn,* and our idea of pornography was centered around *The Droll Stories.* It was obvious that if Raoul de Coude hadn't entered when he did, Tarzan and Olga would have Gone All the Way. A hero could be a fighter and a lover too! Burroughs was breaking all the rules, and we worshiped him for it.

When he wasn't capering in a lady's chamber, the Lord of the Jungle occupied himself with his other multifarious talents. He could follow a three-day-old trail as though it were an eight-lane highway, using only his ultrakeen nostrils. Burroughs explained:

> We may note the garlic and whiskey on the breath of a fellow strap hanger, or the cheap perfume emanating from the person of the wondrous lady sitting in front of us, and deplore the fact of our sensitive noses; but as a matter of fact we cannot smell at all, our olfactory organs are practically atrophied, by comparison with the development of the sense among the beasts of the wild.
>
> Where a foot is placed an effluvium remains for a considerable time. It is beyond the range of our sensibilities; but to a creature of the lower orders, especially to the hunters and the hunted, as interesting and ofttimes more lucid than the printed page to us.
>
> *(Tarzan and the Jewels of Opar, p. 165)*

This interesting effluvium was an open book to Tarzan, who could readily distinguish between the pedal emanations of male and female, white and black, man and beast, Belgian and Arab.

He was fast on his feet and rough in the clinches, and was able to subdue ten burly Left Bank apaches armed with bludgeons, chairs, and knives, working up such a temper that he accidentally clobbered half a dozen gendarmes who had come to his assistance. But that was not his best. He committed jungle mayhem on forty Arabs *in ambuscado,* "bowling them over like tenpins" with no one to help him except a lovesick Ouled Naïl girl who hustled him out the back way after the battle.

His recuperative powers were tremendous. After a hand-to-hand encounter with Bolgani the gorilla:

> A portion of his chest was laid bare to the ribs, three of which had been broken by the mighty blows of the

gorilla. One arm was nearly severed by the giant fangs, and a great piece had been torn from his neck, exposing his jugular vein, which the cruel jaws had missed by a miracle.

(*Tarzan of the Apes, pp. 76, 153*)

After an infusion of mud and healing leaves (known only to the Great Apes) he was as good as new, although he was only ten years old at the time. A short time later, after another rough-and-tumble, "his scalp was in one place half torn from his head so that a great piece hung down over one eye, obstructing his vision." He was carried off a mountain peak by a hungry pterodactyl, supported only by the creature's claws, which were imbedded in his thigh. He swam a river with a crocodile firmly clamped to his leg. He absorbed countless flesh wounds from small arms fire of every caliber, and his handsome skull was dented time and again by clubs, rocks, assegais, and miscellaneous missiles. Once the roof of an ancient temple, constructed entirely of stone, collapsed on his head, leaving him bruised but unhurt except for a temporary bout of amnesia.

How did Tarzan get to be all the things he was? Burroughs had a glib answer for everything. It seems that in 1888, John Clayton, Viscount Greystoke and his pregnant wife Lady Alice embarked at Dover for passage to Africa on confidential government business. Expecting to remain for several years, they took with them all the paraphernalia necessary for bringing into the world and educating a child, plus basic household effects. En route to their destination, they fell afoul of the usual mutiny, and were —yes—marooned with all their luggage on a fertile but unexplored part of the West African coast. (Later in the series this desolate spot would become the Grand Central Station of African marooning activities, as shipload after shipload of castaways were dumped there by murderous lascars.)

Tenderfoot though he was, Lord Greystoke was able to build a strong log cabin and to support his wife with game and fruit. In time she gave birth to a son, John, who was to become both Tarzan of the Apes and the next Lord Greystoke. Soon after, little Tarzan's parents were killed by a band of Great Apes, who would have killed the child too, except for the quick action of Kala, mate of Tublat, the king-ape. She deposited the body of her dead baby in the crib and made off with the little viscount to raise him as her own.

So much for phase one. As he grew older among the apes, Tarzan was surprised and embarrassed to find that he developed more slowly than his companions (although at the age of ten he had "the physical development of a thirty-year-old man"). Moreover, his fur and fangs refused to grow out. He made up for these deficiencies by superior intelligence, and was soon able to equal the apes in hunting prowess and agility.

Now comes his moment of *gestalt*. On a foraging expedition he discovered the old cabin, in which the whitened bones of his parents still lay unburied. He had no idea who they were, but he found a hunting knife which more than adequately compensated for his lack of fangs, and several boxes of fascinating books! These included elementary texts, picture books, and a dictionary. The brilliant lad quickly discerned the frequency relationship between some of the little black insect-like marks printed on the pages and certain pictures, many of which he could recognize as monkeys, elephants, trees, and the like. In no time at all he was building a written vocabulary, and in five years he had taught himself to read and write perfectly. Of course he knew nothing of phonetic connections with the written word, so he could not speak, and was forced to communicate with the first castaways by letter. Speech would come later, and Tarzan's first language was, oddly enough, French.

The books revealed to him for the first time that he was not "ape," but "man," like the contemptible tribe of local cannibals. This was a blow, but he weathered it, to the extent of waylaying a hunting warrior and snatching off his loincloth, leaving him to return to his village nude and very much surprised. Now Tarzan had "clothes" and he began to shave with his knife, to remove the "degrading symbol of apehood." He also affected arm bangles, a spear, a bow and arrows, and a grass lasso.

The next shipment of castaways brought Jane Porter ("white woman"), her father, Tarzan's cousin John Clayton, and others. He was fascinated by "white man" and learned about civilized behavior from peeping at the new arrivals. By the next marooning (an aristocratic and wealthy French naval officer named D'Arnot) he had begun to speak. Rescuing D'Arnot from the cannibals (whose women had stripped the Frenchman nude before preparing to torture him) Tarzan made a lifelong friend. D'Arnot not only taught him to speak flawless French, but later took the Ape Man to Paris with him and changed "man" to "gentleman," introducing him to culture and the better class of bespoke tailors.

D'Arnot brought along the late Lord Greystoke's diary, which contained an entry in which the viscount jocularly referred to a smudge on the page where his infant son had smeared the ink. Fingerprints! D'Arnot sent the page to the Sureté with samples of Tarzan's prints and the secret of his birth was revealed at last. Tarzan was the rightful heir to one of England's most important titles and fortunes, cutting his cousin John Clayton out of the picture entirely.

Meanwhile, Tarzan had paid a quick visit to America

to rescue Jane from a loveless marriage to a scoundrelly millionaire who held her father's debt of honor. He decided to step out of her life in favor of his cousin Clayton when the cablegram arrived

FINGERPRINTS PROVE YOU GREYSTOKE. CONGRATULATIONS.

D'ARNOT

Crumpling the message, Tarzan left Clayton in his fool's paradise. He would need neither money nor title in the jungle—and it was for Jane's happiness. Of course, in *The Return of Tarzan*, Clayton (also an English gentleman) learned the truth, renounced Jane and the title, and the Ape Man was brought to a level of full maturity from which he could embark on the next twenty books.

A great many featured players pass through the books in support of Tarzan's adventures, and some of them are worthy of closer scrutiny. Principal among them was Jane Porter, the Ape Man's mate, whom we first see as a none-too bright but exceptionally pretty American post debutante of nineteen. She steals the heart of the inexperienced Tarzan, who had never seen a girl of his own race before. Except for her physical beauty, Jane was an unattractive character. We readers could never figure out what Tarzan saw in her. She was a snob and an opportunist, with serious qualms about Tarzan because of his background, but she made a rapid *volte face* as soon as she learned he was a British peer. After that, he was "my man" all over again.

Once she had secured her social position by presenting the Lord of the Jungle with a son, she really turned nasty. The boy, Jack (the whole family seemed to be named John), was packed off to a Great Public School to be educated *but she would never allow anyone to tell him of his father's past!* Zoos, menageries, and circuses were strictly off-limits lest the sight of an animal suggest something to him. The kid had to run away to Africa and join the Great Apes on his own before he learned what a winner his old man was. Imagine having Tarzan of the Apes for a father, and having your mother ashamed of it, keeping it a secret from you for fourteen years! *And Tarzan let her get away with it!*

Jane never developed as a character at all, and we never thought of her as a female to be lusted after, in spite of those early kisses on her hot upturned lips. She was a prig and a prude. She never lived in a tree house or wore a leather bikini, as the movies suggested. Instead she coerced Tarzan into dipping into the treasure room at Opar to get money for a huge tract of African real estate, where he was to become a gentleman farmer. There she reigned in feudal splendor, wearing little Worth cocktail dresses and lording it over Tarzan's faithful Waziri warriors, who acted as house servants. She dished out tea on the veranda for visiting dignitaries and generally made a nuisance of herself.

Through the years she kept her figure, and was periodically abducted by lustful Arabs and drooling anthropoids, even after menopause.

La, High Priestess of Opar, was another cup of tea entirely! There was a woman! To us junior grade lechers for whom a skin flick meant Dorothy Lamour in a sarong, La was heady wine. She was:

> . . . an almost naked woman, whose gorgeous beauty was her first and most striking characteristic. Two golden discs covered her firm breasts, and a narrow stomacher of gold and precious stones encircled her hips, supporting in front and behind a broad strip of soft leather studded with gold and jewels which formed the pattern of a pedestal on which was seated a grotesque bird. Her feet were shod in sandals . . . A mass of wavy hair shot with golden

bronze lights . . . half surrounded an oval face and beneath narrow pencilled brows fearless gray eyes regarded them.

(*Tarzan the Invincible, p. 133*)

Wow! How about those golden discs, and those narrow strips of leather in front and behind! A paragraph like that could mean molten white nights to an eighth-grade *tarmangani*, capable of being reduced to helpless tumescence by a flash of white cotton drawers on a windy day or the sight of a blossoming subteen basketball goddess shooting a foul shot in a tight middy blouse and snug gym bloomers. La ("a priestess but yet a woman") was the genuine article. She wasn't interested in social position or her silver pattern. She only wanted one thing— to Do It with Tarzan and she kept trying through twenty-two books, unsuccessfully but with unflagging enthusiasm. Tarzan (to our disappointment) stayed faithful to Jane but we know what *we* would have done, if the opportunity had arisen, and if we had known how. At that time I was still raining kisses on *downturned* faces.

La was not only a beauty, she was action-oriented too. On one occasion she had Tarzan securely bound to the altar of the Sun God, incapable of movement and ready for sacrifice. She raised her flint knife, but suddenly:

. . . La, the woman, collapsed weakly upon the body of the man she loved. She ran her hands in mute caress over his naked flesh; she covered his forehead, his eyes, his lips, with hot kisses; she covered him with her body as though to protect him . . . and in piteous tones she begged him for his love. For hours the frenzy of her passion possessed the burning handmaiden of the Flaming God, until at last sleep overpowered her and she lapsed into unconsciousness beside the man she had sworn to torture and slay. Tarzan, untroubled by thoughts of the future, slept peacefully in La's embrace.

(Tarzan and the Jewels of Opar, p. 147)

Bravo, La! In later years I would meet a few exotic High Priestesses of my own, but there was never anyone like La.

Tarzan's loyal friends and subjects, the Great Apes, had me confused for years until I realized that Burroughs had made them up, and that there was no such species. They were (according to him) fully seven feet tall, weighing 350–400 pounds and more intelligent than gorillas. Other animals were afraid of them. They were carnivorous, and followed a titular leader who won his position by killing his predecessor (like Kipling's wolves). Only one of them, the faithful Akut, had any individuality. He traveled to England as a carnival sideshow attraction in order to find his old friend and master, Tarzan.

The apes did whatever Tarzan told them, since he was their king. Once when immediate water transportation was necessary, Tarzan had them paddling a huge canoe upriver, to the amazement of the local natives. Except for the apes, Tarzan's only other close pal in the jungle was Tantor the elephant on whose broad back the Ape Man frequently rode. He could summon Tantor to help him in times of crisis, and the elephant never let him down. Tarzan had also formed a lifelong attachment to Jad-bal-ja, the Golden Lion, whom he had rescued from death, but Jad-bal-ja was never a real pal like Tantor or Akut, although he did help Tarzan on many occasions. Tarzan kept him at arm's length, because (as Burroughs put it) "a lion is yet a lion."

Tarzan's son, Jack, was not a very successful character,

and Burroughs lost interest in him after one book, reviving him occasionally as a *deus ex machina*. It was hoped at first that he would replace Tarzan as a lover after the Ape Man had become inextricably entangled with Jane, but Burroughs gave up and married Jack off at the end of *Son of Tarzan*.

Jack had a number of adventures, roughly paralleling his father's, and became a king-ape on his own, in the usual violent way. The apes called him Korak, the Killer. He ran away from England at fourteen accompanied by the faithful Akut, whom he disguised as a little old lady to ease his way through customs and immigration. He crossed to Africa, successfully passing his seven-foot companion off as his "sick grandmother." In Africa, he fell in love with Meriam, wooing her in the traditional Greystoke manner (". . . again he drew her close to him and covered her willing lips with his hot kisses").

Meriam was a passionate little French *princesse* who could swing through trees too, but was given to removing her riding skirt to travel in that way, ostensibly whizzing through the foliage in her well-cut riding jacket, panties, and boots. Small wonder Korak made her his She before he enlisted to fight in the Argonne in World War I.

The other characters were only brief moments in the Tarzan saga. They came and went rapidly, unmourned. Professor Archimedes Q. Porter, Jane's father, who bumbled through the jungle in a silk hat and a frock coat, was a Burroughs attempt at humor but came off more as a silly, gibbering loony rather than as a comedy relief. D'Arnot disappeared into Paris society and later became an admiral. Esmerelda, a shrieking, swooning Aunt Jemimah and Jane's faithful mammy, was mercifully put down after the second book. The villains were interchangeable.

One situation has plagued many straight-laced readers for generations. Were Tarzan and Jane married or were they not? Did they live out their love idyll in sin and bear a child out of wedlock? Irving Wallace has reported in his novel, *The Seven Minutes*, that religious groups in California actually invaded libraries and snatched the Tarzan series off the shelves for this reason.

This is a ghost I can now lay once and for all. In the last two pages of *The Return of Tarzan* the Ape Man decided to give an honorable funeral to his parents whose bones had mouldered in the cabin for twenty years. "Professor Porter, *who had in his younger days been ordained a minister*" conducted a simple service. Tarzan wanted to be married near his parents' resting place, and Jane, Miss Goody-Two-Shoes, vouchsafed that she could "think of no other place in which I should rather be married to my forest god than beneath the shade of his primeval forest." With D'Arnot as best man, the Professor united the happy couple in wedlock.

And so Tarzan lives on. Twelve-year-olds and middle-aged dwellers in the past can find him in the Sunday comic supplements, still wreaking mayhem on Numa and Sheeta in his ferocious but dignified way. The original editions of the books are rare now, but the better libraries have recognized him at last. A number of updated paperbacks have been issued, without too much success. Apparently the latest generation of twelve to fourteen-year-olds doesn't thrill to his gymnastics the way we used to, but my contemporaries and I are thankful for the bright moments Burroughs gave us in the dreary Depression days. We will always be grateful for the jewels of Opar, for excursions through the trees, for La with her solid gold brassiere, for half-naked ingenues swooning in the arms of lust-crazed anthropoids, for hunting Numa's hot, fetid breath, for blood and poisoned arrows and cannibals and hidden treasures and murderous lascars and slave traders and burning kisses and elephants and innocent lust and violence and the inimitable Tarzan of the Apes. They just don't write them like that any more.

CHAPTER TWO

THE MARK OF KALI

Imagine a person, tall, lean and feline, high-shouldered with a brow like Shakespeare and a face like Satan, a close-shaven skull, and long, magnetic eyes of the true cat green. Invest him with all the cunning of an entire Eastern race, accumulated in one giant intellect, with all the resources of science past and present. Imagine that awful being, and you have a mental picture of Dr. Fu Manchu.

(Nayland Smith, in *The Insidious Dr. Fu Manchu*)

For a boy who loved to read, there was no joy like being sick. In those days, before someone invented viruses and Asian flu, everybody under the age of fourteen was programed for an annual bout of the "grippe." This indisposition lasted about a week and had few symptoms other than an occasional light cough, the "sniffles," and a moderate rise in body temperature over the normal level of 98.6°Fahrenheit.

To my contemporaries the grippe meant peace and quiet, no homework, and delicate, exquisite meals without too many vegetables (cinnamon toast, lamb chops, chicken, and *tea instead of milk!*). Medication was simple and consisted of aspirin, Brown Mixture, and Ex-Lax or Feen-a-Mint gum. Parents got a kind of superstitious relief out of forcing a laxative down a kid's throat whether he needed it or not, just as in an earlier century they would have sent for the barber to have him bled.

The grippe also meant uninterrupted reading in those pre-television days. My untidy sickbed was always piled high with the adventures of my favorite heroes in their tattered, gaudy dust jackets. It also meant an opportunity —not Christmas or a birthday—to browbeat my worried mother into dipping into her Depression budget to buy me *new* books—books I had not already read a hundred times; and heroes about whom I might never otherwise have known or even suspected. Back at school I would be bitterly envied by my less fortunate friends.

On one memorable occasion, propped up amid a heap of pillows in what Robert Louis Stevenson wetly called "the Land of Counterpane," I was enjoying the superb high produced in pre-teens by a fever of 101°. I had summarily dispatched my nervous mother to Womrath's to "get me something *good* to read." She returned almost immediately (she hated to leave me alone after the Lindbergh kidnaping) with the usual small, flat, rectangular package. No heroes this time. The book was a dark, poisonous green, and displayed on its cover a sinister-looking dragon, spread-eagled in the manner believed by commercial artists in the thirties to be terribly Chinese. The title was *The Insidious Dr. Fu Manchu.* Talk about fever! For weeks I heard the weird, low cries of dacoits outside my window, and the muted "plop" that announced the forced arrival in my room of a deadly Burmese centipede that would inflict on me the agonizing death called the "Zayat Kiss!"

The insidious Doctor, spearhead of the "Yellow Peril," was born in the febrile brain of "Sax Rohmer," pseudonym of an English journalist named Arthur Sarsfield Ward. Ward's dream, and the target of his early studies, was to live and work in Egypt. Not being financially independent, he chose government service as the quickest, easiest way to the tombs of the Pharaohs. He never made it. "I read for a Civil Service appointment in the East," he wrote, "but since throughout my life I have never succeeded in passing the simplest examination, I did not secure this appointment." The failure left him free to pursue a none-too-successful career as an artist, after which he took what he called "A brief canter through the City" (London's financial world). Again a failure, he ended up as a newspaper reporter.

In the meantime, he wrote short stories and tried to sell them, "papering one wall of my room with editorial regrets." One day, heading for a holiday on the Isle of Wight, he mailed off two stories: "The Leopard Couch" to *Chambers' Journal,* and "The Mysterious Mummy" to *Pearson's Magazine.* When he returned to London, both had been accepted. Rohmer was on his way.

The novel *Dr. Fu Manchu* (which I would read in a later American edition as *The Insidious Dr. Fu Manchu*) was published in England in 1913 by World Distributors Ltd., of Manchester. The hottest property in England at the time was Conan Doyle, whose Sherlock Holmes was appearing monthly in the *Strand Magazine.* Rohmer knew a winner when he saw one, and what better insurance could a writer have than a pair of protagonists one of whom was a lean, hawk-nosed, pipe-smoking neurotic who resembled the Frank Wiles illustrations of Holmes in the *Strand,* and the other a literary but not too bright general practitioner? The similarity did not escape the notice of even my highly uncritical circle, but we didn't care. Holmes or Nayland Smith, Watson or Petrie Moriarty or Fu Manchu, we adored them all.

Although the sinister Doctor made him a millionaire, Rohmer grew bored with his money-making offspring. In the years between 1913 and 1948 there were only eight Fu Manchu books, but Rohmer tried valiantly to interest the public in between thirty and forty adventure and fantasy novels, with such tempting titles as *The Yellow Claw, Brood of the Witch Queen, Grey Face,* and *Moon of Madness.* They never caught on with the flair that the

Fu Manchu books had. My contemporaries, after trying one or two, lost interest.

Almost as soon as the first royalty checks arrived, Rohmer moved to White Plains, New York, where the later Fu Manchu books were written. There, far from the swirling yellow fogs of Limehouse, he lived high, enjoying the luxuries he had coveted in the lean years in Fleet Street. He spent money as fast as he made it and the latter books of the series had a kind of grudging quality, as though they had been wrung from him by economic necessity and importunate publishers.

When Doubleday Doran, Inc. took over the American rights, the financial picture cleared again, and inevitably Hollywood got interested. In 1929 Paramount produced *Dr. Fu Manchu*, starring Warner Oland, who would later achieve fame in the role of Charlie Chan. Jean Arthur was the love interest, and the picture was simultaneously released as a silent and an all-talking film, one of the first to be so issued. The following year *The Return of Fu Manchu* came out, again with Warner Oland and Jean Arthur, and co-starring Neil Hamilton as the male romantic lead.

In 1932 Boris Karloff took over the role of the evil Doctor in *The Mask of Fu Manchu*, this time supported by such redoubtable stars as Myrna Loy, Jean Hersholt and Andy Hardy's dad, Lewis Stone. The film prompted CBS to take notice, and in 1933, the deadly Doctor's twentieth anniversary, he was launched as a radio series.

When World War II came along, and the United States and China became allies, the State Department and the Chinese Embassy exerted a great deal of pressure on Rohmer, who had hitherto attributed all Oriental villainy to the Chinese and almost none to the Japanese. He was urged to tone down the Chinese element, and his protagonists' diatribes against "Chinks." Suddenly the sinister

Doctor became a good guy, working with the Allies against the Forces of Evil. With his transformation, the Doctor's popularity began to wane. Nobody wanted to read about a good Fu Manchu.

In the 1950s, when things began to work their way back to normal, the Doctor was permitted to backslide. "He's still villainous and unscrupulous," Rohmer said, "but he's flat out against the communists and trying to help democracy. In the old days, you know, he was all for personal power." The Doctor's recidivism was serialized in *Collier's,* and in 1955 Herbert J. Yates, head of Republic Pictures (and famous as the husband of Vera Hruba Ralston) announced that his studio had bought TV, film, and radio rights for $4,000,000. This, and reprints through the years, kept Rohmer happily solvent until his death in 1959. The yellow Doctor is still available in paperbacks, and in the 1960s he was revived in a movie by Hammer Films, but his great money-making days are over.

The general pattern of the series changed through the years. In the early books—the ones that had my crowd sleeping with the lights on and avoiding Chinese restaurants for years—the action took place in what seemed to be a string of short stories, loosely connected by some thread of plot, like *The Arabian Nights,* or perhaps like *The Adventures of Sherlock Holmes.* Nayland Smith would arrive out of nowhere, bursting into Dr. Petrie's consulting room in a shower of italics and exclamation points, exhorting his friend to take his Browning automatic and head for Limehouse. *"Come Petrie—for God's sake! HE is in London! Providence grant that we get there in time!"* Smith's knowledge of the evil Doctor's arrival usually stemmed from a recent brush with one of Fu Manchu's weird minions.

Smith suddenly stood up and stripped off his coat. Rolling back his left shirt-sleeve, he revealed a wicked-looking wound in the fleshy part of the forearm. It was quite healed, but curiously striated for an inch or so around.

"Ever seen one like it?" he asked.

"Not exactly," I confessed. "It appears to have been deeply cauterized."

"Right! Very deeply!" he rapped. "A barb steeped in the venom of a hamadryad went in there!"

A shudder I could not repress ran coldly through me at the mention of that most deadly of all the reptiles of the East.

"There's only one treatment," he continued, rolling his sleeve down again, "and that's with a sharp knife, a match and a broken cartridge. I lay on my back, raving, for three days afterwards, in a forest that stank of malaria, but I should have been lying there now if I had hesitated. Here's the point. *It was not an accident!*"

(*The Insidious Dr. Fu Manchu, p. 6*)

As the plot thickens, it turns out that an outstanding English government official or professional man has been marked for death by Fu Manchu's secret society, the Si-Fan, which aims to take over the whole Western world and place it under Oriental supervision. Why did M. Jules Furneaux fall dead in a Paris opera house? Because his last speech had shown that he held the key to the secret of Tongking. What became of the Grand Duke Stanislaus? Elopement? Suicide? Nothing of the kind. He alone was fully alive to Russia's growing peril. Why was Sir Crichton Davy murdered? Because, had the work he was engaged on ever seen the light it would have shown him to be the only living Englishman who understood the importance of the Tibetan frontiers. Who is next? Will Smith and Petrie be in time to save him from the Doctor's hideous servants?

Sometimes they made it and sometimes they didn't, but they could always be depended on to stumble into an obvious trap, where they were faced with horrible death at the hands of the fiendish Fu Manchu. Of course last-minute escape was inevitable, with the assistance of a beautiful half-caste slave girl who had fallen helplessly in love with one or both of them or with one of the juveniles introduced in the later books when the aging pair had to be replaced in the love scenes. (Petrie was eventually dropped altogether.) Sometimes Rohmer would write himself into a corner, and people would escape by "a method at which I dare not guess" or some similar evasion.

At the end of each book, Fu Manchu was observed by a crowd of witnesses to be perishing in a fire, explosion, sinking ship, or similar catastrophe, but he was always back in good form for the next volume.

The murderous Doctor never used simple weapons like guns or knives to carry out his dirty work. He had an inexhaustible arsenal of bizarre weapons and hideous servants, dacoits, thugs with strangling cords, trained apes, dwarfs, snakes, spiders . . . you never knew what was coming next. Unfortunately, by the late 1930s Rohmer had run dry and the Doctor began to repeat himself. His methods and hideouts became predictable. To find his headquarters, Smith had only to look for an opium den in Limehouse (or, later, New York's Chinatown) that connected through underground tunnels with the river. Failing that, he could be found in any remote country house with secret panels, passages, and trapdoors. He depended heavily on his favorite weapon, the Golden Elixir, even after Petrie had found the antidote. The Elixir produced artificial catalepsy, simulating all the symptoms of death. The victims were buried by mourning relatives, and after their funerals Fu Manchu would dig them up, revive them, and keep them in slavery for the rest of their lives!

Let's have a look at the fiendish Doctor in action. An example is the murder of Sir Gregory Hale, "whilom attaché at the British Embassy, Peking, who knew the answer to the hitherto unsolved riddle of Tibet." Hale had barricaded himself into his suite at the fashionable New Louvre Hotel on Smith's advice, but our heroes arrived too late to save him. They forced their way into the suite . . .

> . . . from the direction of the bedroom came a most horrible mumbling and gurgling sound—a sound utterly indescribable . . . On the bed a man lay writhing. His eyes seemed starting from their sockets as he lay on his back uttering inarticulate sounds and plucking with skinny fingers at his lips . . . He continued to babble, rolling his eyes from side to side hideously . . . and now with his index finger pointed to his mouth.

> (*The Hand of Fu Manchu, p. 10*)

As anyone can see, it was the "Flower of Silence" that got him. This flower was a rare jungle blossom which concealed under its petals a small thorn charged with deadly venom. Fu Manchu had lowered it through a hole in the ceiling until it rested on the sleeping man's cheek. He had attempted to brush it away, and you can guess the rest.

How about the murder of Sir Crichton Davy, and the aforementioned "Zayat Kiss"? According to Sir Crichton's man:

> . . . [he] suddenly burst open the door and threw himself with a scream into the library. I ran to him, but he

waved me back. His eyes were glaring horribly. I had just
reached his side when he fell writhing on the floor . . .

(The Insidious Dr. Fu Manchu, p. 9)

On the back of the murdered man's hand was a curious
red mark, like a pair of lips. It seems that a beautiful half-
caste slave girl had delivered a "note" to Davy, which,
when opened, was found to contain only a blank piece
of paper, impregnated with some musky scent. This
odor acted like catnip to one of the Doctor's little horrors:

> . . . an insect full six inches long and of a vivid, venom-
> ous red color! It had something of the appearance of a
> great ant, with its long quivering antennae and its febrile,
> horrible vitality. It was a giant centipede of the *scolo-
> pendra* group!

(loc. cit.)

An agile dacoit had climbed Sir Crichton's roof and
dropped the thing down the chimney on a string weighted
with buckshot so he could haul it up again. Of course
it headed straight for the hand that had touched the
perfumed paper.

What about the "Coughing Horror" that tried to elim-
inate Smith himself when he made the mistake of sleeping with his window open? As he later said to Petrie:

> What kind of thing, what unnatural distorted creature
> laid hands upon my throat tonight? I owe my life to . . .
> the fact that I was awakened, just before the attack—by
> the creature's *coughing*—by its vile, high-pitched *cough-
> ing!* Then came a death grip on my throat, and instinc-
> tively my hands shot out in search of my attacker. I could
> not reach him, my hands came in contact with nothing
> palpable. Therefore I clutched at the fingers which were

dug into my windpipe, and found them to be small . . . and *hairy!*

(The Return of Fu Manchu, pp. 85, 95, 99)

The thing was a *Cynocephalus hamadryas,* the sacred baboon of the Amharûn tribe of Abyssinia, an animal whose predominant trait was an unreasoning malignity toward man. It had a tiny dog-like head, little malevolent eyes, and arms fully four feet long that could reach half-way across a bedroom and strangle an unsuspecting sleeper. The coughing? It seems the creatures contracted phthisis in the cold, damp climate of England.

If you were twelve years old how would you have felt after dark? Fortunately my mother subscribed to the school of thought, prevalent at that time, that "the night air is bad for you." She raised no objection to my closing and locking the window at bedtime, but she firmly drew the line at nailing it shut.

Who can forget the Reverend Eltham, the beloved, fighting "Parson Dan," courageous missionary who had been active in the interior during the Boxer Rebellion? He had seen things, a little more than was good for him, and Fu Manchu had reserved the "Wire Jacket" for the good clergyman.

. . . I saw Eltham stripped to the waist and tied, with his arms upstretched, to a rafter in the ancient ceiling . . . The appearance of his chest puzzled me momentarily, then I realized that a sort of *tourniquet* of wire netting was screwed so tightly about him that the flesh swelled out in knobs through the mesh . . .

(The Return of Fu Manchu, p. 21)

One of the Doctor's evil Chinese servants stood by with a razor-sharp knife, cutting off the knobs, one by one.

Surely the "Six Gates of Joyful Wisdom" took the prize. It was a sort of coffin-shaped box, six feet long, two feet high and two feet wide; covered with fine wire netting but opened at the bottom. It was divided into five sections by four sliding, arched partitions which could be raised and lowered at will. Smith was placed in this contrivance and the partitions were fitted over his body. The plan was to empty a leather bag full of starving rats through the first "gate" where they could devour his feet and ankles. Then the next partition would be raised, and they could eat up to his knees. Then the next and the next and so on. Petrie was immobilized nearby and given a samurai sword on a chain just long enough to reach Smith's heart. He could watch his friend's death agonies or put him out of his misery.

These were only a few of the Doctor's toys. There were the bacilli, and the drugs; the elixir that turned Inspector Weymouth of Scotland Yard into a gibbering idiot and another that reduced lovely Kâramenèh to a wrinkled hag. There were the poisonous mushrooms that reacted to light by swelling to enormous size and smothering a whole detachment of Scotland Yard's Flying Squad when they made the mistake of turning on their flashlights. Who can forget the giant, flying bubonic plague flea, developed by cross-breeding with the African tsetse fly? What about poor Forsyth, who met his end when he walked under a tree that sheltered a dacoit holding an ordinary alley cat whose claws had been dipped in curare. The dacoit attracted his attention and dropped the animal on his upturned face. And Swazi Pasha, the Turkish statesman? A murderous dwarf in a suitcase was dropped down the chimney of his hotel suite while he slept. And the laboratory-created Hairless Man that:

. . . had a huge head set upon huge shoulders. The
head was hairless and the entire face, trunk and limbs
glistened moistly like the skin of an earthworm . . . The
hands were misformed, the fingers webbed, and the
thumbs scarcely present. The legs were all out of propor-
tion to that mighty trunk, being stumpy, dwarfed, and
terminating in feet of a loathsome pink color . . . From
the appalling, glistening naked face two tiny eyes, set
close together beside a flattened nose with distended
nostrils glared redly . . .

(*The Bride of Fu Manchu, p. 81*)

Who was the evil genius that contrived these horrors,
nurturing them in his laboratories or collecting them
from their noisome native jungles? In Smith's terms, he
was the most fantastic criminal intelligence the world
has ever known.

"This man, whether a fanatic or a duly appointed agent
is unquestionably the most malign and formidable per-
sonality existing in the known world today. He is a linguist
who speaks with almost equal facility in any of the
civilized languages and in most of the barbaric ones. He
is an adept in all the arts and sciences which a great university could teach him. He also is an adept in certain
obscure arts and sciences which *no* university of today can
teach. He has the brains of any three men of genius.
Petrie, he is a mental giant."

(*The Insidious Dr. Fu Manchu, p. 16*)

Fu Manchu was tall, well over six feet, physically very
strong, and trained in all the Oriental arts of hand-to-hand
combat to the extent that he was able to overcome Inspector Weymouth in a fist fight, the only time in my
memory that a villain overcame a Scotland Yard man.
His brow was high and domed, and his face (as Rohmer

repeatedly informed us) "strongly resembled the mummy
of the Pharaoh Seti I." He always dressed in a plain yellow robe (sometimes sporting the insignia of the Order
of the White Peacock, the highest honor his nation could
bestow) and a small black skullcap with the coral button
that denoted the rank of mandarin. Outdoors he affected
an astrakhan coat, a tweed motoring cap, and dark
glasses. His eyes were uncanny. They were narrow, long,
slightly oblique, and of a brilliant green, and they shone
in the dark. Their "unique horror" according to Petrie, lay
in "a certain filminess that made me think of the
membrana nictitans in a bird." They were also hypnotic,
and on many occasions he reduced a character to help-
lessness with a glance. Once he almost got Petrie to shoot
Smith under the influence of post-hypnotic suggestion, but
Smith had taken the precaution of unloading Petrie's
Browning, just in case.

He had "an indescribable gait, cat-like yet awkward"
walking with his high shoulders slightly hunched. His
hands were large, bony, and parchment-like, with long,
narrow fingernails. His voice, in any of the languages he
spoke with such facility, was both sibilant and guttural.

In the first books he was a member of "an old Kiangsi
family," but by the eighth book he was described as a
relative of the Imperial family with the rank of Prince.
He also had the right to and frequently used the title of
Marquis. In spite of these advantages, he was not the
head man of his organization, the Si-Fan (or "The
Seven"), but was merely a kind of European regional di-
rector, his mission being (as Smith put it) "to *pave the
way!*" For this purpose he had unlimited funds at his disposal. On one occasion when the Doctor lost out in a
struggle of office politics and the Si-Fan cut off his credit,
he unearthed an ancient formula for making pure gold
out of base metal, and in doing so precipitated (although

only a select few knew about it) the financial chaos of the 1930s. The only problem he had with his gold formula was that he needed human bodies for fuel. This was no hardship for Fu Manchu, but it did make an unpleasant smell around John Ki's Joy Shop in Limehouse, and led Smith and Scotland Yard to his underground refinery.

He was a superb toxicologist, and his knowledge of insect life, especially the venomous kind, was unparalleled. He knew all about fungus growths, and developed several new species of his own. Before becoming an arch-criminal, he had administered the province of Ho-Nan under the Dowager Empress, and he held degrees from four universities, both as a Doctor of Philosophy and a Doctor of Medicine. He was adept at several branches of medical specialization, and was able to direct Petrie and Sir Baldwin Frazer, the finest brain surgeon in Harley Street, in an operation on his own brain, after his slave girl Kâramenèh had fired a .38 slug into his head (Petrie and Frazer were blackmailed into saving his life).

By Smith's calculations, Fu Manchu was 160 years old. He kept himself alive by annual infusions of a strange compound which (Rohmer said) was made of such simple, readily obtainable ingredients that you would laugh in amazement if you knew what they were. However, it wasn't the ingredients, but what you *did* to them that gave them their power.

Toward the end of the series, the Doctor began to abandon his weird insects and plants in favor of electronic marvels. He was able to create life (e.g. the terrible Hairless Man), and he was one of the first fictional villains to use wire tapping and concealed television cameras for surveillance. He knew all about explosives and on two occasions escaped by blasting his enemies with an aerial torpedo of advanced design dropped from a Si-Fan bombing plane.

For all his miracles, the Doctor was one of the great bunglers. Time and again he was foiled by simple police methods and by marvels no more advanced than Petrie's Browning. Women were a great cross for him to bear, and no one ever had a larger staff of beautiful but treacherous half-caste slave girls working in his household. The girls always set his captives free with stolen keys, warned Petrie and Smith of his next move, and tipped off Scotland Yard about the location of his secret laboratories. He never caught on. The girls' underhanded actions left him open to a great deal of criticism from his own superiors in the Si-Fan, but he never seemed to realize that they were disloyal. Even his own daughter, the wickedly beautiful Fah Lo Suee, betrayed him again and again.

At the age of 158 the Doctor decided that he would like to perpetuate his dynasty, and chose a bride whom he had kidnaped when she was six months old and trained carefully in the proper attributes of an arch-criminal-cum-world-emperor's wife. Fleurette was just nineteen and the banns had been posted when, like all half-caste girls, she fell madly in love with one of Petrie and Smith's young aides and the project fell through, to the accompaniment of much sibilant, guttural invective.

In one of the later books the Doctor went through an entire public relations campaign with a Si-Fan trained candidate who very nearly became President of the United States (Smith was able to swing the electorate with a last-minute revelation that the candidate was an unfrocked priest). The Doctor went on and on, agelessly welding the forces of wickedness into tools for his search for power, and in 1957 he was ready to come out of retirement in yet another book, while Smith and Petrie got grayer and grayer and younger juveniles and half-caste girls who could have been their grandchildren took over the leading roles.

In the opposite corner was Nayland Smith, an obscure
colonial police official ("Burmese commissioner") who
dedicated his life to foiling the Doctor and the Si-Fan.
Smith was tall and lean, and had the kind of crisp, graying, English hair that every boy imagines he will have
when he is older. He wore a long leather coat and a well-
worn tweed suit throughout the whole series. He was a
pipe smoker, and had a favorite charred old briar that
was always clenched between his firm white teeth. Petrie
called him "the most untidy smoker I ever knew," and
he was constantly spraying burning bits of tobacco and
ash over the carpet in Petrie's consulting room.

At first Smith had no fixed address. He would appear
suddenly, with an out-of-season tan, and camp in Petrie's
quarters for a few hundred pages. Later, when his anti-
Fu Manchu activities had earned him a knighthood and a
baronetcy, Sir Denis Nayland Smith would stay at the
New Louvre or some other fashionable hotel; and when
he had been transferred from Burma to head up a secret
division in Scotland Yard (with the rank of Assistant
Commissioner) he took a house in Whitehall near the
Yard and employed a manservant named Fey.

The years were kind to Smith, bringing titles and an
O.B.E. Petrie was not as lucky. He had to sell his practice
and move to Egypt because he fell in love with and married Kâramenèh, a girl with mixed blood. His only reward
was that her beauty and his skill as a doctor eventually
earned them grudging social acceptance from the British
colony in Cairo.

Smith's powers, in spite of his relatively obscure official
position, were amazing. Apparently the Crown recognized
the peril of the Si-Fan, and Sir Denis had *carte blanche*.
He carried in his breast pocket for thirty years a certain
letter which we readers were never privileged to see, but

which he flashed in times of crisis. This letter enabled him
to pressure a French Préfet de Police into summoning
naval forces to prevent the yacht *Lola* from leaving port,
so Smith could search it for the Doctor. On one occasion
he leaped into the middle of a London street and commandeered a chauffeur-driven Rolls-Royce. One glance
at the letter and the affluent citizen in the tonneau sur-
rendered his place to Sir Denis and continued his journey
by bus. Petrie notes on another occasion that "Dreadful crimes had marked Fu Manchu's passage through the
land. Not one-half of the truth (and nothing of the later
developments) had been made public. Nayland Smith's
authority was sufficient to control the press."

He stopped people's luggage in customs, commandeered and rerouted railway trains, and played fast and
loose with Scotland Yard and the British Navy. In America
he carried a simple card that said *Federal Agent 56*, but
written across the bottom of it was the signature of the
President of the United States.

Even the frigidly correct Home Secretary was not
immune to Smith's powers. Sir Denis burst into the Cab-
inet Minister's sitting room one foggy night demanding
that Scotland Yard send a detachment to break into a
cemetery and disinter a corpse that had been buried
that afternoon (the Golden Elixir again). The Home
Secretary replied that the whole business was "irregular—
wholly irregular. I shall be bothered by the Roman Catho-
lic authorities, and you know how troublesome they can
be."

"It is perhaps unfair of me to remind you that I can
bring pressure to bear."

"You are not suggesting that you would bother the
Prime Minister with this trivial but complicated affair?"

"I am suggesting nothing. I only ask for your signature.

I should not be here if the matter were as trivial as you suppose."

"Really—really, Smith . . ."

Five minutes later the police car was stealing through a mist, yellow, stifling, which closed in remorselessly, throttling London.

(*The Trail of Fu Manchu, p. 37*)

Smith's background was always a mystery to his fans. Where he came from, and how he got to the Far East in the first place no one ever knew. There were hints of a scandal, a broken love affair out there, a woman. Whatever happened, Smith came off badly, and it left him a lifelong misogynist. "She's only a woman, old boy, and women are very much alike—very much alike from Charing Cross to Pagoda Road" he would say to Petrie whenever Kârameneh turned nasty under the influence of one of the Doctor's drugs. Under the mask, the bitter, hard, authoritarian baronet had Heart. One day when Fleurette, Petrie's daughter, was left alone in Smith's study and browsed through his books, she found that:

> Those works which were not technical were of a character to have delighted a schoolboy. Particularly Fleurette was intrigued by a hard-bitten copy of *Tom Sawyer Abroad*, which had obviously been read and reread. Despite his great brain and his formidable personality, what a simple soul he was at heart!

(*The Trail of Fu Manchu, p. 118*)

Smith was no desk soldier. Whenever it became necessary to raid the Doctor's premises, as it did two or three times per book, he was always the first to enter, regardless of the danger. Scotland Yard always waited outside for the signal to break in. In order to carry out these pene-

trations, Smith (and Petrie) resorted to a number of
clever disguises. Thus we find him dressed as a "rough-
looking citizen" in a Limehouse pub, and later as a "man
with a claret-colored nose." On a visit to the Cafe de
l'Égypte, "a hang-out of artists and Bohemians," he and
Petrie were "transformed into a pair of Futurists, oddly
unlike our actual selves. No wigs, no false mustaches
had been employed; a change of costume and a few deft
touches of water color paint had rendered us unrecog-
nizable by our most intimate friends."

To the end Smith battled the Si-Fan, always a little
ahead, always winning, pulling the lobe of his left ear
(a habit of his when mulling over the best countermove to
a Fu Manchu gambit) and chaffing Petrie good naturedly.
Over a period of some thirty years he and the Yellow Doctor came to have a grudging respect for each other, and
in the crises they shared one noble trait. Each of them
was as good as his word, and on many occasions Smith
and Petrie were set free after facing horrible death, because the Doctor had made some inviolable promise.

Dr. Petrie was as faceless and as heartily bumbling as
the good Watson. In all the books there is only one actual
description of him, and that is limited to the simple sentence "He was definitely a handsome man, gray at the
temples and well set-up." No charred old briar or well-
worn tweeds for him. No yellow robe or astrakhan coat.
He was a cipher, and could have been made of pure cardboard for all Rohmer cared, but it was he who was the
love interest, not Smith, and he whose heart "fluttered
like a captive bird" in the throes of tender emotion. It
was well set-up old Petrie who turned Kâramenèh's
knees to water the first time she set eyes on him, and made
her risk her life repeatedly to save him over several
thousand pages. He was dependable and gave off a kind
of sense of security. At first he was an impecunious prac-

titioner, but in later volumes he became an expert in rare tropical diseases and was able to vie with the evil Doctor himself in the affair of the flying bubonic plague flea.

The early books were written in the first person, with Petrie as narrator, but after the fourth book Rohmer began to introduce new blood, on the grounds that Petrie was getting old. Young American and Canadian juveniles took over and Petrie's appearances got fewer and fewer until he dropped out of sight. We missed him. He was the perfect foil for the nervous, snappish, asexual Smith who would readily have consigned a lovely ingenue to the "Green Mist" or the "Scarlet Brides" if it meant getting Fu Manchu before the Assizes. Petrie was a sentimental fool sometimes, but the stories badly needed him. Imagine Holmes without Watson.

Kâramenèh, delicious half-Bedouin slave girl, who was forced to serve Fu Manchu because he kept her brother in a constant state of artificial catalepsy, was Petrie's love and later his wife. The first time Petrie saw her, his "heart fluttering like a child" he describes her . . .

> A girl wrapped in a hooded opera cloak stood at my elbow, and as she glanced up at me, I thought that I never had seen a face so seductively lovely nor of so unusual a type. With the skin of a perfect blonde, she had eyes and lashes as black as a Creole's, which, together with her full red lips, told me that this beautiful stranger, whose touch had so startled me, was not a child of our northern shores.
>
> (*The Insidious Dr. Fu Manchu*, p. 13)

Around the house she affected gauzy harem costumes, and little red high-heeled slippers. Rohmer saw to it that all pretty girls in the books wore little red high-heeled slippers, although Fah Lo Suee once switched to green. Zarmi of the Joyshop wore them, as did Fleurette. They were as much a personal insignia as white hats in a cowboy film.

Kâramenèh was a confusing character. She was constantly tricking Smith and Petrie into some disastrous situation, and then appearing at the last minute to get them out again. This habit irritated the waspish Smith:

> "She is one of the finest weapons in the enemy's armory, Petrie. But a woman is a two-edged sword, and treacherous. To our great good fortune, she has formed a sudden predilection, characteristically Oriental, for yourself. Oh you may scoff, but it is evident."
>
> (*The Insidious Dr. Fu Manchu, p. 15*)

She was my first introduction to Oriental women and I liked what I read. The girls I knew never formed a sudden predilection for oneself. They had an irritating habit of looking through you as though you were invisible. What wouldn't I have given for a subteen Kâramenèh with velvet eyes and a fascinating musical accent, who would say, clasping her hands in wild abandon, "Throw me into prison, kill me if you like for what I have done, but do not torture me, try to drive me mad, with your reproaches!"

Kâramenèh and Petrie lived happily in Cairo after their marriage, and she stayed just as lovely as ever although Petrie's hair got progressively grayer. Their union was blessed with a little daughter, Fleurette, who died at the age of six months to their great grief. Petrie never suspected that it was the Golden Elixir again. Fleurette was exhumed and spirited to Fu Manchu's island headquarters near Monte Carlo, where she was carefully trained to be the evil Doctor's bride and the eventual Empress of the World. This plan was frustrated when she fell in love with Alan Sterling, a junior Petrie-surrogate. She was a carbon-copy of Kâramenèh except that she had blue eyes instead of velvety black ones. Petrie, who hadn't seen her in nineteen years, recognized her immediately as his daughter.

Fah Lo Suee was Fu Manchu's daughter, and she too had been educated for a special purpose, to be the "Lady of the Si-Fan," a half-legendary character, a kind of female Dalai Lama. Once again love intervened, when she fell head over heels ("in true Oriental fashion") with Smith. This infatuation caused her to betray her sinister father on at least fifteen occasions, and resulted in her untimely death, when he fed her into the blast furnace he used for his gold transmutation experiments. Poor Fah Lo Suee (the name meant "sweet perfume" according to Rohmer) was no better than she should have been, and she was the only sexually inclined character in the series. She attempted to seduce not only Smith, but Alan Sterling as well, and even Sir Bertram Morgan, Governor of the Bank of England. She was also the only nude in any of the books, and was hung up by the thumbs to have her smooth, ivory body whipped by one of her father's dacoits after one unusually blatant betrayal.

The evil Doctor's servants deserve some notice here. The wrinkled, pigtailed little old Chinese, John Ki, also called "Singapore Charlie" and a number of other names, who always kept an opium den for the Doctor's headquarters, turns out to have been the governor of a province under the Dowager Empress. The dacoits were Burmans, squat, ugly, squint-eyed, and physically very powerful. Between their eyes they bore a religious brand called "the mark of Kali." They could climb like monkeys, and were trained stranglers. Before each kill they uttered the weird, minor key call that froze Petrie's marrow again and again. Their most endearing trait was the ability to sneak about the crowded corridors of fashionable London hotels, dressed only in Ghandiesque loincloths, without attracting notice. For special duties, the Doctor also had *thugs, phansigars* (the dwarf in the suitcase was one), *hashishin,* and for maritime activities, sea-Dyaks from Malaya.

A good many years after my first adventure with the Doctor and his minions, when my pre-teens were behind me and I was old enough for military service, I found myself in London, bored, lonely, but wearing the smug assurance that olive drab carried in those days. With time on my hands, I hailed a taxi and directed the driver to take me to Limehouse, so that I could see for myself the locale of the Doctor's sinister machinations. The driver looked me over carefully. "I wouldn't go down there if I was you, mate," he said (olive drab or no I was still a man taxi drivers called "mate" at that period). I persisted, but he would not be moved. When I asked him what was lurking there that was so dangerous to curious American soldiers he could not explain. He just "wouldn't go down there" if he were I. I no longer pressed the point. He knew best. By mutual consent we turned and headed for the Rainbow Corner and the blacked-out lights of Mayfair. From behind me, the direction of the East End docks, I dimly heard what could have been a weird, minor key call, and something flapped against the rear window of the cab that just might have been a giant flying bubonic plague flea. Thirty years after the Doctor's appearance, Limehouse was still a place to stay away from. I never did get there. Perhaps it was for the best. You never can tell.

CHAPTER THREE

THE SECRET OF NANCY DREW:
Pushing Forty and Going Strong

> *"We will crash! Oh—oh—"*
> *An ashen-faced middle-aged man leaned across the aisle of the four-engined transport plane toward Nancy Drew.*
>
> *The attractive blonde girl smiled reassuringly. "Please don't worry," she said gently. "Only one motor has stopped. We'll be all right. And we'll soon reach River Heights."*
>
> (*The Scarlet Slipper Mystery*)

A few karmas ago, circumstance compelled me to raise a small daughter, without benefit of wife and mother, in the insecure atmosphere of a large hotel. Emily was ten, and because of my busy schedule, she had to spend a great deal of time alone, inventing her own amusements. One evening I observed her curled up in a ball on the sofa, shoes off, face unusually serious and preoccupied. Interrogated, she answered in a manner so vague, so ruminative, that if I had been a husband of ten years instead of a father I would have been certain she had taken a lover. She had discovered Nancy Drew.

In a local bookstore, mixed in among out-of-date Little Golden Books and the misadventures of improbable animals, my daughter had found a row of blue-jacketed volumes, each bearing in a printed medallion the intrepid girl detective's seductively *nice* face. Emily bought *The Secret of the Old Clock*, identified as the first in the series by the small numeral (1), and promising countless hours of pure happiness ahead. By the time she was ready for *The Hidden Staircase* (2), she was hooked, like so many bored, lonely kids before her. "So many" means 30,000,000 reading Nancy's adventures in seventeen languages over a period of thirty-eight years.

My daughter is grown now, and oriented toward more sophisticated pleasures, but Nancy's magic still galvanizes the nine to eleven-year-old set in the same wonderful way. The dauntless, bewitching girl detective is still happening, while other favorites dwindle and disappear. Bomba the Jungle Boy crumbles into dust. Tom Swift is replaced by Tom Swift, Jr., but Nancy is still a smash at the box office. In a world of gaudy exhibitionism, subteens find refuge in Nancy's enviable, secure, conservative world.

Nancy is written in East Orange, New Jersey, by "Carolyn Keene," who is really a grandmotherly lady named Harriet S. Adams, abetted by her partner Andrew Svenson and four anonymous ghost writers. This group also writes the "Tom Swift, Jr." series, the "Hardy Boys," the "Bobbsey Twins," and a number of others. Mrs. Adams has written forty-three Nancys, the latest of which will appear this year. The girl sleuth is the financial star of the list. Last year Nancy sold 1,500,000 copies compared to 1,000,000 for the Hardy Boys and a paltry 250,000 for the Bobbseys. Mrs. Adams's publisher, Grosset & Dunlap, is understandably reticent about how much actual cash Nancy has brought her creator, but simple arithmetic tells us that since 1930 she has probably netted her author considerably more than $1,000,000.

Augmenting this profit, Nancy came to the attention of Warner Brothers in 1938, and they decided to film her, with Bonita Granville in the title role. There were four films in all, beginning with *The Hidden Staircase*, loosely based on the book of the same name. The other three, dreamed up and "improved" by contract script writers, were *Nancy Drew, Detective* (1938); *Nancy Drew, Reporter* (1939); and *Nancy Drew, Trouble Shooter* (1939);

after which the series petered out, having failed to achieve the popular following of, say, Andy Hardy or Charlie Chan. What Grosset & Dunlap calls "contract complications" have prevented Nancy from appearing as a TV series, although she would probably make a good one.

A girl usually gets her introduction to Nancy Drew from someone else; a gift or loan from some friend or relative. After initial exposure, she mounts a campaign of wheedling and cajoling until she has extracted the other forty or so from her parents. Advances are begged on allowances. Hints are dropped before birthdays and Christmas. Once a kid is hooked she has no scruples about infecting her friends and classmates, and Nancy reaches epidemic proportions in the fourth, fifth, and sixth grades. Strict reciprocal trade agreements are drawn up, and woe to anyone who tries to slip in a "Dana Girls" or a "Judy Bolton."

A parent who tries to fathom the secret of Nancy's success is doomed to failure, because, strictly speaking, Nancy is terribly square. Yet she appeals to subteeny-boppers today just as she did in the 1930s. Apparently there is a rock-ribbed streak of conservatism in the nine-to-eleven group. They will participate in outlandish fads for the sake of show, but they like things simple, basic, well-organized. Just as the brashest smart-aleck will still gulp down a massive lump of anguish when Beth, in *Little Women*, comes in out of the snow and says, "Jo, the baby's dead . . .", the loudest little cynic will retire to her room, curl up among the psychedelic posters and "Legalize Pot" buttons, and devour some forty Nancy Drews in a row with deep concentration and heartfelt involvement.

Parental permissiveness is thought to be a major factor in Nancy's longevity. Women of my generation passed their worn copies to their daughters fondly and with (as Nancy would say) a suspicious moisture in their eyes. Mothers who have never read the series examine it and find it harmless if not downright wholesome. Parents who don't care one way or another tolerate Nancy because she keeps the children quiet and arouses in them an interest in books and reading. These reasons do little to explain Nancy's attraction. On the contrary, any one of them is sufficient to poison a little girl's mind against the series. Nancy appeals to her readers in spite of parental approval, not because of it.

The books have an odd, timeless quality. I looked for anachronisms in our 1930 first edition of *The Secret of the Old Clock*. Except for Nancy's roadster with its running boards and rumble seat there were none. Like the Land of Oz, Nancy Drew Country is in another time dimension, untouched by the outside world. The Depression came and went, followed by three wars, but they passed unnoticed in Midwestern, suburban River Heights, where Nancy and her chums and their well-to-do country-clubbing parents live. Teen-agers all have new cars there. They buy unlimited pretty clothes, and they summer at fashionable resorts. They give lovely parties. At the height of World War II Nancy went on a pleasure cruise to Buenos Aires, untroubled by U-boats in the sea lanes. There was always plenty of gasoline for her convertible. Hungry kids, shattered by the announcement of bubble gum rationing, drowned their sorrows in Nancy's world.

When I asked my daughter why she had loved Nancy, she thought for a moment, and then said simply, "You can *identify* with her." She meant that a little girl can plausibly pretend to be Nancy. She is an example of the fantasy world in which pre-pubescent girls live in daydreams. A boy can imagine that he is swinging from tree to tree, ululating the victory cry of the bull ape, but he knows in his heart it will never happen. Nancy, on the other hand, is within reach. She is pretty but not beautiful ("like a quaint little princess"). Her hair is a lovely golden color, and naturally wavy. She is small, with a slight but good figure at sixteen. She is graceful, the result of ballet lessons; and she dresses well, with as many changes of costume as any paper doll. She is respected by difficult grownups, such as salespeople, waitresses, and policemen, all of whom address her courteously as "Miss Drew."

Lest any reader think her keen mind is restricted to solving mysteries, it should be noted that Nancy also has a rich vein of pure culture, although at sixteen she shows no signs of attending school or preparing to enter a university. Invited by the parents of her beau, Ned Nickerson, to accompany them to the big Thanksgiving Day football game at Emerson College, where Ned is on the team, Nancy replies that she will enjoy going to the game, but she will "also enjoy the Shakespearean play the Drama Club is presenting afterwards." A clue appears in an obscure document, and:

> George and Bess studied the paragraph to which Nancy had pointed. It was a quotation in Old English and they could not make it out. Nancy, who had learned to read the works of the old English poet Chaucer in school, eagerly translated it.
>
> (*The Clue in the Crumbling Wall, p. 130*)

Asked to a college weekend, she is just as much at home in a deep discussion with a young faculty member on "the subject of bringing lost relatives together" as she is on the dance floor. She is not above pausing in her gardening to instruct a family servant:

These larkspurs are also called "delphinium" because they were the sacred flower of the temple at Delphi, Nancy explained. I believe they have other names too.

(*Passport to Larkspur Lane, p. 7*)

For all her intellectual attainments, Nancy is no bluestocking, as we shall see. She rides and swims in Olympic style, not only besting the Amateur Champion of fashionable Sylvan Lake, but on one occasion leaping into a bayou with all her clothes on and doing a rapid 500 yards to the shore. She can fix a balky outboard motor with a bobby pin. With no effort, she climbs a rose trellis to the second floor. Pursuing an escaped crook, she puts the police on his trail by drawing a perfect likeness of him for them. When the River Heights Women's Club charity show faces disaster because of the defection of its leading lady, Nancy steps in at a moment's notice and wins general kudos with a creditable ballet, although she is recuperating from a sprained ankle. At 100 yards, she plugs a lynx three times with a Colt .44 revolver. Her delphiniums win first prize at the flower show. She floors "Zany" Shaw, a full-grown lawbreaker, with a right to the jaw. She is always a barrel of fun at a party, and she ". . . received a lot of applause for her impersonation of Helena Hawley, a motion-picture star who played parts in old-time Westerns."

What hero or heroine of modern fiction can top that?

One of Nancy's greatest victories comes at an Emerson College dance, when the master of ceremonies announces:

"Now, as you all know, it is our custom to select each year a beautiful young lady to preside over this event—one who will wear the Festival Robe and Crown. After

careful consideration, a choice has been made by a com-
mittee of faculty and students."

"Gosh, I wonder who the lucky girl will be?" Bill Tomlin
commented. "It always goes to the prettiest and most
popular one in the audience."

"Will Miss Nancy Drew please come to the stage?" he
requested. Everyone began to clap and whistle, for beyond question the choice was a pleasing one.

(*Passport to Larkspur Lane, p. 139*)

Put that in your daydream if you dare, no matter how
old you are. Poor Nancy doesn't wear the Festival Robe
and Crown very long, because the auditorium lights are
suddenly extinguished, and she is abducted, Robe, Crown
and all, and hustled away in a speeding car by a masked
man and a hard-faced woman.

Nancy's mysteries follow a simple but inflexible pattern. First there is an anonymous warning to her to get
off the case or face dire consequences, which she bravely
ignores. In every one there is a wild chase, either on
foot through crowded streets or in Nancy's convertible.
Nearly all are concerned with the withholding of sums
of money or jewelry from deserving people by thieves or
embezzlers. There are missing wills, treasure maps, hidden rubies, secret codes, long-separated relatives reunited. Occasionally there is an oddball crime like the
forgery of ancient Chinese porcelains, or the plagiary of
popular tunes. There are several attempted arsons to conceal evidence, but murder is never allowed.

Kidnaping abounds, and in almost every book someone, usually Nancy, is spirited away, bound and gagged,
and abandoned. Rescue is swift. No one is ever permitted
to die. Even the unlucky lynx, shot by Nancy in *The Secret at Shadow Ranch*, staggers off into the underbrush,
presumably to get well after having learned his lesson.

Violence in the series usually takes the form of atrocious assault on Nancy's person. Again and again, just as she sees an important clue, and reaches for it, everything goes black as she is sapped from behind with a blunt instrument. There are more than thirty occasions on which Nancy is bludgeoned into unconsciousness by blows on the head, enough to reduce her to a lifetime of hanging around Stillman's Gym looking for odd jobs. She is struck by lightning, hurled down a flight of stairs, and even blown through a plaster wall by a charge of dynamite. None of this seems to have any effect, and she always bounces back, bright as a button, to foil the caitiff responsible.

The protagonists in the stories are generally poor, but well-educated, having seen better days. They are patient and deserving, people of family, who have nice but run-down old houses with a few good antiques. They are ladies and gentlemen in every sense. Crooks are easily identifiable, because they are vulgar, bad-tempered, and have an unfortunate tendency to raise their voices to people. They have red or coarse, bushy black hair, and nicknames like "Spike," "Red," "Snorky," or "Flip." They further identify themselves by their regrettable preference for checkered suits, yellow overcoats, elevator shoes, and (for the oilier, better-educated crook) striped pants, spats, and goatees. Criminals always have a physical oddity; a long nose, or a missing middle finger.

The surest clue to an evildoer in the series is grammar. A Nancy Drew felon reveals himself at once by his garbled syntax. In *The Quest of the Missing Map* Nancy receives an anonymous letter:

Dear Miss Drew: I tuk yere boat cos I need money but I can't sell it. You kin hev it bak fer five dollars. It says

sumthin importent inside. Don't tell the perlice and come
alone on foot to 47 White Street.

(The Quest of the Missing Map, p. 48)

Who but a miscreant would write such a letter? Nancy
hurries to the White Street address, is captured, bound,
gagged, and shoved in a broom closet from which she is
eventually rescued by her father and Ned.

"Are you hurt, Nancy?" her father asked apprehen-
sively. "No, I'm all right, Dad," she reassured him, "but
I'm afraid the worst has happened."

(op. cit., p. 55)

It is characteristic of Nancy that this remark is never
for a moment interpreted as meaning that her abductor
has taken liberties. Her rescuers assume at once, and correctly, that she means the crooks have stolen her half of
the missing treasure map.

In addition to bona-fide felons with long police records,
each book contains an evil couple, a shrewd, wickedly
handsome man and a hard-faced, overdressed woman.
Every volume also contains a homily of some sort, a little
lecture on some obscure but marginally educational subject: Ming Dynasty porcelains, the impasto technique in
modern painting, conchology, old ships figureheads, New
Orleans trade and commerce, dye-making from whelks,
button manufacture, stained-glass painting—all are woven
painlessly into the plot to instruct the curious little reader.

The characters who support Nancy in her adventures
seem pallid compared to their heroine. Her beloved and
indulgent father, Carson Drew, a "noted lawyer engaged
largely in mystery cases," discusses his law practice with
her and finds her opinion to be "astonishingly sound for

one so young." He supplies her considerable logistical needs, replenishing her wardrobe and her private savings and checking accounts; and buys her a shiny new convertible when crooks disable hers (as they do periodically) by sawing through its brake or steering mechanism. When he is not engaged in uttering platitudes ("Success is one tenth inspiration and nine tenths perspiration"), he is usually on his way out of town on a business trip. He looks distinguished, carries a cane, worries a lot about whether Nancy will get hurt, and always listens with interest to what she has to say. From the pre-teen point of view, this makes him a perfect Daddy. Nancy adores him, and shows it by tweaking his distinguished ear mischievously, or ruffling his well-brushed gray hair.

Left motherless at an early age, Nancy was raised by elderly Hannah Gruen, who does the cooking and the heavy housework. Hannah and Nancy never depart from their servant-mistress relationship, and there is no doubt about who is the boss. Hannah is too old, too plain, and too working-class to pose a threat to Nancy's freedom or her relationship with her father, as a real mother might. When the chores get too hard for Hannah, she is assisted by her niece, Effie, a giggling cretin about Nancy's age.

Ned Nickerson, Emerson College football hero, is Nancy's sincerest admirer. Big and good-natured, malleable and self-effacing, he knows Nancy is smarter than he is and doesn't care. An Emerson sophomore for the past thirty-two years, Ned easily beats out Lord Fancourt Babberley for the all-time undergraduate longevity record. Although he makes it plain in his blunt, outspoken way that he expects to make Nancy his bride some day, Ned is allowed no physical contact or visible sign of affection. Occasionally, pursuing a hot clue in Nancy's car (faster and larger than Ned's) he will make a leading remark, pointing out that they are alone and there is moonlight. This boldness makes Nancy blush to her finger-tips (a frequent habit of hers) and change the subject to "something less personal."

Poor unkissed Ned is unceremoniously brushed off in most of the books; brought in for a chapter only when a strong back is needed. Often he is a mere mention. "Where is Ned?" someone will ask. "Oh, he is in South America," Nancy will reply, without further embellish-ment. During the school year he is conveniently away at college, and in the summer he works as a camp coun-selor. In one horrid sequence the reader is led to believe that he has shown a little gumption and asked another girl to the big Emerson dance. Nancy bears up well ("After all, he has a perfect right to"), but it turns out to be a mistake and the two are reunited.

Nancy is helped in her detective work by her dearest chums, George Fayne and Bess Marvin. George, (who is a girl) has short hair, a boyish voice, and a boyish figure. She hates frilly clothes, jewelry, and people who call her "Georgina" or "Georgette." Bess is pretty but slightly plump, and is terrified by rats and spiders, a feminine weakness that causes endless merriment to her bolder companions. George has an unfortunate tendency to fall into wells, creeks, bayous, and other muddy water holes. Sometimes the girls are joined by Helen Corning, but she is a weakling and too lah-de-dah to contribute anything to the excitement.

Nobody ever tells a lie in the series, and there are none of the commoner vices. Whiskey only appears once, in *The Bungalow Mystery,* in which a silly watchman allows himself to be seduced into taking one too many by would-be burglars, and abandons his post. He is roundly pun-ished for this transgression. Parents don't drink at dinner parties, and Nancy and her chums are never exposed to

beer, even at the numerous fraternity functions held at
Emerson College. No one smokes cigarettes. Nancy herself eschews stimulants to the extent of substituting milk
or cocoa for morning coffee.

There is some sex in the series, but nothing that would
have caused Colette a moment's envy. It is all of the pre-
pubescent giggly kind, which doesn't need boy and girl
contact to titillate. In *The Clue in the Crumbling Wall*,
George falls into a lily pond, and, soaked to the skin, lays
out her clothes to dry. She is forced to pop into a summer
house with nothing on when a naughty twelve-year-old
boy comes prowling around and steals all her garments,
leaving her in a fine pickle indeed until Bess comes to the
rescue with a raincoat. In *The Scarlet Slipper Mystery*,
Nancy spots a suspect during a ballet class, and rushes
into the street in a revealing leotard, unaware until she is
reminded of her improper costume by the disapproving
stares of passers-by. In *The Hidden Window Mystery*, a
sneak thief rifles the girls' luggage and makes off with not
only an important clue, but intimate bits and pieces of
their underwear as well. This sort of harmless, pre-teen
ribaldry serves to relieve the routine of the mysteries
with an occasional blush and titter.

Negroes in the earlier books were minstrel-show stereotypes with names like Mandy and Beulah. They said
things such as "Lawsy me!" and "Yassuh" and spoke a
kind of pidgin English:

> "Scuse me, sah, but de bank am closin'. Ah jest natcherly
> got to shet de do'."
>
> (*Nancy's Mysterious Letter, p. 78*)

By 1957, although they still drop their consonants,
Negro characters have become articulate and informa-

tive. Uncle Rufus, bayou dweller and voodoo practitioner, says:

> "It was my ancestors that invented the first long distance com-mun-i-cations. We made drums that could carry sounds for miles and miles. The folks in one place sent signals an' messages by beatin' on the drums with their hands. Then the next village would pick it up an' send the signal on to another place far away. That's how they get all the members of a tribe together for special meetin's and for fightin' wars."

(*The Haunted Showboat, p. 88*)

Uncle Rufus is still being patronized, but there is an improvement. By the 1960s the earlier books had been rewritten to expunge objectionable matter (also cleaning up vulgar, pushy Johnny and Kitty Blair, who had changed their name from Sellerstein, and smirking, cringing, disbarred lawyer Abe Jacobs).

Mrs. Adams is presently engaged in writing *The Invisible Intruder*, forty-third in the series, and undoubtedly the sixteen-year-old girl detective will go on forever. My daughter will never read *The Invisible Intruder*, and neither will many other girls who have achieved puberty and have begun to notice boys and create another fantasy world of a very different kind. But they are expendable in Nancy's world. There is a whole new generation of stupefied pre-teens, with puffy, red-rimmed eyes from staying up too late so that they can finish one more chapter. They can *identify* with Nancy. Following them is another generation of first-graders, spelling out their A-B-C's with no idea of the thrills and joys in store for them. A day will come when each of them will discover, either on her own or through the instrument of some fond relative who remembers her own girlish past, the irresistible girl detective and *The Secret of the Old Clock,* and will turn to chapter one, page one, and read:

THE LOST WILL

"It would be a shame if all that money went to the Tophams! They will fly higher than ever!" Nancy Drew, a pretty girl of sixteen, leaned over the library table and addressed her father, who sat reading a newspaper by the study lamp . . .

and the cycle will start all over again.

(AUTHOR'S NOTE:) When this chapter first appeared as an article in the *Saturday Review,* I was traveling abroad. When I returned home, I found the usual odd assortment of mail that follows the publication of this kind of essay in that kind of magazine. There were honey-and-vinegar notes from nice old lady English teachers, taking issue with my placement of commas and semicolons, and there were a number of dissertations on word meanings and literary usage. There was also some nostalgia from people who had liked the Nancy Drew series, and a few dissents from people who thought I had been unkind to the Dana Girls, Judy Bolton, Beverly Gray, and others.

Conspicuous in the jumble of mail was a small, flat package which, when opened, turned out to contain a brand-new edition of *The Invisible Intruder.* I opened it and discovered that it was inscribed to me and signed by no less a personage than Carolyn Keene herself. I thought it was a practical joke until I found that there was a letter too. Out of natural curiosity, I had opened the package first without realizing the letter was there.

It was a strange feeling, communicating with an immortal. The letter was typewritten, but without the rigid, flawless formality that marks the work of a highly trained

executive secretary. One or two strikeovers indicated that
Miss Keene—or Mrs. Adams—had taken the trouble to
type it herself, probably using two index fingers as I do.
She had liked the article, and praised it with much kind-
ness. She was touched at the paragraph in which I said
my daughter was grown and would probably never read
The Invisible Intruder, and had paused in her busy day
to send it to me. She also pointed out a few errors that I
had made, and brought me up to date on recent changes
in Nancy's career. I wrote at once to thank her, and was
invited to lunch in East Orange, where I found her working at her desk, under a large portrait of Nancy which
had appeared earlier as the cover of *The Mystery of the
Fire Dragon.* I spent the day with her and her partner,
Andrew Svenson, at the offices of the Stratemeyer Syndicate, and was able to inspect their wonderful library of
old Bobbsey Twins, Nancy Drews, Tom Swifts, Hardy
Boys, Bomba the Jungle Boys and many, many others,
all in their original covers. It was quite a day.

Nancy has aged slightly over the years, and is now
eighteen years old, to conform with motor vehicle laws
in most of the states. It was that or give up the shiny blue
convertible, which would, of course, have been unthink-
able. She has become less formal as dress standards
have changed, and now does her wall-climbing and
underbrush-prowling in blue jeans and a boy's shirt, a
costume which would have been impossible thirty years
ago, when her more strenuous activities were carried out
in neat frocks turned out on Hannah Gruen's sewing
machine, and set off with snap brim felt hats and white
gloves. Ned Nickerson has a more important role in the
new books, and Carson Drew no longer carries a cane.

Her relationship with Hannah has mellowed with time,
and Hannah herself has ceased to be a lower-class drudge
and has become a warm, motherly person with whom

Nancy can maintain a cheerful and quasi-maternal accord.

In recent years Mrs. Adams has been approached by numerous racial and religious pressure groups who persist in screening each book with great thoroughness. There have been demands that some characters, including poor, good-hearted Uncle Rufus, the voodoo practitioner, be removed entirely. Mrs. Adams has seen to it that all the books conform to current rules of good taste, and that no individual or group is insulted or denigrated in any Stratemeyer Syndicate book. However, she has not yielded entirely to pressure or overreaction. I hope Uncle Rufus stays. He never did anybody any harm. Nancy liked him, and so did I.

Mrs. Adams pointed out that my remark about Nancy being written by her, Mr. Svenson, and "four anonymous ghost writers" was incorrect. Although the Syndicate uses contract writers for some of its series, she does all the Nancys herself, and has done so since the death of her father, the late Edward Stratemeyer, who was Nancy's creator, and who wrote the first three books of the series. Mr. Svenson writes "The Happy Hollisters" and others.

I suppose in a way I was unfair to the Dana Girls and the others, but not entirely. According to Grosset & Dunlap they have a strong following, but Nancy still leads in sales. In fact, even now, a year and a half after the first appearance of my article, her sales have increased, ignoring, as the books did, recession, tight money, war, television, and the other burdens of our decade.

Most other books about girls which appeared in the last twenty years or so followed the Nancy Drew pattern. The "gothic novel" had not yet become popular, and girls in literature involved themselves in solving "mysteries" of one kind or another. The Danas were written by Mrs.

Adams, using her Nancy Drew pseudonym of Carolyn Keene. They were very much like two Nancys, and the fact that there were two of them removed the need for steady chums or foils, although many of their friends reappeared in several of the books. The very title of their first book, *By the Light of the Study Lamp,* recalls the first paragraph of the first Nancy book. Remember the Tophams and how Nancy addressed her father on the subject of their inheritance as he sat reading by the study lamp?

The Danas appeared in 1934, not too long after Nancy's early successes. They lived in Oak Falls, a carbon copy of Nancy's own suburban, Middle-Western River Heights, a community of nice people and pleasant environs. Although Nancy never seemed to go to school at all, the Danas attended a posh boarding school, the Starhurst School for Girls, which gave them leeway for much dormitory fun, and for the discomfiture of what passes in girls' boarding schools as bullies. There were restrictions, however. Nancy had complete freedom, but the Danas had to cope with rules and a benign but strict headmistress whose approval had to be sought even for so simple a move as a trip downtown.

Louise Dana was seventeen and dark, and her sister Jean was sixteen and blonde in 1934. They were both pretty, and in true Carolyn Keene fashion the girls had been relieved of parental interference with their adventures. They lived with attractive, unmarried Aunt Harriet and good old Uncle Ned Dana, a sea captain who made frequent voyages away from home. The girls had Aunt Harriet completely subjugated and the servants, stupid Cora Appel and stuttering Ben Harrow, were caricatures who adored Jean and Louise and did pretty much as they were told. As a rule, the girls could solve mysteries to their hearts' content, except during the school day.

Like Nancy, the Danas were upper middle class. They had a soft spot for the poor but honest, and a distaste for the rich and pushy (and in those days rich kids were generally depicted as snobbish, arrogant, flashily dressed and dishonest). The Danas' allowances were vast by the standards of the thirties and forties. Their mysteries, like Nancy's, depended in large part on the return of money, jewels, and legacies, to deserving folk who had somehow lost them. Villains followed the general subteen pattern of what evil men ought to look like, for example, Jake Garbone in *Study Lamp:*

> He was a stout, swarthy individual with beetling eyebrows, dark eyes that glittered strangely, a nose like a beak, and a thin, cruel mouth. He rubbed his fat hands together as he moved stealthily behind the counter.
>
> *(By the Light of the Study Lamp, p. 17)*

Could Dickens have described him better? He was obviously a desperado from the word go, and no girl would ever doubt it for a minute. The Danas were plagued throughout the series by their wealthy classmate Lettie Briggs, who had a "pinched, disagreeable face" and did what she could to put them down, always unsuccessfully. Like Nancy, they triumphed every time because of their quick wits and their ability to make and carry out decisions.

Judy Bolton was another kind of girl entirely. Simple and practical, with both feet planted squarely on the ground, she was half a social class or so below Nancy and the Danas, although her father was a doctor. There were no fancy boarding schools or country clubs for Judy. She attended a good solid public high school in her town of Farringdon, and at the outset of her series she was a senior.

Judy had no glamorous sea captain uncle or doting daddy to raise her differently from other girls. She had a proper small-town family. Her father's office and residence were the same and he was there for dinner every evening; a dinner, moreover, which was prepared by Judy's intelligent, practical, decision-making mother. She also had an older brother, Horace, who worked as a newspaper reporter and was very useful to have around at mystery-solving time. Unusually gregarious, Judy let her whole gang of chums help her solve her mysteries, and even had mystery-solving parties for twenty or thirty kids equally divided among boys and girls.

Unlike Nancy and the Danas, Judy had a very real and red-blooded boy friend, her high school classmate Peter Dobbs, a no-nonsense kid. When Judy, who had suspected him of a practical joke, found that he was quite innocent, she murmured:

"How can I ever make up for being stupid enough to think it was you?"

"Like this," he said and kissed her right in plain sight of all the curious people who lived in that shabby row of houses almost at the end of upper Grove Street.

(*The Mysterious Half Cat, p. 138*)

No Stratemeyer Syndicate heroine ever got grabbed and kissed in public like that. Ned Nickerson would never have had the courage.

Peter Dobbs had a rival, Arthur Farringdon-Pett, not too bright but fantastically rich. He had a huge car and an airplane and all the other trappings of fictional riches in the early thirties. Judy never considered rich people snobbish or cruel. Money was there to be used, and if a mystery could be solved more rapidly by using Arthur's plane, she commandeered it, even though her heart belonged to Peter. Arthur never minded. He was a good sport.

As far as social amenities went, Judy could not have cared less. The Danas and Nancy were very careful about proper dress and behavior, but Judy, on the night of her high school graduation dance

> . . . stood before the mirror in her room dressed in white, like a bride. She couldn't decide between Arthur's orchids or Peter's gardenias, so she wore them both.

(The Mysterious Half Cat, p. 202)

Nancy would have died first.

Politically Judy stood rather far to the right of Nancy. She had no patience with the poor, and felt that they ought to pull themselves up by their bootstraps. Discussing a shabby row of houses in a poorer section of Farringdon, her friend Scottie says with a sigh:

> "People actually live in them! They bring up children in them.
> "They bring up crooks and gangsters and scrubwomen and when you look at these houses, can you blame those who have to live in them for being what they are?" asked Judy philosophically.

(op. cit., p. 87)

So much for the poor. Judy's creator was (and is) Margaret Sutton, a lady who is not (so Grosset & Dunlap tell me) a syndicate. The series began in 1936, some years after Nancy's early successes, and two years after the Danas appeared, and is apparently still doing well, but never as well as Nancy.

Judy is accompanied by other girl detectives in the girls' series market, like Connie Blair and Beverly Gray, girls whose popularity assured their creators a comfortable income but who were never quite able to take the wind out of Nancy's sales. A couple of professionals, Vicki Barr, airline stewardess and Cherry Ames, crisp, efficient nurse, have a considerable following, but are too remote for little girls to really identify with them. Glamour is fun to read about, but Nancy is the real loved one.

In Linda Craig, the Stratemeyer Syndicate tried to fashion a Nancy Drew on horseback, a winning combination if there ever was one, but for some reason she never caught on. The syndicate hasn't given up hope, pointing out wisely that it takes five years or more for a series to take hold. They were more successful with Kay Tracey, their first paperback girl sleuth.

One of the great joys of researching this book was the rediscovery (or discovery on my part) of the Camp Fire Girls, brought out in the first years of the twentieth century by Hildegarde G. Frey. They were perfectly splendid. Older than most (they were eighteen or nineteen) each of them was as lovely as a flower. No pert prettiness for them, they had grown-up good looks. They glowed with good health from their outdoorsy activities, but at the same time they were entirely feminine with the kind of femininity that began to vanish after World War I and the beginning of the Jazz Age. Nonetheless, they carried on an unending guerrilla war against both the Boy Scouts and the Girl Scouts, and bested both at such activities as kite flying contests and drill team activities. They had superb *esprit de corps* without being prigs or gym teacher types, and their books are surprisingly well-written.

Ruth Fielding, a creation of Edward Stratemeyer under one of his female pseudonyms (Alice B. Emerson), brought a theatrical flair into the early girls' series. Ruth, like Nancy Drew, was invariably successful in her activities, and ended up with her own film company in which she wrote scenarios, acted, directed, and produced. She was, as far as I know, the only film star in any series, but it never kept her from being a simple, down-to-earth American girl.

My researches also brought back into my life that treacly little mushmouth, the Little Colonel, maundering to her beloved pony:

> "Oh Tarbaby! Everybody has forgotten that it is my birthday! Even Papa Jack has gone off to town without saying a word about it, and he nevah did such a thing befo' in all his life!" . . .
>
> "It isn't the presents I care about," she whispered, choking back a heartbroken sob; "but oh, Tarbaby, it's the bein' forgotten! Of co'se mothah couldn't be expected to remembah, she's been so ill. But I think grandfathah might, or Mom Beck or *somebody*. If there'd only been one single person when I came downstairs this mawnin' to say 'I wish you many happy returns, Lloyd deah', I wouldn't feel so bad. But there wasn't and I nevah felt so misah'ble and lonesome and left out since I was bawn."

> (*The Little Colonel's Hero, p. 11*)

Of course 1902 ideas about girls' literature differed from what they were in 1911 or 1919 or 1934, but the Little Colonel, in print or played on the screen by Shirley Temple, was unbearable. If, as some biographer has suggested, Lewis Carroll was really a dirty old man and far too fond of dainty golden-haired nymphets, and if God saw fit to punish him for this aberration, I have no doubt that he is in a No-Exit room in some purgatory, imprisoned for eternity with the Little Colonel.

Eighteen months after I had answered the last letter about my Nancy Drew article, and had put the series away forever or at least until I should be presented with a granddaughter to start the cycle again, one more letter arrived, from a little girl in Oakland, California, who had somehow turned up an obsolete copy of the *Saturday Review*.

Dear Sir,

My name is Geri and I'm eleven years old. I'd like to point out that in the January 25, 1969 issue of Saturday Review, your article called the "Secret of Nancy Drew" is incorrect in some places. Perhaps this is due to incorrect data, or perhaps an error in the writing, or maybe you just haven't read Nancy Drew books lately. In any case, the part about no killings in Nancy Drew is wrong. Quote "No one is ever permitted to die. Even the unlucky lynx, shot by Nancy in The Secret at Shadow Ranch, staggers off into the underbrush, presumably to get well after having learned his lesson . . ." Unqoute (sic) Wrong! Quote: "You got him all right," George observed with satisfaction. "What a wicked old fellow too! Come on girls, and have a look!" Unqoute. There's your statement and mine. Thank you for listening to my argument. (page 82)

I still like to think he got well. As for Geri, I wrote and enjoined her to save her allowance up and buy this book. The world can't be such a bad place to live in as long as there are eleven-year-old girls in it to put us straight.

CHAPTER FOUR

RASCALS AT LARGE

*"I have reason to believe
that one of the biggest
groups in crime is operating
under our very noses,"* he
burst forth.

*"You mean right here in
Bayport, Dad?"* Joe ex-
claimed.

(*The Clue of the Broken
Blade:* a Hardy Boys
Mystery.)

If reading maketh a full boy, I was as *farci* as any Christmas turkey by the time I was fourteen years old. There was a myth prevalent at that time that the junior male population could be divided into two categories, "outdoor" boys and "indoor" boys. The outdoor species were red-blooded young American activists, typified by Mickey Rooney or Jackie Cooper. The indoor ones were generally depicted as thin, stoop-shouldered, sallow little toadies with prescription eyeglasses. They were sissies and crybabies. They always got good marks in school, and they read a lot.

There wasn't a word of truth in it. My own peer group, careening into puberty at a time when Lou Gehrig and Babe Ruth were at the apexes of their careers, numbered among its members some of the great sports fans of history. There were still empty lots in the New York City limits then, and the arrival of the vernal equinox saw winter dreams give way to baseball, bicycles, tree-climbing, and the endless quest for active physical mischief of all kinds. We spent as many winter evenings rubbing linseed oil into fielder's mitts as we did in literary pursuits, and there was plenty of time for both.

Whatever the season, when night fell, we read hungrily and omnivorously, hauling home armfuls of library books and saving our scanty allowances for magazines; *G-8 and His Battle Aces, Weird Tales, Blue Book,* and many more. Although none of us had ever been farther from home than Rockaway Beach, we read hunting and fishing magazines from cover to cover, hotly debating the merits of the sleek, deadly rifles advertised in them. We read *Argosy* and *True,* and pored over the colorful, seductive maps and photographs in *National Geographic.*

We sank our money into boys series books, Tarzan, the Hardy Boys, Jerry Todd, Poppy Ott, Don Sturdy, the X Bar X Boys, and all their fascinating contemporaries. Our parents tried to wean us away from these, and from the Street & Smith magazines ("trash") by subtly subjecting us to a strategic bombardment of approved literature, which we found to our amazement to be bearable and even enjoyable. *She* and *King Solomon's Mines, Kim, The White Company, Ivanhoe, Treasure Island, The Three Musketeers,* an endless parade of them were introduced into our lives to keep us in a constant state of euphoric make-believe. Best of all, books were cheap. They made the selection of birthday and Christmas presents simple and painless for our harassed parents, who cooperated heartily.

For people like my family and the families of my friends the Dow-Jones Average was always low. It was always tight money at our house, and so the Depression did not affect my small corner of the family very much. I was faced with decisions such as the relinquishing of newspaper subscriptions (we always took the *Graphic,* the *World* and the *Journal*). I followed the comics religiously and it was hard to sacrifice Captain Easy in favor of Tailspin Tommy, but I did it manfully. Occasionally my parents would indulge in a histrionic display that would not have been out of place in a Japanese movie, on the general theme of where the next meal was coming from, but somehow it always came, and somehow it was always an excellent one. The threatened spectre of my father selling unemployed apples never did come into being, and there was always money for a book for me.

It was during a period of winter inactivity when I was suffering one of my literary bereavements—the death of Sherlock Holmes, the last book in the Tarzan series, or something of the sort—that I came across the Hardy Boys. At that time I had never heard of Nancy Drew (and would not have admitted it if I had) but the boys were more or less counterparts of Nancy's in the teen-ager *qua* detective school of children's literature. They solved mysteries, discomfited bullies, beat up grown criminals, carried firearms, rode motorcycles, camped out, and did as a matter of course almost everything that was forbidden to me and my friends. I asked my mother for money for *The Tower Treasure,* and as soon as I had finished it, for *The House on the Cliff.* Covertly glancing at the inside cover to determine that even then there were more than twenty titles in the series, she sighed her well-known sigh and went to get her pocketbook. I was off on another one. What next?

The early Hardy Boys were written, as I was not to find out until many years later, by the redoubtable Edward Stratemeyer, the uncontested champion of children's series writers, using the pseudonym Franklin W. Dixon. Stratemeyer was a Newark stationer with literary longings who wrote his first story on wrapping paper during a business lull. He was twenty-six at the time. It was 1886, and he sold his story to a shrewd publisher for $75. After that it was good-bye to the stationery store for him. He had started on a career that made his name a household word to kids all over the world—or would have if he had not used more than sixty pseudonyms through the years until his death in 1930.

Stratemeyer thought them up faster than he could write them, and had to form a syndicate and employ contract writers to help him, as Alexandre Dumas had done two generations earlier. Before he died he turned out 800 books, all of which he plotted, outlined and edited himself. They made him a rich man. When he died, his stricken publishers prevailed on his daughters to carry on the syndicate, and a Stratemeyer daughter (Mrs. Harriet S. Adams) is carrying on to this day along with her business partner, Andrew E. Svenson, turning out Bobbseys, Hardy Boys, Nancy Drews, and dozens of others for new generations and generations yet to come.

A shrewd businessman as well as a man with sensitive insight into children's reading needs and wants, Stratemeyer chose his subjects well. Who else would have announced a new thriller for boys entitled *Under Dewey at Manila* soon after Dewey's victory? His plots followed closely the heroes and major events of the period. His pseudonyms were also carefully chosen. For example, "Arthur M. Winfield" (the Rover Boys) was selected because (Stratemeyer said) the books were going to "win the field" in sales. And what did the "M" stand for? The "M" was for million, the author assured his interviewers.

A few of his triumphs are worthy of mention here. As "Victor Appleton" he wrote the Tom Swift series, Don Sturdy, the Moving Picture Boys, and the Movie Boys. ("Victor Appleton II" was to appear after his death to carry on with Tom Swift, Jr.) He was both "Horatio Alger, Jr." and "Oliver Optic," competitors who attacked the rags-to-riches market after the real Alger and Optic died. As "Lester Chadwick" he created Baseball Joe. As "James Cody Ferris" he wrote the X Bar X Boys' experiences out West and as "Lt. Howard Payson" he brought the Boy Scouts series into being. Under the name of "Roy Rockwood" he created Bomba the Jungle Boy, the Speedwell Boys, and the Great Marvel Series (*Under the Ocean to the South Pole, Five Thousand Miles Underground* and others). In the guise of "Franklin W. Dixon" he wrote the Hardy Boys and the Ted Scott flying stories.

Not one to overlook the lucrative female reading public, he tried his hand at girls' books with great success. He was "Annie Roe Carr" (the Nan Sherwood series) and "Laura Lee Hope" (the Bobbsey Twins, Bunny Brown and His Sister Sue, the Blythe Girls, the Moving Picture Girls, the Outdoor Girls, and the Six Little Bunkers). As "Margaret Penrose" he wrote the Motor Girls series, and as "Helen Louise Thorndike" created Honey Bunch. He was "Grace Brooks Hill" (The Corner House Girls), "Alice B. Emerson" (Betty Gordon, Ruth Fielding), "Mabel C. Hawley" (The Four Little Blossoms), "Carolyn Keene" (Nancy Drew), and many more.

The Hardy Boys were in their teens at the start of the series. Frank was sixteen, with dark, straight hair, and his brother Joe was a year younger, pink-cheeked with blond curly locks. Joe's eyes were blue and Frank's dark, and both had "firm, good-humored expressions of the mouth." Frank, moreover, had a "clever, good-natured face" although no such claim is made for Joe in any of the books.

The brothers were always on excellent terms with each other, and their teamwork in solving mysteries was well coordinated. No sibling rivalry there. They lived in suburban Bayport, a thriving metropolis of 50,000 souls that rivaled Virginia City or East St. Louis as a lodestone for criminal activities of all kinds. Never were so many assorted felonies committed in a simple American small town. Murder, drug peddling, race horse kidnaping, diamond smuggling, medical malpractice, big-time auto theft, and even (in the 1940s) the hijacking of strategic materials and espionage, all were conducted with Bayport as a nucleus.

The town (which had the worst weather in modern literary history—every mystery reached its climax in a thunderstorm) was on the Atlantic coast, close enough to New York for easy access. It was located on a sheltered bay about three miles inland, and surrounded by cliffs which were liberally riddled with caves that figured importantly in every book. The caves served as criminal hideaways, headquarters and storerooms, often overlapping from book to book, so that the diamond smugglers were able to use the same cave that the car theft ring had used after the latter had been unmasked and jailed by the Hardys.

In 1927 Dr. Sigmund Freud, six years older than Stratemeyer, was practicing in Vienna. It is unlikely that the two men ever met, but the author of the Hardy series understood the fascination that caves have for boys, and used it with his usual lavish hand. The Bayport caves were reached by long, narrow tunnels through which Frank and Joe could crawl unnoticed and eavesdrop on the nefarious plans of their criminal enemies. In a number of the books the caves had entrances (or exits) in innocent-looking buildings, where they were disguised as bookshelves or storage cupboards. Joe (or Frank), about to give up, would lean wearily against a shelf, and a section of wall would swing slowly forward revealing the yawning mouth of yet another tunnel to adventure.

On several occasions, the boys traveled far from good old Bayport—to Mexico and once to the Deep South— but the inevitable caves were there too, for the boys to crawl, eavesdrop, and get captured, bound and gagged in, with the usual hairsbreadth escape.

The Hardy family lived in a large, well-appointed but not luxurious frame house. They kept no servants, but there was plenty of yard and a roomy two-story garage in which Frank and Joe were able to maintain a home-made modern crime laboratory. (This facility was later moved to the cellar for security reasons.) The boys were the sons of the nationally celebrated Fenton Hardy, who had served many years on the New York City police force, and had retired to Bayport to begin a highly successful career as a private detective at the age of forty. Mr. Hardy was tall, with graying hair, keen blue eyes, and a shrewd, clean-cut face. He wore neatly pressed tweeds, and was inordinately proud of his boys. By the third book of the series (*The Shore Road Mystery*) he was regarded as "one of the greatest American criminologists," and numbered among his clients millionaires, generals, high government officials, and notables of all kinds, none of whom seemed at all dismayed when the busy detective handed their cases over to his fifteen- and sixteen-year-old aides.

At first Mr. and Mrs. Hardy wanted Joe and Frank to study law and medicine, but after the boys had displayed their detecting skills and earned several handsome rewards the family relented and the boys were permitted to follow in their father's footsteps.

An example of the astounding deductive powers that brought Fenton Hardy to the top of his profession is revealed in *The Tower Treasure*. Referring to a certain Mr. Norton who taught at the Bayport High School, he told the boys:

> "As a matter of fact, Mr. Norton is bald and he wears a chestnut wig. You never noticed that? He belongs to the Elks, and his favorite author is Dickens."
>
> The boys looked at their father in amazement.
>
> "But Dad, you've never met him."

"I've never been introduced to him, but I've passed him in the street a number of times. When your powers of observation have been trained as mine have been, it's no trick at all to take away a mental photograph of a man after seeing him once. If you are specially observant it isn't hard to notice such details as that regarding the wig. A wig never has the same appearance as natural hair."

"But how do you know he belongs to the Elks?" asked Joe.

"He wears the lodge emblem as a watch chain."

"And how do you know his favorite author is Dickens?"

"On three separate occasions that I met Mr. Norton I noticed that he was carrying a book. Once it was *Oliver Twist*. Another time it was *A Tale of Two Cities*. The third time it was *David Copperfield*. So I judge that his favorite author must be Dickens. Am I right?"

"He always talks Dickens to us at school," said Frank.

"It's simple enough once you get the habit," remarked Mr. Hardy.

(*The Tower Treasure, p. 36*)

And get the habit they did, for the boys were not far behind their famous father in deductive powers. Following a suspect to his quarters, they were forced to admit their error and give him a clean bill of health when he reached his destination.

Frank and Joe exchanged glances. It was scarcely likely they realized, that a crook would belong to the YMCA . . .

(*What Happened at Midnight, p. 166*)

Deductive reasoning was not Fenton Hardy's only qualification, as the following circus vignette will prove:

"Hey fellas! Buy a balloon! Only a nickel!"

"We don't want a balloon!" replied Frank with an

emphatic gesture, but when he endeavored to push past the man the latter blocked his way.

"It looks as if we'll have to call out the Reserves to get rid of this fellow," said Joe under his breath. "If you don't mind," he added aloud, "we aren't the least bit interested in your balloons."

"No?" The vendor's face bore a hurt expression. "You no likea my balloon? You no wanta buy for some poor leetle kiddie? Look, I show you something special!"

Despite the boys' irritation their curiosity got the better of them. The man had transferred his string of toys to one hand while he fumbled in a torn pocket with another. As Frank and Joe watched mystified, the vendor drew forth a crumpled sheet of paper which he held toward them.

"What's this?" snorted Joe, staring at the man.

Suddenly his jaw dropped. He started to utter an exclamation but caught himself and reached for the paper.

"Come on, Frank," he whispered, pulling his astonished brother through the crowd and off to one side. "Didn't you recognize him? What a disguise. Why even mother wouldn't have known Dad!"

(The Clue of the Broken Blade, p. 169)

Whether or not Mother would have known him is hard to say, since the reader was never allowed to get close enough to the elusive Mrs. Hardy to find out anything about her at all, except that she had the ability to turn out hearty, delicious meals at the drop of a hat. She was probably in her thirties, but she is never described, and she must have been as much a master of disguise as her distinguished husband, since we find him addressing her as "Laura" in the early books, and as "Mildred" in the later ones. Whether this was the same Mrs. Hardy or whether a divorce and remarriage had taken place is never revealed. In any event, if it was a different Mrs.

Hardy, she loved the boys as much and her skills in the kitchen never faltered.

The remaining member of the family was Aunt Gertrude, an eccentric old lady who

> was one of the pepperiest and most dictatorial old women who ever visited a quiet household. She was a rawboned female of sixty-five, tall and commanding, with a determined jaw, an acid tongue and an eye that could quell a traffic cop. She was as authoritarian as a prison guard, bossed everything and everybody within reach, and had a lofty contempt for men in general and boys in particular . . . Underneath this rough exterior was a kindly heart. Her bark was worse than her bite. Joe always said she looked as though her clothes had been chosen by a color-blind saleslady and put on her by a cross-eyed maid with only one arm.
>
> *(What Happened at Midnight, p. 57)*

This strange relative spent her time dropping in on her kinfolk for visits of indeterminate length, and her brother Fenton and his family had their share. And didn't the boys brush their hair and mind their manners when the old lady was around! In several of their cases she was able to help them by applying feminine intuition to a knotty problem, and she made the best cookies on the Eastern Seaboard.

The Hardys were rarely alone in solving their mysteries, even when Fenton and Aunt Gertrude Hardy were not available. A gregarious pair, they had numerous chums their own age who always seemed to be free to make one of the zigzag, high-speed Odysseys that were essential to mystery-solving in the environs of Bayport. Their set included an ethnic mixed bag worthy of the World War II cinema. There were WASP American farm boy Chet

Morton, stout-hearted Phil Cohen, dark, curly-haired Tony Prito, and Biff Hooper in major roles, and a few others in less prominent ones.

There seemed to be a notable lack of Negroes; and Irish Catholics were used only for comedy in those days. The books have all been rewritten now, and reissued in smart, colorful, washable plastic covers, and it can only be hoped that the Hardys have annexed a black chum or two in recent years. The villainous Felix Polucca of *The House on the Cliff* in his 1927 edition has had his name changed to Pollitt in the revised edition, and Frank's remark "I have a sort of hunch that there's a nigger in the wood pile" has become "The boys felt uneasy."

According to Andrew E. Svenson, Stratemeyer partner in charge of revising the series, today's readers will miss the old gunplay of yore, the horseplay and the snide remarks about dumb cops. Now the Hardys respect the police, eschew sidearms in favor of judo, and never make minority groups the butt of jokes. All of the early books have been rewritten. In many cases an entirely new mystery appears under an old title. *The Flickering Torch Mystery* is now about an isotope theft ring at Kennedy Airport and a rock group. *The Clue of the Broken Blade* is now about fencing and voiceprint techniques. *The Mystery of the Flying Express* now deals with hydrofoils and astrology. Aunt Gertrude now appears as a modern woman in her forties but she has, alas, lost much of her pepper.

Principal among the Hardy chums was Chet Morton, who served as the comedy relief for the series. Chet is described as a "fat-cheeked roly-poly youth," and he was possessed of a huge appetite and a vast capacity for trouble of all kinds. Everything happened to Chet. If he took a picture with his new camera, he was certain to

step backward right over a cliff. When he sat in a rocking
chair, it tipped over. An attempt to put a dead fish in Joe's
desk at school resulted in his being caught by the teacher
and made to stay after school. When he bought firecrackers
for the Fourth of July, they exploded prematurely, scaring
the daylights out of a Bayport policeman. On several
occasions Chet's proverbial bad luck got him into more
serious trouble. He was arrested (falsely) for a movie box
office robbery because a wounded and delirious accom-
plice of the real robber kept mumbling that his colleague's name was Chet. On another occasion, when the
boys were off to solve a mystery in Mexico, Chet was
denied a passport temporarily because a fugitive felon
with numerous offenses just happened to be named Chet
Morton.

These trials did nothing to dampen Chet's good spirits
and justly celebrated reputation as a boy humorist. No
matter what his situation, Chet could always be depended
on to come up with a humdinger. A few examples of his
humor are worth repeating here.

> The lads could see a faint winding path leading up the
> side of the hill back of the cottage.
> "I know what they call this place," said Chet gravely.
> "I don't think it has a name," said Biff.
> "Oh yes, they call this place Fish-hook."
> "Fish-hook? Why?" asked Biff, neatly falling into the
> trap.
> "Because it's at the end of the line."
>
> (*The Secret of the Caves, 1929, p. 66*)

The Hardys laughed so hard at Biff's discomfiture that
they had to stop their motorcycles. Another Chet Morton
sally referred to an eccentric spinster, one Miss Applegate,
who, he declared, "used to be a blonde, but she dyed."

On another occasion, when he was tardy in attending a meeting with the boy detectives:

> "You'd be late for your own hanging, Chet Morton," said Frank.
> "Then they'll just have to wait. I'd like to see them hold it without me," grinned Chet.

(op. cit., p. 79)

Biff Hooper was the biggest of the chums, strong, athletic, and slow. He was, of course, the natural foil for Chet's humor, but slow or not, Biff was not stupid, and when the chums were graduated from Bayport High in 1930 (*The Great Airport Mystery*) it was Biff who was chosen to deliver a recitation. Tony Prito rendered an accordion solo. A girl (wouldn't you know) was class valedictorian, and the Hardys and Chet were lumped together in a skit. Academic honors were not for the boy detectives, but they didn't care. They were satisfied (as their father put it) to "use their heads for something more than to hang their hats on."

Tony Prito and Phil Cohen, who were "noted at school for their fearless, at times even reckless, dispositions" were practically interchangeable, with Tony slightly more in evidence than Phil. Tony had a starring role in one book (*The Clue in the Embers*, 1955) in which he inherited a curio collection which was promptly stolen by sneak thieves, but Phil remains in the background in the series, content to be mentioned from time to time. He is never described, although Tony is revealed as having "dark hair, olive skin, and sparkling eyes" which "indicated his Italian parentage even more emphatically than his name."

No mention of chums would be complete without a mention of Callie Shaw and Iola Morton, Frank and Joe's special girl friends. Callie, brown-eyed and brown-haired, was "an object of special enthusiasm for Frank," while Iola (Chet's sister) was "all right as a girl in Joe's opinion." In 1927 (*The House on the Cliff*) Iola is described as a plump, dark girl, but by 1950 (*The Secret of the Lost Tunnel*) she has become "slender and good-looking," presumably after twenty-three years of low-calorie meals.

The boys had a hearty, comradely relationship with Callie and Iola (it was Callie, incidentally, who was class valedictorian, and "won the hearts of all by her valedictory address") which included ice-cream soda dates, dancing to phonograph records, parties, and picnics for which the girls prepared the food. There was never any physical contact between them, and certainly no kissing, spooning, lollygagging or similar foolishness. During one group picnic, when Callie and Frank had gone for a walk in the woods and their classmates heard Callie scream, no one suspected for a moment that Frank had been guilty of attempting to steal second base. Everyone knew instinctively that the boy sleuth had been abducted by a pair of red-hots, bundled into the boot of their speedy roadster, and carried off in the direction of the Shore Road caves.

Let's eavesdrop on the conversation that soared over the ice-cream sodas at one of the foursome's rendezvous in the Bon Ton, Bayport's most exclusive pharmacy:

"I wish I were a boy," sighed Callie Shaw.

Iola Morton looked up from her ice-cream soda. "Me too."

"It's tough luck that you're not," said Joe Hardy. "We'd like to have you along on the trip with us."

"Boys have all the luck. Girls have to stay at home."

(*The Secret of the Caves, p. 43*)

But whether they had to stay at home or not, the girls were always loyal throughout the forty-odd years of the series. They, or at least their recognition and admiration, were a part of the handsome rewards the young heroes received at the end of each adventure. For example, there was the incident when the town bullies, Ted Carson and Ike Nash, attempted to injure the Hardys' homemade ice boat and succeeded in smashing their own boat and placing themselves in a perilous position from which Joe and Frank had to rescue them. Callie said:

"If that Ike Nash or Ted Carson ever dare speak to me again, I'll go past them with my nose in the air. Won't you, Iola?"

"I certainly will. And I'm going to tell the other girls about it too. I think it was mean of them, and I'm glad their old boat got smashed."

"Oh, I guess they've suffered enough," said Frank. "No use rubbing it in."

"If they had smashed your boat they would have told the story all over Bayport. I'm certainly glad it turned out the way it did," said Callie.

"Drat that Chet!" muttered Frank, after the girls had gone on down the street. "Why can't he keep quiet? He'll be making me out a hero if he keeps up. I didn't want anything said about that affair."

"Well only two girls know about it now," returned Joe comfortingly.

"*Only* two girls!" snorted Frank. "He might as well have published it in the newspaper."

(*The Mystery of Cabin Island, 1929; p. 19*)

But the usual post-mystery dialogue that kept the boys going and sped them on their way into danger and glory again in each volume, ran more like this excerpt from *The Shore Road Mystery:*

CALLIE: Oh I think Frank and Joe are too wonderful for anything!

IOLA: I never thought Joe could be so brave!

PAULA ROBINSON: They sure are a pair of heroes!

TESSIE ROBINSON: I really think they ought to be in a book!

What more could a boy want?

One of the boys' most outstanding characteristics was high-speed mobility. In the first books the Hardys and their chums all had motorcycles, on which they tore in and out of Bayport and the nearby villages, seemingly without arousing the local populace. In those days a teen-ager on a motorcycle was the norm rather than an object of community terror. They were, if truth be told, a juvenile motorcycle gang, although not the first one to appear in boys' books. Stratemeyer had preceded himself (in his guise of Roy Rockwood) with the Speedwell Boys, and (as Andrew Carey Lincoln) the Motorcycle Chums, both pre-World War I, and both very similar to the Hardys. The Motorcycle Chums even had a fat, food-oriented, comical chum to accompany them on their speedy excursions.

Soon after the beginning of the series, the boys put their motorcycles aside in favor of a sleek (but not too dependable) convertible, which they had used in 1928 to trap the members of an automobile burglary ring. The car served them well until 1943, when World War II gasoline rationing had them reduced to bicycles for the duration.

With the reward from one of their first mysteries, Joe and Frank had invested in the *Sleuth*, the fastest motorboat in the Bayport area. They spent a great deal of time afloat, roaring up and down the cave-ridden coast, rescuing drowning women and children (they never embarked without a rescue in the offing somewhere) and nearly losing their lives in Bayport's numerous thunderstorms. As soon as the *Sleuth* appeared, it seemed to stimulate local bullies (who had their own motorboats) to try to run the Hardys down and ruin their boat. They always failed, ending up in the bay amid the splinters of their own ill-fated craft. The Hardys, gentlemen always, would fish the miscreants out and set them ashore with stern admonition to avoid dangerous violence in the future. The same fate seemed to attach itself to their homemade ice boat, the *Sleuth*'s winter replacement, which attracted homicidal maniacs as frequently as its summer counterpart.

When they weren't manning their own vehicles, the boys still traveled fast, and by the early 1930s they had discovered airplanes, making one of the first parachute jumps in boys' literature (*What Happened at Midnight*). Whatever the vehicle, no book ever ended without a smash-up. Motorcycles went off the road, over cliffs, into trees. Cars skidded and spun. Boats rammed other boats. Airplanes sputtered, stalled, and headed for forced landings in wild country. Thrills and more thrills, but the boys (shaken up, knocked about and bruised) always came out in shape for the next chapter.

Lack of official status was the only handicap that prevented the young detectives from functioning with total efficiency, and they frequently tangled with obtuse small-town cops who imagined that their breathless requests for emergency action were boyish practical jokes. After the series was well under way, and newspaper publicity had made the boys famous in and around the Bayport area, it was easier for them to commandeer official help. The Bayport Police Department consisted at first of fat, stupid, nervous Chief Collig, Traffic Officer Riley, another dolt, and Detective Smuff, slow, but friendly. The whole department smarted at being outwitted by the teen-age detectives time and again. The local cops felt that the Hardys' success in mystery solving was due almost entirely to luck. On one occasion, Smuff remarked (re: the Hardys):

> More amatoors (he sighed). What chance has a regular officer on a case like this when everybody else in town is puttin' their oar in?

As the years progressed the police force expanded, and by 1955 Chief Collig was able to field large-scale dragnets and surveillance operations whenever the boys asked for them. Described in 1930 as a "fussy little man with a vast sense of dignity", he had become "fat, genial Chief Collig" by 1955, after having unaccountably been replaced by "fat, genial Chief Finch" in 1941. Today this description has been replaced by a more timely image. Collig is now a keen-eyed vigorous man with iron gray hair, and a veteran of many battles with Bayport's criminal elements.

A typical Hardy case began in one of two ways. Either Fenton Hardy, too busy with other work to pursue a new and urgent assignment, passed it to the boys, or Joe and Frank spotted a suspicious character in Bayport's streets and followed him right smack into the middle of a new mystery. In either event, the action usually began with a warning, phoned, mailed, or tossed through a window of the Hardy domicile by a person or persons unknown. In *The Secret Warning* (1938) it was simply a scribbled "Leave town at once or there'll be trouble." In *The Secret of the Lost Tunnel* (1950) the crook was a little more formal:

Hardy Boys:

Clear out and go back to Bayport if you want to stay healthy. Kids who don't mind their own business end up in the graveyard. If Smith finds the gold, he can't claim it regardless.

(p. 153)

Or en route to Mexico: (*The Mark on the Door* 1937):

To Senor Fenton Hardy, Private Detective from the United States: This is to warn you and your sons that you must not set foot upon Mexican soil. If you disregard this warning, there will be but one penalty, and that penalty will be—Death!

(p. 44)

Or this one from *The Flickering Torch Mystery* (1943):

YOU TWO HARDY BOYS THINK YOU ARE PRETTY SMART BUT YOU AREN'T FOOLING ANYBODY. IF YOU DON'T MIND YOUR OWN BUSINESS YOU ARE GOING TO GET HURT. SO LAY OFF THE GRABLE CASE. I MEAN THIS. LAY OFF. STAY AWAY FROM THE GREENHOUSES AND GO BACK TO BAYPORT WHERE YOU BELONG.

(p. 102)

The Hardys, of course, were not to be frightened by this kind of fiddle-faddle. They launched into phase two without batting an eye. This usually consisted of some kind of fortuitous coincidence. They met someone on the street who looked like a crook, they overheard two men talking about a crime in a restaurant booth, or some similar evasion. Once a suspect was spotted, they followed him right to the gang's headquarters, and then moved into phase three, trouble.

A favorite device for starting things off was telephone exposition. Sighting a suspicious-looking fellow with little close-set eyes, the boys sneak up on him as he telephones a colleague and blows the whole caper. Here is a phone conversation on which Joe and Frank eavesdropped after secreting themselves in a candy store whose proprietor had criminal features:

"What's that?" the proprietor hissed into the telephone. "Does anyone suspect *me?* The police? No! Everyone thinks just what I want them to think—that this is a candy store and I am the dumb shopkeeper. Hah!"

They (Frank and Joe) could hear a sharp *crack* as Hinchman slapped his thigh in an explosion of laughter. Then came a long silence, finally followed by the man's voice again.

"Yes, it's too bad you didn't get away with the Liberty Company boxes, Gordon, but never mind. Next time we'll do better. So long as nobody knows this little candy store is the headquarters for our trucking business! Ha, some joke, eh? Listen, Gordon, I'll tell you something . . ."

The boys exchanged triumphant looks as Hinchman's voice sank to an inaudible whisper . . .

(*The Clue of the Broken Blade, p. 35*)

Now the boys are sure they have found the true criminals, but who will believe them. *Prima facie* evidence is needed, and throwing caution to the winds, they follow the miscreants a little too closely. A favorite surveillance method of theirs is for Joe (or Frank) to lock himself in the trunk of the felons' car.

During their pursuit, a number of extraneous dangers threaten them, and no one, even Nancy Drew, was ever so accident prone as Joe Hardy. In *The Clue of the Broken Blade* Joe is knocked down and hospitalized by a speeding fire truck. In *The Secret Warning* he faces death, and is once again hospitalized by a firebomb explosion in a dry-cleaning establishment. Cattle almost stampede him to death in Texas in *The Mark on the Door*. A drunken pilot buzzes his car off the road in *The Great Airport Mystery*. He falls out of a second-story hotel window in *A Figure in Hiding*, and goes right through a glass canopy, staggering off with superficial cuts. There are car, boat, and motorcycle crashes. In other books Joe is attacked by a giant octopus while deep-sea diving, and drinks water from a poisoned cactus. None of these perils ever seems to affect Frank, who stands by, powerless to do anything except check on hospital visiting hours, and report the latest bloodshed to their father.

There is deliberate mayhem too. The boys are shot at, blinded with a water pistol full of ammonia, and left bound and gagged to starve in caves. An attempt is made to electrocute them by thugs who leave a rifle in the grass after connecting it to a power line. The lifeline on Joe's diving suit is cut. Somehow they always bounce back in good shape for the next rough-and-tumble.

Unlike the Nancy Drew books and other juvenile detective series, the Hardy books had plenty of violence. The boys often carried pistols, and people (always criminals) were shot and killed or wounded. On one occasion the boys dug up a mouldering corpse and then reburied it. There are plenty of heads bashed, jaws punched, and teeth rattled. Frank and Joe, for all their tender years, were always able to overcome full-grown men, because both were adept at the manly art of boxing, and both recognized the superiority of science over brute strength. Time and again, dodging ponderous, heavy blows from some bull-necked hoodlum, Frank (or Joe) darts in with fancy footwork and plants a scientific left hook that leaves his opponent *hors de combat* for at least fifteen minutes.

Phase four in the books is capture. After peril and mayhem, the boys overstep the bounds of good sense and tumble right into the hands of their enemies.

"It's them! The very same pair of spyin' brats." A rough hand seized Frank's shoulder and swung him around. "I'd know them anywhere. Fenton Hardy's kids."

The name of Fenton Hardy made a distinct impression on the gang. There were mutterings of anger and fear.

"The detective's boys, eh?" growled one. "What are you doin' here, boys?"

"That's for you to find out," replied Frank, shortly.

"Is that so? Well you've got no business here. You know that, don't you?"

"Your own business here doesn't seem any too lawful."

"Never mind about us. You come spyin' around here and you've got to take the consequences. What'll we do with 'em, Gus?"

"They're not goin' out of here, that's certain. We're not goin' to let them go back home and tell what they've seen."

"Or what they heard. How long were you two boys hidin' in that tunnel?"

"You can try to find that out too," retorted Frank.

"Smart, aren't you?" snarled Montrose. "You won't be so smart when we get through with you. Anybody got a rope?"

(*The Shore Road Mystery, p. 174*)

Somebody did, and the boys were trussed up to wait for the end, and, of course, rescued in the nick of time by their chums.

In Mexico, Frank and Joe faced torture as well as death at the hands of the cruel Pedro Vincenzo.

"Remember, if you try to escape it will be that much worse for you. I'll turn you over to the natives in charge of the Ceremonial of the Fire. Do you know what that will mean?"

His face was ugly with malice and cruelty.

"Don't take a chance on being branded with the mark of the P and the fire!" warned Vincenzo. "You wouldn't want to go back to your friends in Bayport with that sort of decoration on your foreheads. Besides, it's said to be very painful."

"We're not afraid of your threats," Joe answered.

"Brave boys!" jeered Vincenzo. "You're not so clever now, are you? And you won't think your father is so clever either, when he is thrown in here to keep you company."

"Our father is worth twenty of you."

(*The Mark on the Door*, p. *174*)

That Pedro Vincenzo was a man of his word was brought home to the Hardys soon after by the arrival of lovely Pepita, who brings them their rations. She bore the fearful brand right in the middle of her forehead. When Frank questioned her about it, Pepita "a dark-skinned gypsy-like young creature with big eyes"

. . . did not understand. Frank leaned forward and lightly touched the branded symbol. A look of terror crossed her face. She glanced over her shoulder as if fearful of being overheard.

"Eet was Pedro," she whispered.

"He branded you!" Joe exclaimed in horror.

"Pedro—not please wit' me," she answered.

"He branded you because he was angry with you?" Joe asked.

The girl nodded her head vigorously.

"So that's the sort of fellow Pedro Vincenzo is," muttered Frank indignantly.

(ibid., p. 190)

But once again, rescue, abetted by Fenton Hardy and several mounted companies of *federales,* intruded on Pedro Vincenzo's nefarious plans, and Joe and Frank, luckier than the flawed Pepita, returned unbranded to Bayport. As always, Frank had to have the last word.

> "I see the game is up," he [Vincenzo] said bitterly. "But if it hadn't been for those American boys I'd have had my revenge on you, Macheta."
>
> "Thanks to the Hardys," replied the Mexican gentleman with dignity, "my family will now know peace and security."
>
> ". . . We didn't do it for money," said Frank. "We had a million dollars worth of adventure out of it."

(ibid., p. 217)

But they accepted the money anyway, for how else do detectives live? And so the final phase of each book began with escape and retribution, punctuated by whines and muttered invective from sniveling felons, and ended with a reward—five hundred dollars, two hundred dollars, a gold watch and chain, a movie camera, the usufruct of a vacation island in the bay, a new vehicle of some kind. No adventure ever ended for Frank and Joe without cash profit and a pat on the back.

> "Boys," said Fenton Hardy in the living room of their home the night of his sons' return, "you've done your best job yet! That's one of the most exciting stories I ever listened to, and I've been in the detective game all my life!"

"*Too* exciting, I think." Their mother shivered. "I hope you boys will decide to stay home now and lead a peaceful life for a change!"

Joe looked at Frank with a sly smile. His brother winked back.

(*The Secret Warning, p. 220*)

Peaceful life indeed! Fat chance! We readers knew (and if we hadn't known Mr. Stratemeyer would have told us—he always advertised the next book in each series at the end of the last one) that the young sleuths were already planning their next battle against crime. In all probability a warning note had been tucked into the mailbox, even as Mrs. Hardy sat simpering. Rascals were at large, and the Hardys would fight on until the very last criminal was behind bars. The old readers are grown up and scattered now, and Stratemeyer has gone to whatever special Heaven exists for people who make children happy, but the boy detectives go on thrilling new generations, rewritten, brought "up to date," but still fearlessly making their dad proud of them.

CHAPTER FIVE

PERIL: THE MOTHER OF INVENTION

> "What do I care for prin-
> ciples of science?" cried
> Tom . . ." Some of the sci-
> entists said it was totally
> opposed to all natural laws
> when I planned my electric
> rifle. But I made it, and it
> shot. They said my air glider
> would never stay up, but she
> did."
> "But Tom, this is different.
> You are talking of sending
> light waves—one of the most
> delicate forms of motion in
> the world—over a material
> wire. It can't be done!
>
> (Tom Swift and his
> Photo-Telephone)

In my day boys were supposed to be conversant with and fascinated by mechanical and electrical devices of every kind. Given half an hour, a few ells of copper wire, and some complicated and mysterious-looking metal parts, any normal twelve-year-old was expected to be able to construct a workable radio with the same speed and expertise that American GIs were to display a generation later in building shower baths out of coconut shells and bamboo. The arcana of automobile engine repair were thought to be the dearest hobby of every red-blooded pre-teen.

The theory that mechanical genius was endemic to my contemporaries was supported by the giant intellects of Hollywood, who celebrated the abilities of any given group of urchins to build a serviceable tree house using only shirt cardboards and Scotch tape. How many broken collarbones can be attributed to those departed movie moguls?

All these talents were said to be latent in the male offspring at birth, to blossom like secondary sex characteristics, along with incipient whiskers and a changing voice. It was, alas, another myth. In our crowd there was one kid who bought a Model A Ford at sixteen, and was able, so they said, to cope with its simpler crotchets, like flat tires. Another kid knew how to develop his own photographs. The rest of us subsided into slack-jawed idiocy at the sight of anything more complicated than a roller skate.

I was presented with the usual equipment boys were supposed to pine for at Christmas and birthdays. There were Erector sets, tool kits, junior chemistry laboratories, and build-it-yourself devices of all kinds. I enjoyed them in a passive way. They filled in rainy afternoons when baseball was impossible. They bridged the gaps that occurred when I had outpaced the writers of the Stratemeyer Syndicate, but they always held a low priority. Sports and books came first, and sometimes even daydreaming.

My initial trauma with respect to the mysteries of science centered around our first radio, a huge console from which we gleaned many hours of enjoyment from the Horn & Hardart Children's Hour and Major Bowes's amateurs. I rapidly became addicted to Buck Rogers and Chandu the Magician, and sat soberly with my parents to drink in Eddie Cantor's little sermons. We chortled over Fred Allen, Phil Baker, and Colonel Stoopnagle and Budd. The set became a part of our lives, but it knew its place and never tried to take over, as television was to do in later years. It allowed itself to be turned off when it wasn't wanted, very much like a beloved old dog, goodnaturedly complying with an order to get off the couch.

Our radio was powered by a wet cell (a lot of American consumers' houses still weren't wired for electricity). This battery was a massive, threatening black box bursting with corrosive acid and deadly volts which (I was told) could reduce a small boy to a smoldering crisp. "Don't touch!" my mother said, punctuating her injunction with the traditional *commedia del'arte* finger and eyebrow business that always accompanied such strictures.

The cell was concealed behind our living-room sofa, and since the mysterious world underneath large pieces of furniture was a favorite domain of mine, it played an important role in my solitary games. It sat there, ugly and squat, ready to rain destruction like an anarchist's bomb. I never did touch it, and one day it vanished with the arrival of an Atwater Kent that plugged into the wall, but I never forgot it. To this day I always shrink a little when I turn on a radio. As for repairing one—not me; and I don't even like to think about what goes on inside a television set.

Mechanical inability and fear on the part of my contemporaries did not keep us from developing a lively interest in the literature of boys and machines. We never missed an issue of *Popular Science, Popular Mechanics,* and other scholarly journals of the period. You could build a speedboat in your own cellar! You could surprise your mom and dad by turning their bedroom into a vasty balanced aquarium, complete with indirect lights and oxygen pumps! Just around the corner was a happy world in which everyone would own a car that would take off and fly when the traffic was heavy. People would harness cosmic rays (whatever they were). Telephones would let you see the people you were talking to. Space ships would land on Mars, to discover strange plant and animal life and even humanoid beings. I was never able to distinguish between a ripsaw and a crosscut, but oh how I wanted to *invent* something.

The mysteries of machines and their attraction for boys who didn't understand them were obvious targets for Edward Stratemeyer and his aides and imitators. Spurred by the success stories of Thomas Edison, Cyrus McCormick, and Samuel F. B. Morse, Stratemeyer and his gnomes got to work and brought forth the brilliant young inventor-industrialist Tom Swift. He was a smashing success immediately. Tom and his pals and his inventory of weird devices slid effortlessly into the hearts and libraries of boys everywhere, to the tune of six million copies.

The thirty-eight books of the series were written in a rollicking, bouncy prose, rhythmic and jolly, crammed with adverbs that led to the "Tom Swifties" of a later generation. Never was there so much dialogue, and almost every sentence included the name of the person addressed, like the patter of vaudeville comedians. Tom lasted until he was superseded by the era of electronics and moon landings. He was allowed to marry his boyhood sweetheart, Mary Nestor, and go into honorable retirement, to be replaced by Tom Swift, Jr., and a whole new series. The younger Tom is now coping with the intricacies of rockets, robots and bathyspheres, and is written, appropriately, by "Victor Appleton II," the "nephew" of the original author, Victor Appleton, a Stratemeyer pseudonym.

Tom was a red-blooded American youth in his late teens, hailing from upstate Shopton, New York. He had a brilliant, inventive turn of mind and kept his eye, as the Rotarians used to say, on the doughnut instead of the hole. Combining good solid horse sense with sticktoitiveness and broad technical know-how, he parlayed his first motorcycle into a complex of industries supported by fat government and utilities contracts. Unlike many other boy heroes (the Hardys for example) he progressed and expanded in each book, like any smart young pre-income tax capitalist.

He was a "bright-looking young fellow with an alert air and a rather humorous smile," not offensively handsome, and decently dressed in sober, neat three-piece suits and jaunty tweed caps or snap-brimmed Fedoras. He certainly was not a round-shouldered, pale-faced grind, peering through glasses like the bottoms of Coca-Cola bottles, but "possessed all the mental vigor and muscular energy that a young man should have," since he had "not neglected his athletic development while he made the best use of his mental power." Moreover, Tom was a scrapper, and could topple a bully with the best of them. We are told that:

> If there was anything Tom Swift liked, it was a good fight. The clash of diverse interests was the breath of life to the young fellow.

> (*Tom Swift and His Electric Locomotive, p. 6*)

Where his mental powers came from is something of a mystery, for Tom never attended a university, and his formal training in the sciences stopped at high school level, where, if I remember correctly, boys were given the option of one year of physics or chemistry, and a few semesters of "shop." His tremendous store of information about every known scientific discipline seems to have come almost entirely from magazines and the local newspapers, and from association with his father, who was also an inventor.

Our hero had not spent all of his time culling the scientific pages of periodicals, however, and we are informed in *Tom Swift and His Electric Locomotive* that he was something of a ladies' man, until Mary Nestor came into his life and then:

> Mary Nestor was a very pretty girl, and Tom thought

she was just about right in every particular. Although he had been about a good deal for a young fellow and had seen girls everywhere, none of them came up to Mary. None of them held Tom's interest for a minute except the girl whom he had been around with for years, and whom he had always confided in.

(op. cit., p. 22)

Whatever he may have been in the boudoir or on the porch swing, there was no nonsense about Tom at the office. After his rise from backyard workshop to executive suite, he ruled his workers with the hearty benevolent despotism of a turn-of-the-century robber baron. The Swift Construction Company, which by 1922 was "broadly known not alone throughout the U.S. but in several foreign countries," employed a large number of workmen, all fiercely loyal to Tom.

> "The young boss is mulling over something new," the men said, and grinned at each other. They were proud of Tom and faithful to his interests.
> Time was when there had been traitors in the works; but unfaithful hands had been weeded out. There was not a man who drew a pay envelope from the Swift Construction Company who would not have done his best to save Tom and his father trouble. Such a thing as a strike or labor troubles of any kind, was not thought of there.

(op. cit., p. 73)

No Molly Maguires or Pinkertons needed. These splendid craftsmen worked a twenty-four-hour day, since Tom got most of his inspirations in the wee hours; and their leader, Garrett Jackson, an engineer of the college graduate type, lived on the premises. They were skilled in any known type of "construction," and could manufacture a dirigible, a locomotive, a super-speed army tank, or a submarine with equal ease. They had pride in achievement, and worked in happy harmony with management to turn out a superior product. What a different place the world might have been if Nikolai Lenin had been born in Shopton, New York!

Barton Swift, Tom's father, "had spent so many years investigating chemical and mechanical mysteries that he saw more clearly and more exactly into and through most problems than other people." For all of this, he did not have a single invention worth talking about to his credit. Nevertheless, he had a number of potentially lucrative patents lying around the house where villainous competitors were readily able to find them and steal them until they could be recovered by patient, long-suffering Tom. From time to time the old gentleman got himself kidnaped (as did Mary Nestor's father and other principals in the series) but Tom never complained. He was always willing to interrupt some important and fascinating project and rush to the rescue in one of his bizarre, homemade vehicles.

Swift *père* became a semi-invalid as the series progressed, and his health caused Tom a good deal of worry. He was proud of his boy, and even at the very beginning he foresaw a bright future for the young inventor.

> "You have, by your inventions, shoved the clock of progress forward. I am proud of you, my boy. I know that no matter what may happen to me, you will make an enviable mark in the world of invention."
>
> (*op. cit., p. 75*)

Notwithstanding this confidence, he played the role of a cranky iconoclast in many of the books, explaining in painful detail why Tom's latest brainstorm couldn't be done.

Mr. Swift chuckled silently, gradually breaking into a louder laugh. Instead of being angry, Tom only regarded his father with an indulgent smile and continued.

"All right, Dad. Go ahead and laugh!"

"Well, Tom, I'm not exactly laughing at *you*—it's more the idea than anything else. The idea of talking over a wire and at the same time having light waves as well as electrical waves passing on the same conductor!"

"All right, Dad, go ahead and laugh. I don't mind," said Tom good-naturedly. "Folks laughed at Bell, when he said he could send a human voice over a copper string; but Bell went ahead and today we can talk over a thousand miles by wire. That was the telephone.

"Folks laughed at Morse when he said he could send a message over the wire. He let 'em laugh, but we have the telegraph. Folks laughed at Edison when he said he could take the human voice—or any other sound—and fix it on a wax cylinder or a hard rubber plate—but he did it, and we have the phonograph. And folks laughed at Santos-Dumont, at the Wrights, and at all the other fellows who said they could take a heavier-than-air machine and skim above the clouds like a bird; but we do it—I've done it —you've done it."

(Tom Swift and His Photo-Telephone, p. 3)

What parent could rebut so impassioned a speech? As always, unhealthy Mr. Swift was wrong and Tom came through with flying colors.

Tom's mother had died when he was very young, and the rest of the cadre dwelling in the Swifts' "fine house" in Shopton consisted of the aforementioned Garrett Jackson, Mrs. Baggert, a cardboard housekeeper who was rarely seen and never heard, and Eradicate "Rad" Sampson, a minstrel-show Negro retainer with his mule Boomerang. In the thirteenth book of the series (*Tom Swift in Captivity*), Tom ventured abroad and was imprisoned by a strange jungle tribe of nine-foot giants. Escaping, he brought one home with him to Shopton, and so Koku joined the household as a kind of servant-bodyguard and a source of constant irritation to Rad.

In most of his peregrinations, Tom was accompanied by his two closest chums, Ned Newton and Mr. Wakefield Damon. Ned was a natty dresser with a quick wit, who majored in business administration and got a job in the local bank. As the series progressed, he became "an important bank official" and the comptroller-general and chief fiscal officer of the Swift Construction Company, investing Tom's rewards, bonuses, hidden treasures, and royalties in gilt-edged securities and tax free municipals. Both Tom and Ned were turned down for military service in World War I because the government felt that they were too valuable turning out inventions to be used in the front lines, but both contributed heavily to the Red Cross and invested in Liberty Bonds. Tom refused to accept any profit from the War Department for his giant war tank, his silent airplane motor, and other sophisticated weaponry.

Mr. Wakefield Damon was considerably older than Tom and Ned, and hailed from Waterfield, a town not far from Shopton. He was constantly blessing himself or some part of his anatomy, and was apparently of independent means, since he was always able to take off on an adventure, in spite of the presence of a shadowy Mrs. Damon at home. Notwithstanding their close relationship, Tom never addressed him by his first name, although he was always "Tom" to the older man. Both Ned and Mr. Damon took great joy in joshing Tom about his romance with Mary Nestor. On one occasion the old gentleman surprised the young couple *en tête à tête* at Mary's house.

"Who's this?" queried Tom, puzzled.

A sharp voice suddenly was raised in an exclamatory explosion.

"Bless my brakeshoes! Is that Tom Swift? Just the chap I was looking for. Bless my mileage-book! This saves me time and money."

"Why it's Mr. Wakefield Damon," Mary cried with something like relief in her tones. "You can ride home in his car, Tom."

"All right, Mary. Don't be afraid for me," replied Tom Swift, and ran down the walk to the waiting car.

"Bless my vest buttons! Tom Swift, my heart swells when I see you—"

"And is like to burst off the said vest buttons?" chuckled the young fellow, stepping in beside his eccentric friend who blessed everything inanimate in his florid speech.

"I am delighted to catch you—although, of course," and Tom knew the gentleman's eyes twinkled, "I could have no idea that you were over here at Mary's, Tom."

"Of course not," rejoined the young inventor calmly, "seeing that I only come to see her just as often as I get a chance."

"Bless my memory tablets! Is that a fact?" chuckled Mr. Damon.

(Tom Swift and His Electric Locomotive, p. 26)

Ned was no less a tease than Mr. Damon, and never missed a chance to needle his inventor pal about his pretty inamorata. When the three chums had finished the planning phase of a voyage to the City of Gold:

"Good!" exclaimed Tom. "I hope we can bring back some of the [gold] images."

"Yes, I know who you'll bring one for," said Ned with a laugh, and he took care to get beyond the reach of Tom's fist. "Her first name is Mary," he added.

"You get out!" laughed Tom, blushing at the same time.

"Oh what a thing it is to be young!" exclaimed Mr. Damon with a mock sigh.

(Tom Swift in The City of Gold, p. 46)

When the chums, and Mr. Swift, senior, were not poking good-natured fun at their young idol, they served as foils at whom Tom could reel off pseudoscientific jargon that was very close to the real thing, and which we *aficionados* could repeat in school to lord it over our less literate friends. In response to a question from Ned about the workings of one of his inventions, Tom explained:

> "I have only had rigged here one trolley wire. There must be two attached alternately to the catenary cable. Such a form of twin conductor trolley will permit the collection of a heavy current through the twin contact of the pantagraph with the two trolley wires, and should assure a sparkless collection of the current at any speed. You noticed that when I took the sharper curves there was an aerial exhibition. I want to do away with the fireworks."

(Tom Swift and His Electric Locomotive, p. 111)

Sweet Mary Nestor was the very model of a sprightly country lass, brimming with good humor, loyal, affectionate, but terribly shy. She made the best apple turnovers in Shopton, and put up her own jams and jellies, and she blushed every time Tom or anyone else addressed her. Between the blushes she had a pawky sense of humor, and could match Tom with a one-liner any time. Let's eavesdrop on the lovebirds in one of their dialogues, when Tom has invited Mary to take a spin in his air scout.

The young man leaned over the edge of the padded cockpit and clasped in his rather grimy hand the neatly gloved one of the young lady. And though the glove was new, and fitted the hand perfectly, there was no attempt to withdraw it. Instead, the young lady seemed to be very glad indeed that her hand was in such safekeeping.

"Mary!" exclaimed the young man, "if it wasn't safe—as safe as a church—I wouldn't dream of taking you up!" and at the mention of "church" Mary Nestor blushed just the least bit.

"Shall I have to wear all those things—such as you have on?" asked Mary, blushing again.

"Well, you'll be more comfortable in a fur-lined leather suit," asserted Tom. "And if it does make you look like an Eskimo, why I'm sure it will be very becoming. Not that you don't look nice now," he hastened to assure Mary Nestor, "but an aviation suit will be very—well, fetching, I should say."

"If I could be sure it would 'fetch' me back safe, Tom—"

"That'll do! That'll do!" laughed the young aviator. "One joke like that is enough in a morning. It was pretty good, though. Now go on and tog up."

(*Tom Swift and His Air Scout, p. 2*)

Never one to take this sort of thing lying down, Tom was always ready with a sockdolager of a retort. After a close call in his electric locomotive, he got back at Mary.

"Tom, are you all right?" Mary asks.
"No. Half of me is left," grins Tom.

(*Tom Swift and His Electric Locomotive, p. 16*)

Good old Rad, Tom's black man-of-all-work was one of the worst Uncle Toms in the history of children's literature, and they really had them in those days. He persistently referred to himself as "dis ole coon" and functioned willingly as the butt of all sorts of practical jokes. He was thoroughly convinced of the inferiority of the black race according to the popular beliefs of the early decades of the twentieth century, and accepted racism with stoicism and good nature. When Tom asked him to stand before the device housing his photo-telephone, so that he could test its prototype, the invention turned out (at first) to be a failure.

> "Massa Tom, I reckon I knows what's wrong."
>
> "Yes Rad? Well, what is it?"
>
> "Mah face am too black—dat's de trouble. You done want a white-complected gen'man to stand in dat booth an' look at dat lookin' glass plate. I'se too black! I suah is!"
>
> "No that isn't it, Rad," laughed Tom hopelessly. "If the thing works at all it will send a black man's face as well as a white man's."
>
> (*Tom Swift and His Photo-Telephone, p. 49*)

Bravo, Tom! Yet for all his comic quality, Rad was allowed to be brave and strong, and unlike the stereotypes of the time he pitched in and struck a few blows when enemies were after Tom's inventions. There was no "Feet! Let's go!" about Rad when the going was rough. He was a chum insofar as the letter of the law would permit, and outside of Shopton he bore Jim Crow with resignation. When he accompanied Tom and Ned to Africa on an ocean liner, he "ate with a party of colored persons whose acquaintance he had quickly made" while Tom and Ned dined in the first-class lounge. The chums accepted this without protest. After all, you can't fight the system.

About the worst and most persistent of Tom's numerous enemies was Andy Foger, a red-haired bully his own age who spent all his time trying to frustrate our hero's plans and destroy his inventions. Andy and his father, a

senior-grade bully, turned up all over the world, anywhere the Swift ménage happened to be operating. Of
course Andy was defeated every time, either by Tom or
one of his aides.

Andy had a little scientific knowledge of his own, and
always knew exactly where to cut a wire or plant a bolt
that would cause a near-lethal malfunction. Tom always
escaped and gave the bully his comeuppance. Here is a
typical sequence, in which Tom comes up behind Andy
(who is on a bicycle) and gives him a good fright with
his speedy monoplane, the *Butterfly*. (Tom shuts off
his motor and volplanes down within a few feet of the
bully who is pedaling along the road. He lets out a terrific yell, almost in Andy's ear. Andy shouts, vaults over
the handlebars, and Tom lands.)

"Is it—is it gone?"

"Is what gone?" asked Tom grimly. At the sound of his
voice, Andy looked up.

"Was that you, Tom Swift?" he demanded. "Did you
knock me off my wheel?"

"My monoplane and I together did," was the reply; "or
rather we didn't. It was the nervous reaction caused by
your fright, and the knowledge that you had done wrong,
that made you jump over the handlebars. That's the scientific explanation."

"You—you did it!" stammered Andy, getting to his feet.
He wasn't hurt much, Tom thought.

"Have it your own way," resumed our hero. "Did you
think it was a hobgoblin in a chariot of fire after you,
Andy?"

"Huh! Never mind what I thought! I'll have you arrested for this!"

"Will you? Delighted as the boys say. Hop in my airship and I'll take you right into town. And when I get
there I'll make a charge of malicious mischief against you

for breaking the propellor of the *Butterfly* and slashing her wings. I've mended her up, however, so she goes better than ever, and I can take you to the police station in jig time. Want to come, Andy?"

This was too much for the bully. He knew that Tom would have a clear case against him, and he did not dare to answer. Instead he shuffled over to where his wheel lay, picked it up, and rode slowly off.

"Good riddance," murmured Tom—

(*Tom Swift Among the Diamond Makers, p. 46*)

A typical Tom Swift book began with an idea, born in the young inventor's fertile brain and brought into maturity in his workshop. The idea was compromised through some coincidence or other, and attempts were made to steal it or capitalize on it in some way. The enemies were not above using attempted murder, arson, kidnaping, bribery, and blackmail as well as simple larceny. There was always a thrilling chase, usually in a weird vehicle of Tom's own design, and final retribution accompanied by financial gain for Tom. Only once in the series did his giant intellect fail him, and that was in *Tom Swift Among the Diamond Makers*, in which another scientist designed a method for making artificial diamonds, using the electricity in lightning bolts. Tom tried again and again without success to duplicate the process.

Tom first appeared in *Tom Swift and His Motorcycle* in 1910. Mr. Wakefield Damon, later to be his comical sidekick on many an adventure, collided with a tree while riding his motorcycle past the Swift home in Shopton. The eccentric gentleman was hurt, but not badly. Tom bought the machine, repaired it, and had a number of adventures on it including a thrilling chase after a gang of thieves who had stolen a valuable patent model belonging to Mr. Swift.

In the next book (*Tom Swift and His Motor Boat*) it was hot pursuit of patent thieves once again, this time on the water. En route Tom, Ned, and the elder Swift rescued one John Sharp from a burning balloon. In gratitude, Sharp helped Tom build the *Red Cloud*, a combination biplane and dirigible that could hover, and contained a plant for manufacturing its own balloon gas. The airship held ten people but only two were needed to operate it. It had a sitting room, a dining room, a kitchen, and a number of bedrooms as well as a motor compartment and a control tower. This led Tom into book three (*Tom Swift and His Airship*) in which he, Sharp, and Mr. Damon used the dirigible to capture a gang of bank robbers and clear themselves of the charge of having stolen $75,000, suspicion having been thrown their way by Andy Foger and his father.

Book four finds Tom searching for buried treasure in his submarine, and captured by a foreign warship, but not for long. He escaped in time to return to Shopton and manufacture an electric automobile with which he won an important race and saved from ruin a bank in which his father and Mr. Damon were interested.

Switching from vehicles to communications, and venturing out of Shopton, Tom (who was now the possessor of a national reputation) accepted an invitation to serve as consultant to a Mr. Hosmer Fenwick of Philadelphia in the construction of another airship. On its maiden test, the airship was blown out to sea by a hurricane, and wrecked on an island in the West Indies. Tom discovered seven castaways there, shipwrecked when the yacht *Resolute* foundered during the same hurricane. Among them were Mary Nestor's parents. With salvaged electrical apparatus, Tom built a wireless station and sent out SOS messages that were intercepted by a steamer which rescued them just before the island was destroyed by an earthquake.

One of the castaways, a Mr. Barcoe Jenks, was the owner of the artificial diamond process mentioned *supra*. Tom's failure to produce diamonds was followed by a voyage to the Caves of Ice, and a wonderfully fast trip in the Sky Racer to bring a doctor to Shopton in time to save Mr. Swift's life. Then he was off to Africa with his electric rifle to hunt elephant, and amazing adventures with animals, pygmies, and savages. Two missionaries, rescued on this voyage, steered Tom and his pals to the City of Gold and a race to liberate a number of solid gold statues. In this adventure Andy Foger and a German companion followed in an airship of their own, and Tom saved Andy's life, but this gesture had no effect on the bully's character. As Rad sagely put it, "Dat meanness neber will done git whitewashed outer him—dat's a fact!"

With the coming of World War I Tom reached his zenith. In rapid succession he turned out his wizard camera, his air scout, his war tank, his great searchlight, his giant cannon and his aerial warship, refusing to accept any profit at all from Uncle Sam.

Our hero turned his attention back to business after the Armistice and devoted his researches to fire-fighting equipment, submarine exploration, tunneling and railroads. In 1922 he scornfully turned down an offer from a rival railroad of $20,000 a year, not at all bad for a teenager of that period, and built an electric locomotive in time to collect a $100,000 bonus. Small wonder he was able to present Mary with a $1500 diamond brooch on her birthday.

And so Tom continued through the series, always a little ahead of the rest of the scientific community, always on the go, and always flanked by his seedy dad, his two chums and his loyal sweetheart. We loved him, although we rarely understood his inventions, but we could never really identify with him. He was too smart, too secure, too levelheaded. He never did a darned-fool thing in his life, or wasted time or daydreamed. None of *us* ever "shoved the clock of progress forward."

> "The world do move," said Ned. "You believe that you have the edge on all other inventors?"
> "Along the line of this development—yes," said Tom. "I am taking up the work where former experimenters ended theirs. Why shouldn't I find the right combination?"
> "Oh Tom," cried Mary with clasped hands. "I hope you do."
> "I hope I do too," said Tom grimly. "At least if trying will bring it, success is going to come my way."
>
> (*Tom Swift and His Electric Locomotive*, p. 114)

That kind of determination was foreign to us. Tom was to invent the house trailer and television years before they became commonplace items, and we had no doubt that the rest of his inventions were or could be real. They were so plausible, so obvious. We cherished the young inventor and his friends, and gave them our boyish faith.

Edward Stratemeyer was never a man to put all his eggs in a single basket. The success of Tom Swift led him to hedge his investment and to create other mechanically inclined boys to pick up the slack in case Tom's popularity should wane. Vehicles and scientific wonders were the order of the day, and Stratemeyer and his cohorts and rivals turned them out by the dozen. Oddly enough, nobody ever produced another omniscient boy inventor. There was only one Tom Swift. The other mechanical and scientific boys specialized in a single discipline, usually associated with a vehicle. Young Ralph Fairbanks struggled upward from engine wiper to switchman to locomotive engineer to chief dispatcher and further toward an eventual vice-presidency of the Great Northern Railroad. The Speedwell Boys started, like Tom Swift and the Hardys, with motorcycles, and added racing cars, power launches, ice boats, submarines, and other wonders to their repertoire. The Motor Boys and the Motorcycle Chums zoomed through high-speed adventures. The Radio Boys delved into the mysteries of wireless communication. Ted Scott, lanky air pioneer, flew the Atlantic, the Pacific, and carried the airmail too.

A favorite of mine was the "Great Marvel Series," written by Stratemeyer as "Roy Rockwood," the same name he used as the author of *Bomba, the Jungle Boy.* I don't know why I liked the Great Wonder books so much. They had no hero to speak of. The protagonists were interchangeable and had little or no individuality of character. There was no one to identify with, and there were no female characters at all. Stratemeyer had taken a mixture of Jules Verne and Edgar Rice Burroughs (in his science fiction period), toned them down to subteen level, and created a series in which, for the first time, the locales upstaged the people.

The central figure in the stories was Professor Amos Henderson, a faceless and ageless bachelor who was able to build any known type of super-vehicle. His "general helper and companion" was Washington White, a standard boys' book comedy Negro given to excellent cooking and absurd dialogue ("Yas sir, Perfesser, I'se goin' t'saggasitate my bodily presence in yo' contiguous proximity an' attend t'yo immediate conglomerated prescriptions at the predestined period. Yas sir!"). The professor's constant companions were Mark Sampson and Jack Darrow, a pair of two-dimensional eighteen-year-olds whom it was impossible to tell apart. The boys were orphans, down on their luck, who had hopped a freight that was

wrecked near the professor's laboratory. The scientist befriended them, invited them along on his first voyage,
and the series was on its way.

Accompanied by Andy Sudds, an old hunter, and a pair
of farmers whom Stratemeyer uncharacteristically named
Tom Smith and Bill Jones, the chums boarded the wonderful electric airship *Monarch* and headed *Through the
Air to the North Pole,* battling fierce animals, hostile "Es-
quimaux," and bad weather. The professor then built a
submarine, the *Porpoise,* which took the group *Under the
Ocean to the South Pole,* by a route which led them into
trouble via the Sargasso Sea, a sea of boiling water, and
deadly ice fields. En route they were presented with
diving suits, something that fascinated every boy of the
period who had ever read about Captain Nemo or peeped
into the strange silent world under the sea in the movies.
Just reading about the "graveyard of lost ships" or giant
swimming monsters was a major thrill.

After the successes of the *Monarch* and the *Porpoise,*
the professor could do nothing but combine the two and
make a flying submarine, the *Flying Mermaid,* to descend
into a yawning vaporous hole which he believed was
the gateway to the center of the earth. In *Five Thousand
Miles Underground: Or the Mystery of the Center of
the Earth* Stratemeyer, with the scientific pseudo-
knowledge that had served him so well in the Tom Swift
books, invented jet propulsion in 1908. The *Flying
Mermaid*

> . . . moved forward or backward by means of a novel
> arrangement. From either end of the lower hull there pro-
> jected a short pipe working in a ball and socket joint so
> it could be turned in any direction. By means of strong
> pumps a current of compressed air could be sent out from
> either pipe. Thus, when floating above the earth the ship

was forced forward by the blast of air rushing from the pipe at the stern. It was the same principle as that on which a skyrocket is shot heavenward, save that gases produced by the burning of powder in the pasteboard rocket form its moving impulse.

(*Five Thousand Miles Underground, p. 14*)

Thank God the Kaiser never read the Great Marvel Series. The Allies had enough trouble with submarines. The professor took his intrepid little band of adventurers to Mars, Venus, and the moon, and into fantasyland to the City Beyond the Clouds where they were plagued by impish red dwarfs. They also visited a vast island in the air which had floated off into space after a "tremendous convulsion of nature."

Stratemeyer wrote eight of the series, but eventually it petered out, overshadowed by the more lucrative giants of the period. Nevertheless it was fun to read, and omitted much of the corn that was chronic in similar series of the pre-war era.

Another of the lesser but beloved series was the Ralph Fairbanks saga. The affinity of boys and trains was a likely money-maker to Stratemeyer, and young Ralph was a railroader to the very marrow of his bones. The Ralph stories centered around the Great Northern Railroad, a beleaguered line sorely beset with spies, "sorehead strikers" and unscrupulous competitors who used every kind of skullduggery to wreck its schedules. If it wasn't timber felled across the track, it was caustic soda in the boilers. Ralph had to face danger after danger to get through "on time," and every book had a runaway engine that the intrepid young railroader stopped in the nick of time.

Ralph was a bit too goody-goody to really get to us kids, already turned cynical by the Jazz Age. He bore

traces of an earlier period, when Stratemeyer had served
his time both as "Oliver Optic" and "Horatio Alger, Jr."
in the rags-to-riches field. The prose style was still over-
formal and stilted, and had not warmed up to the Tom
Swift-Hardy Boys-Nancy Drew level.

> "Those men will bear watching—they are up to some
> mischief, Fairbanks."
> "I thought so myself, Mr. Fogg. I have been watching
> them for some time."
> "I thought you would notice them—you generally do
> notice things."
> The speaker with these words bestowed a glance of
> genuine pride and approbation upon his companion Ralph
> Fairbanks.
> They were a great pair, these two, a friendly loyal pair,
> the grizzled old veteran fireman, Lemuel Fogg, and the
> clear-eyed, steady young fellow who had risen from
> roundhouse wiper to switchtower service, then to fireman,
> then to engineer, and who now pulled the lever on the
> crack racer of the Great Northern Railroad, the Overland
> Express.
>
> (*Ralph the Train Dispatcher, p. 1*)

Ralph's meteoric rise covered every branch of railroading, in simple, understandable terms. Our hero had
"taken to railroading as naturally as does a duck to water."
His late father had been one of the pioneer builders of
the Great Northern, whose untimely death had left his
son the sole support of a widowed and destitute mother.
In volume one (*Ralph of the Roundhouse*) he left school
to get a job, and won laurels as the best engine wiper in
the business while foiling village magnate Gasper Far-
rington, who was trying to rob his mother of her little
home.

From then on it was onward and upward, with the admiration of his colleagues and the assistance of Mr. Adair, the railroad detective, and the benevolent favoritism of the president of the Great Northern.

Ralph was never too busy to reach out and help a deserving fellow less fortunate than himself, and we find him riding a handcar to inspect a wreck with the railroad claims agent. The wreck contained a number of crates of chickens, and at the site of the collision Ralph discovered ragged young Glen Palmer.

"You talk clear and straight and earnest, my lad," here broke in the claims agent. "What's your name?"

"Glen Palmer."

"Do you live near here?"

"Yes, sir—in an old abandoned farmhouse, rent free, about a mile north of here."

"With your folks?"

"No, sir, I have no folks, only an old grandfather. He's past working, and, well a—a little queer at times, and I have to keep close watch of him. That's what's the trouble."

The claims agent took out his notebook.

"Look here," he spoke, "if Fairbanks will vouch for you, I'll tab off the chickens to you at fifteen dollars, due in thirty days."

"Oh—oh!" gasped the lad, clasping his hands in an ecstasy of hope and happiness. "I'll be sure to pay you— Why, with what I know I can do with those chickens, I could pay you ten times over inside a month."

"Mr. Fry," said Ralph, studying the boy's face for a moment or two, "I'll go security for my friend here."

"Say—excuse me, but say, Mr. Fairbanks, I—I—"

The boy broke down, tears choking his utterance. He could only clasp and cling to Ralph's hand. The latter patted him on the shoulder with the encouraging words:

"You go ahead with your chicken farm, Glen, and if it needs more capital come to me."

(op. cit., p. 23)

A little laughter, a few tears, that was the formula until the 1930s made it all obsolete. We wanted stronger meat and more thrills, but Stratemeyer never missed a chance to shove in a ragged orphan. Mercifully they got fewer and fewer as the years passed. Horatio Alger had become a joke by the time I was twelve.

Ralph was not only a real sweetheart vis-à-vis the less fortunate. He was tough and gutsy as well, and handy with his dukes, a true product of the rough and tumble life of the roundhouse. Captured in a tunnel by hired thugs out to wreck the Overland, he was, unfortunately, outnumbered.

Ralph swayed and swung to and fro, struggling actively to break away from his captors.

"What now?"—rang out at his ear.

"Run him forward."

"He won't run."

"Then give him his quietus."

Ralph felt that a cowardly blow in the dark was pending. He had retained hold of the cane. He tried to use this as a weapon, but the clasp on either wrist was like that of steel. He could only sway the walking stick aimlessly.

A hard fist blow grazed one ear, bringing the blood. Ralph gave an old training ground twist to his supple body, at the same time throwing out one foot. He had succeeded in tripping up his captor on the left, but though the fellow fell he preserved a tenacious grip on the wrist of the plucky young railroader.

"Keep your clutch!" panted the other man. "I'll have him fixed in a jiffy. Thunder! What's coming?"

"A train!"

"Break loose—we're lost!"

Ralph was released suddenly. The man on the right, however, had delivered the blow he had started to deal. It took Ralph across the temple and for a moment dazed and stunned him. He fell directly between the rails.

The two men had darted ahead. He heard one of them call out to hug the wall closely. Then a sharp grinding roar assailed Ralph's ears and he tried to trace out its cause.

"Something is coming," he murmured. His skilled hearing soon determined that it was no locomotive or train, but he was certain that some rail vehicle of light construction was bearing down on him . . . Then there sounded out upon the clammy blackness of the tunnel an appalling, unearthly scream . . .

(op. cit., p. 56)

It wasn't until 1918 that an enterprising general practitioner discovered a heart murmur that kept the young railroader out of the Army, although it never prevented any hairsbreadth thrills and chills in his incessant quest for spies on the troop trains of the Great Northern.

A lily-white union policy on the Great Northern Railroad kept the usual black stereotypes out of the Ralph series, but there had to be comedy relief of some kind. Sausage-and-sauerkraut-eating German-Americans suddenly stopped being funny when they were popped into detention camps for sabotage and other subversive activities, and so Stratemeyer had to settle on the good old money-grubbing Jewish businessman, waving his arms as he spoke, his battered derby shoved down over his ears. The laugh of the Great Northern line was "Ready-Cash" Cohen, always ready to turn a fast nickel on salvage.

At a crossing a man came tearing towards them, arms waving, long beard flying, and his face showing the greatest urgency and excitement.

"Mishther Fry! Mishther Fry!" he panted out, "I haf just heard—"

"Nothing for you, Cohen," shouted the claims agent.

"I hear dere vas some boxes. Shtop! Shtop! Shtop! I've got the retty gash."

"'Ready-Cash' Cohen," exclaimed Fry to Ralph. "Always on hand when there's any cheap wreck salvage lying around loose. That fellow seems to scent a wreck like a vulture."

"I've heard of him," remarked Ralph with a smile.

(*op. cit., p. 17–19*)

Oh, that smile. There wasn't a subteen Jewish reader in the country who didn't know that smile; who hadn't seen it on friend and foe alike in all its damning, superior, excruciating mockery. It was a time of restricted neighborhoods and beautiful landscaped country clubs that Jewish kids longed for and knew they would never see the inside of. We accepted it as the Law. There were places some of our gang could play where others could not. The grown-ups accepted it and we took it as a matter of course. It wasn't the kids' fault. It was the fault of "Ready-Cash" Cohen and his ilk. The gentile kids thought he was funny, but the Jewish kids hated his guts. As for Stratemeyer and his associates, they toyed with him briefly and then after the war replaced him with bold, good-looking young Phil Cohen, the Hardy Boys' chum. Perhaps they were assisted by Jewish pressure groups and public opinion, but the stereotypes disappeared, buried in their own obsolescence.

By 1922, "Allen Chapman," author of the Ralph books, had terminated the series. Railroads were old stuff. The

new craze was radio, and Chapman-Stratemeyer created
a whole new series around it, the Radio Boys. It wasn't
easy to build thrills around stationary apparatus instead
of zippy vehicles, but the boys did very well, first building
a prize-winning wireless, then saving ships in distress,
making midnight calls for assistance, solving mysteries,
and working with the forest rangers. It was a tight, ade-
quate little series, though no world-beater from the financial standpoint.

The boys lived in Clintonia, a thriving town of ten
thousand inhabitants about seventy-five miles from New
York City. The town was located on the Shagary River,
which afforded many opportunities for fishing, speedboats,
drowning rescues and the other mainstays of boys' reading. Bob Layton was the son of the town's leading drug-
gist. He was fifteen, tall, dark, and well-developed, an
athlete and an outdoor boy. He was a "live wire," quick-
tempered, not a trouble seeker, but neither was he a boy
to avoid a scrap with a bully. Joe Atwood, Bob's special
chum, was the son of the town's most prominent physician. He was fair and blue-eyed, and athletic too. Note
the resemblance to Frank and Joe Hardy? All they needed
was a fat, food-loving chum, like Chet Morton.

> Jimmy Plummer was fourteen, round, fat, lazy, and
> good-natured, and a great lover of the good things of life.
> His father was a carpenter, thrifty, respected and a good
> citizen.
>
> (*The Radio Boys' First Wireless*, p. 21–23)

The cast was completed by Herbert Fennington, son of a
prosperous merchant. The boys shared an interest in
science, and all had marked mechanical ability. They
spent the whole of the first book building a wireless set

under the guidance of their local pastor, a radio ham, and winning the coveted Ferberton prize with it.

Of course there were chases and daring rescues, and attempts by infamous bullies to destroy the boys' apparatus, but the wonders of wireless, as explained by genial Dr. Dale, launched the boys on thirteen volumes of fun and adventure.

> The boys watched him [Dr. Dale] breathlessly as he handled two of the knobs at the side of the box. A moment later they heard the clear, vibrant notes of a violin playing a beautiful selection from one of the operas. The music rose and swelled in wonderful sweetness until it filled the room with the delicious melody and held all the hearers entranced under its spell. It was evident that only the hand of a master could draw such exquisite music from the instrument.
>
> The doctor waited until the last notes had died away, and smiled with gratification as he saw the rapt look on the faces of his visitors.
>
> "Sounds as if it were in the next room, doesn't it?" he asked. "But that music came from Newark, New Jersey."
>
> (*op. cit.*, *p. 33*)

Of course nothing ever went smoothly in the world of Stratemeyer people, and a particularly loathsome trio of bullies was invented to plague the radio lads in their work.

> There was a loud guffaw behind the lads accompanied by snickers, and the friends turned around to see three boys following them.
>
> One of them, who was apparently the leader of the trio, was a big, unwieldy boy of sixteen, a year older and considerably larger than Bob and Joe. His eyes were close together, and he had a look of coarseness and arrogance

that denoted the bully. Buck Looker, as he was called—
his first name was Buckley—was generally unpopular
among the boys, but as he was the son of one of the rich-
est men of the town he usually had one or two cronies
who hung about him for what they could get. One of
these, Carl Lutz, an unwholesome-looking boy somewhat
younger than Buck, was walking beside him, and on the
side nearer the curb was Terry Mooney, the youngest of
the three, a boy whose furtive eyes carried in them a
suggestion of treachery and sneakiness.

(op. cit., p. 12–15)

As far as new-fangled contraptions were concerned,
the bullies were as right-wing conservative as could be.

"The whole thing is bunk, if you ask me," [said] Buck
with the confidence that so often goes with ignorance.
"Telephoning without wires! You might just as well talk
of walking without legs."

This argument seemed to him so overpowering that he
swelled out his chest and looked triumphantly at his two
companions, whose faces instantly took on the same expression.

"You made a ten-strike that time, Buck," declared
Lutz, clapping him on the shoulder.

"Hit the target right in the bull's-eye," chimed in Terry
with a smirk.

Bob and Jimmy and Joe looked at each other and, despite their resentment, it was all they could do to keep
from breaking into laughter.

Buck noticed their amused expression, and his coarse
face grew red and mottled.

"Well," he demanded, "what have you got to say to
that? Am I right or ain't I?"

"You're wrong," replied Joe promptly. "Dead wrong.
You're so far from the truth that you couldn't see it with a
telescope. You're talking like a ham sandwich."

"Look out what you're saying, Joe Atwood, or I'll make you sorry for it," threatened Buck as he clinched his fist, an ugly look coming into his eyes.

"I apologize," said Joe. "That is, I apologize to the ham sandwich."

Bob laid a restraining hand on his friend's arm.

"Easy, Joe," he counseled. "Listen, Buck," he went on, "did you ever hear of Marconi?"

"Sure I did," replied Buck. "He's the fellow that had the fight with Julius Caesar. The one that Cleopatra was dippy about."

(loc. cit.)

Combine the Radio Boys with the Speedwells and add a dash of the Motorcycle Chums, and you end up with the Hardys. The Speedwell Boys were very similar to the Radio Boys, except that in the Speedwell series our old friend "Roy Rockwood" had discovered the value of girls and vehicle crashes. The girl friends, Mildred and Lettie, accompanied the Speedwells everywhere, adding squeals and flutters and heartfelt adulation. The crashes came periodically, since the Speedwells concerned themselves primarily with the construction of racing vehicles.

Dan and Billy Speedwell were the sons of a small dairy farmer whose spread was adjacent to the town of Riverdale on the Colasha River. They were seventeen, and attended Riverdale High School, working between school sessions to help out at home. By a series of fortuitous coincidences the boys acquired motorcycles, a racing car, and a power launch. Then the discovery of a buried treasure made the family independent. They bought more land and some luxuries. A nest egg of twenty thousand dollars was wisely invested for Dan and Billy. Riches did not spoil the Speedwells, and they continued to live simply, going to school and delivering milk to the dairy

farm's customers in the Riverdale area, to the amusement
of certain rich and snobbish boys, Barrington Spink for
one.

The series ran to five books and included a submarine
and an ice boat as well as the vehicles aforementioned.
The boys were mechanically inclined, and could break
down an automobile engine and repair it in no time at all.

The Motorcycle Chums were almost a carbon copy of
the Speedwells. Freckles, the leader of the pack, was once
again the son of a prominent physician, and Budge was the
same lovable fat boy, provokingly slow but good-natured
and jolly. Jack Kinkaid was the troubled chum, the son
of an inventor whose patent for a lucrative invention had
been stolen by a disgruntled employee, thus giving the
chums a grail to search for. Alec was a fine, manly looking chap with a "resolute face, brown curly hair and dark
eyes." He was an orphan and lived with a well-to-do and
generous guardian who gave him the *Comet*, his souped-
up Reading motorcycle, much envied by the other lads.
The chums tooled around New England, catching criminals, trailing runaway tigers escaped from circuses, and
behaving in general very much like their fictional contemporaries.

There was competition from Dave Dashaway, from the
Motor Boys and from a number of other vehicle-oriented,
mechanically inclined, invention-prone heroes, but those
of us who learned to read in the 1930s found them
a little old hat. Radios and automobiles soon became commonplace. After all, we had grown up with them. Motorcycles were still special, and so were speedboats, and few
of us had ever seen an ice boat except in the Fox Movietone Newsreels. But there was something new, something
so exciting that it took your breath away just to see one
go by. Airplanes! On spring afternoons my father would

break out his Essex Super Six and drive me out to Roose-
velt Field to stand behind a fence and look at them poised
on the tarmac, ready to fly away. We'd seen countless
movies about test pilots, barnstormers, intrepid con-
querors of the air played by Richard Dix or Richard Arlen.
They would fly the airmail through pea soup fog, carrying
the mandatory cup of coffee, perched on a knee so the
pilot could tell whether his plane was level in those pre-
needle-and-ball days.

Airplanes were magic, and a ball game would stop in
the middle so that we could look up and watch a lone
biplane until it disappeared over the horizon. Glamour
and romance. Speed and danger. What more could a boy
want?

Grosset & Dunlap called in their first team and plunged
into the new airplane career field with young flying heroes
Andy Lane and Rex Lee. Flanked by the usual *cuadrilla*
of fearless chums, Andy set a new endurance record for
air-to-air refueling, won a race to the South Pole, fought
air pirates, and hunted buried treasure using a giant
autogyro. Andy's author, according to the book jackets,
was "Eustace L. Adams," himself an aviator who had had
"many thrilling adventures in the air—both as a member
of the Lafayette Escadrille and in the United States Naval
Aviation Service."

Not to be outdone, the author of Andy's rival series,
(the Rex Lee Flying Stories), one "Thomson Burtis,"
described himself on *his* book jackets as follows:

"During my five years in the army, I performed nearly
every sort of flying duty—instructor, test pilot, bombing,
photographing pilot, etc., in every variety of ship, from
tiny scout planes to the gigantic three-motored Caproni."

Not only had this author had many experiences as an army pilot, Grosset & Dunlap went on to assure us, but he had also been "a postal clerk, hobo, actor, writer, mutton chop salesman, preacher, roughneck in the oil fields, newspaperman, flyer, scenario writer in Hollywood, and synthetic clown with the Sells-Floto Circus." Rex himself flew with the border patrol, the sky rangers, and served a stint with the airmail service, solving a few mysteries and experiencing the usual narrow escapes.

These luminaries paled before the brilliance of the Stratemeyer Syndicate's top aviator, Ted Scott. Although Stratemeyer himself had little to do with the actual writing of the series, Ted was a true creation of the master himself. Why waste time when there was ready-made material to use? Why build a whole new character who might not be a success, when real heroes were available to use as models? Ted Scott, intrepid airman, was a lanky, soft-spoken Middle-Westerner of twenty-one who had achieved world celebrity (and the nickname the "Lone Eagle") by making the first flight across the Atlantic solo from New York to Paris.

Ted was the first international hero in boys' literature. Although many others, like Tom Swift, Tarzan, and the Boy Allies, were widely known, they could still walk down the street unmolested. Not so Ted Scott. Wherever he went he collected cheering, yelling mobs of well-wishers. This had not spoiled his simple charm, and he remained plain old Ted, avoiding, as far as possible, public displays of adulation. On a jaunt south of the border, he chose to go incognito because of

. . . his desire to avoid a public and official reception when he should arrive at Mexico City. If it were known that he was coming, there would be thousands to greet him. Then there would be the mauling and pounding by the crowds, the formal dinners and receptions, the parades through the streets while the people showered his car with flowers, the thousand things that were the penalty of such fame as his.

(*Ted Scott South of the Rio Grande, p. 44*)

What a bore! Fortunately the United States Ambassador to Mexico got to him in time, and convinced him to change his mind with an impassioned plea worthy of old Daniel Webster himself.

"For years relations with Mexico have been strained. More than once the two countries have been on the verge of war. Things are better now, but there is yet much to do. The oil question, the land question, the agrarian question, are pressing for solution. You've come just in time to help me, and in helping me you are helping our country. Mexico is a sensitive nation. Other countries have given you great ovations. Mexico wants to do the same. If you slight it, the people will think that it is because of indifference or contempt. That would hamper my negotiations. On the other hand, if you fall in with their plans, the Mexicans will be carried away with enthusiasm for you, and I shall come in for a share of the popularity and my work will be made easier. Do you see?"

Ted Scott's response was instant. He loved his country with all his heart. Not for a moment would he let his personal wishes stand in the way of helping her.

(*op. cit., p. 69*)

Ted got his ovation, complete with the President and the Mexican Army Band. It can only be hoped that from then on the oil question, the land question and the agrarian question were rapidly to become moot.

It was not only in the world's great capitals that Ted was known and revered. In the tiny backwoods villages of Middle-Western America he was an idol. On a forced landing in a remote cow pasture, Ted was forced to spend the night at a small farmhouse. As soon as he introduced himself:

> "Ted Scott! The man the President decorated! The one the whole country went crazy about! And in my house! It seems to me I must be dreaming. Just wait till I tell Pa! He'll be the proudest man in the country!" exclaimed Mrs. Wilburton.
>
> "Probably he knows already," remarked Ted.
>
> "And you've shaken hands with kings!" exclaimed Mrs. Wilburton in tones of awe.
>
> "Yes," smiled Ted. "But I've found that their hands were very much the same as anybody else's. Each one has five fingers."
>
> (*Over the Rockies With the Air Mail, p. 30*)

Ted, who was a "lithe, muscular young fellow without an ounce of superfluous flesh on the frame that was surmounted by a well-shaped head from which looked out a pair of frank brown eyes," was twenty-one at the outset of the series. Like Bomba, the Jungle Boy, he had little knowledge of his parents or of his life before the age of two or three. A foundling, his earliest memory was when he found himself in the poor but honest care of James and Miranda Wilson, a "worthy couple whose hearts had been touched by the plight of the little waif, and who had taken him into their household."

When Ted was ten, the Wilsons died simultaneously. Again an orphan, Ted was discovered by childless Eben and Charity Browning who "welcomed the forlorn little fellow into their hearts and home." Thus Ted became the first *double* orphan in children's literature, with four rather than two kindly foster parents. Stratemeyer was nothing if not lavish with Ted Scott.

Eben kept a hotel, the Bromville House of Bromville, Ohio, formerly the most prominent caravanserai of that thriving town. Unfortunately industry (the Devally-Hipson Aero Corporation) brought upheaval as well as prosperity to Bromville, and new modern hotels in its wake, and the Bromville House lapsed into shabbiness and decay. Unscrupulous Brewster Gale was the proprietor of the new Hotel Excelsior, which stood on land which Gale had cheated out of Eben by "legal hocus-pocus—reorganizations, holding companies and the like."

Out of school, Ted got a job with the Aero plant where industry, skill and a special aptitude for mechanics brought him rapid advancement. Working on planes made him want to learn to fly. One day a flying circus came to town, and from then on flying was an obsession with our hero.

Instead of annexing the usual chums, Ted chose more wisely. His closest sidekicks were a couple of money men, rich Paul Monet, and well-to-do young businessman Walter Hapworth. They lent the money that saw Ted through flying school and into the airmail service. One day the newspapers announced a prize of $25,000 for the airman who would make the first non-stop flight from New York to Paris. Ted, with financial help from his chums, supervised the building of his monoplane, the *Hapworth*, and took off across the Atlantic.

". . . in the haze of a rainy morning Ted mounted into the skies for his flight to Europe—the fog, the sleet and storm with which he battled over the surging wastes of the Atlantic—the final swooping down of the lone eagle on

Paris—the tremendous ovations that greeted him there
and which reached their climax on his return to his native
country as a national idol— . . .

(*Over the Ocean to Paris, introduction*)

Now Ted had powerful friends and a Name, and he
was able to return to Bromville, defeat Brewster Gale in
the courts, and reimburse Eben for his kindnesses. Gale's
twin sons, Gregory and Duckworth—Greg and Duck for
short—appeared in the second book, and plagued Ted
from then on.

Each of the twins was as big as Ted, and they were
several years older. But they were flabby from soft and
dissipated living and wind and muscle failed when the
test came.

Apart from physical disqualifications, Greg and Duck
had a yellow streak. They could not "stand the gaff." Yellow was one color with which Ted had no acquaintance.

(*Over the Rockies With the Air Mail, p. 67*)

Ted was able to handle them with no trouble, and usually
beat them up together, scorning to waste his time thrashing them individually.

After his marvelous transatlantic flight, Ted volunteered
as a Red Cross aviator, rescuing flood victims in Arkansas,
and then went back to the airmail, but not for long. There
were other laurels to be gathered. He won the great
Trans-Pacific Race from San Francisco to Honolulu and
made the first flight to Australia in record time. During
this period he cleared up the mystery of his birth and
vindicated the memory of his dead father, who had been
falsely accused of murder.

There was no female character waiting at home for
Ted (except, of course, for good old Charity who fol-

lowed him with a mother's prayers). Ted had no sweetheart, although everywhere he went he was the idol of
pretty girls. He just didn't have the time for them.

"Women is curious creatures," ruminated Mr. Wilbur-
ton, blowing his nose vigorously.
As Ted's own experience of women had been greatly
limited, he could only murmur a polite assent.
"Cry when they're sad an' cry when they're glad," continued his host. "How're you goin' to take 'em?"
"Way they're made, I suppose," replied Ted, trying to
direct the conversation into a different channel.

(*op. cit.*, *p.* 39)

In Mexico on a later adventure, Walter Hapworth pre-
sumed to tease his chum about a dark-eyed señorita who
was more than a little interested in our hero.

"Seem somewhat absent-minded this morning, Ted,"
remarked Hapworth. Then he added with a mischievous
glint in his eyes:
"Thinking perhaps of the fair Conchita?"
"No," replied Ted with a smile. "She's a charming girl
and will make somebody a lovely wife. But as for me, I
have only one sweetheart. Eh, old girl?" and he patted
the *Silver Streak* caressingly.

(*South of the Rio Grande*, *p.* 215)

The rapture of the skies was sufficient substitute for the
raptures of the boudoir, as far as old Ted was concerned,
and the series continued through twenty-odd books,
progressing with the aviation industry until it met the fate
of most long-run series. Its little readers grew up and got
involved in the apocalyptic events of the 1930s and 1940s
and Ted Scott ceased to be an "active property." His

author, "Franklin W. Dixon," still turns out the Hardy Boys, but airplanes are no longer exciting.

And so the mechanical boys, and their mighty industrial revolution, fade into memory, except, of course, for Tom Swift, Jr., and his rockets and electronic space vehicles. They gave us a taste of power, of the thrill of invention, the dim rattle of a foreign land in the earphones of a homemade radio, the trembling of a joystick in the treacherous updrafts of the Rockies, the excitement of a technological breakthrough in the backyard lab. The recent landings on the moon were anticlimactic compared to some of Tom Swift's adventures. After all, the astronauts simply got into their capsule, went to the moon, and came back again. No bullies dropped bolts into the machinery. No unscrupulous inventors tried to steal their mortgaged homes. No one was kidnaped or locked in a burning barn. They were all married. Not one of them was a gallant teen-ager. Good luck to those brave astronauts, but if I had not known Edward Stratemeyer was dead these thirty years I would have sworn he was writing their dialogue. One Great Leap Forward for Mankind indeed. How he would have loved that line.

CHAPTER SIX

BEATING THE BOCHE

(Then came a sharp exclamation from Joe and they turned in time to catch him as he fell.

"Let me go, fellows!" he cried, his face drawn with pain. "I'm done for. Save yourselves. Hurry—"

"Don't be a fool," rasped Blake, gathering all his strength for one last, mighty effort and slinging Joe over his shoulder. "It's going to hurt you, old man, but it—can't—be helped . . .")

(The Moving Picture Boys on French Battlefields)

Those of us who were born in the intermission between the two World Wars were hawks in every sense of the word. A boy with dovish tendencies would have been drummed out of my gang in short order, as would anyone who played with dolls or hated baseball. To us pacifism was equivalent to effeminacy. We held the First World War to be our own personal property, and equated Ypres and Verdun with Crécy and Agincourt. After all, our *fathers* had been in that war. There wasn't an attic in our neighborhood that did not contain a battered cartridge belt or some other fascinating item of olive drab equipment stamped with the proprietary insignia of the United States forces.

Our militant attitude was supported wholeheartedly by Authority. It took very little pleading to evoke a war reminiscence (usually much inflated) from our parents. Sunk as they were in the Depression, they remembered the recent hostilities as the happiest days of their lives. Youth and adventure and *Roses of Picardy* it meant to them, although they were careful to explain that it was all over now and there would never be another one.

In school we were bombarded with the literature of gallantry in action. We had to learn by heart the effusions of Rupert Brooke, Joyce Kilmer, and their genre. A classroom recitation about the grey spires of Oxford and the gallant young students who laid their good lives down never failed to bring a tear of envy to every boyish eye. How we would have loved to take the khaki and the gun instead of the fustian cap and gown that seemed to loom ahead for all of us. There were war memorials in every public park—determined-looking, square-jawed bronze doughboys pointing their bayonets down at some invisible cringing Hun. And we had missed it. It would never happen again.

This martial spirit did not escape the eternal vigilance of the publishing and film decision-makers, and they kept us at a white heat of militarism that would have done credit to a Samurai. We poured our nickels and dimes into the box office as always, and sat wide-eyed through *What Price Glory, The Cockeyed World, The Big Parade, Wings,* and *Hell's Angels. All Quiet on the Western Front,* both book and movie, exploded on our little world with stunning impact. As for *Dawn Patrol*—well, the less said about *Dawn Patrol* the better. It was *Dawn Patrol* and not Adolf Hitler or Pearl Harbor that drew me inexorably into the Air Corps, and very nearly got me blown to pieces, when wiser boys were scrambling for the Quartermaster Corps.

My crowd of junior-grade warhawks knew more about international military insignia and equipment than any Assistant Chief of Staff (G-2) in the civilized world. We could reel off verbatim statistics on artillery capabilities, fighter curves, and tank maneuvers. We could discourse in scholarly terms on turning a flank or "crossing the T." We knew the intricacies of a "falling leaf" or an Immel-

mann turn. With a little encouragement, I could list
chronologically every one of the air victories of Baron
Manfred von Richthofen, for each of which he had ordered a small silver cup (engraved with the date and a
few significant particulars) to place in his trophy room.
Oh that trophy room! How I longed at the age of twelve
for a chance to kill somebody and start a trophy room of
my own.

Of course the juvenile spirit of the times was reflected
in the juvenile literature sold to us. Many of our heroes
whose series were begun before 1914 had served honor-
ably in the forces. Tarzan was the most merciless Hun-
hunter of them all, cleaning Germans out of Africa almost
singlehanded. His son John ("Korak the Killer") served
in the British infantry at Verdun and the Argonne. Tom
Swift turned his inventive genius to war matériel. New
series had sprung up in the postwar years that we devoured with sanguine joy. The Boy Allies, still in their
teens, hobnobbed with Haig, Pershing, and Winston
Churchill. The Submarine Boys captained warships at
fifteen. And Tom Slade . . . Tom Slade whose most noble
exploit had been a summer at Boy Scout camp, served as
mess boy aboard a troop transport, carried dispatches in
the Motorcycle Corps, and then became a pilot and shot
down an Albatross night-fighter.

Ralph Fairbanks left the throttle of the Overland
Express and joined Mr. Adair, the railroad detective, in
tracking down dynamiters trying to blow up the troop
trains of the Great Northern line. Even the Camp Fire
Girls did their bit, engaging in counterespionage and
falling in love with dashing lieutenants in polished boots
and Sam Browne belts. The Moving Picture Boys dodged
whizzbangs and mortar shells, filming the hostilities for
posterity. Ned Newton led the Liberty Bond Drive in
Shopton, New York. Everyone pitched in with laudable

spirit, to beat the Boche. Only the Rover Boys, mysteriously, failed to join the action, after all that military schooling at Putnam Hall. Perhaps they were too young (a factor which did not seem to hinder Tom Slade or the Submarine Boys), and of course they were too old for World War II, in which the Hardy Boys were able to expose a spy academy right there in Riverdale.

With so many heroes helping out (and heroines too) the AEF soon put the Kaiser to flight, and the War and His Imperial Majesty were only memories when I was old enough to know about them. The Kaiser had become a shrunken little old man, living out his exile chopping wood in the Netherlands; appearing periodically in the Fox Movietone News ("The Eyes and Ears of the World") between Lew Lehr ("Monkies is de cwaziest people!") and girls water skiing at Cypress Gardens. I found him disappointing, as reality often is compared with fiction. I much preferred Sir Basil Zaharoff, described in the newsreels as the "mystery man of Europe," although what he was mysterious about I was never able to determine. He had style. Sax Rohmer would have approved of him, and so would Edward Stratemeyer. I had no doubt that he knew the answer to the "hitherto unsolved riddle of Peking."

Tom Slade was the brainchild of Percy Keese Fitzhugh, a prolific (more than a hundred titles) writer of boys' books and probably the greatest propagandist the boy scout movement ever had. He grew interested in the scouts in 1917, and they appeared in every one of his juvenile books. He contributed greatly to the growth of the movement and had the full blessing of scout officials, who reacted with some coolness to the Stratemeyer Syndicate's Boy Scouts series. When the Tom Slade books achieved success, Fitzhugh broke up Tom's troop, and wrote a series about each member. The result was the

Roy Blakely series, the PeeWee Harris books, Westy Martin, Lefty Leighton, Wigwag Wiegand, Spiffy Henshaw, and many more.

Fitzhugh, who hailed from Oradell, New Jersey, died in 1950 at the age of seventy-three, after an attempt to write a serious novel for adults (*The Wolves in the Barber Shop*). It was something less than a critical success, and he died, rich, and if unfulfilled at least (as far as my gang was concerned) beloved.

Tom Slade was Fitzhugh's incontrovertible proof that a boy with scout training can accomplish anything, even escape from a German prison camp. He scoffed at simple lore like moss growing on the north side of trees. Tom's command of nature's esoterica was so profound that it is a wonder he didn't capture the whole German Army singlehanded. He did pinpoint the location of a camouflaged Big Bertha cannon by the fact that a dud shell fired by the big gun carried with it a splinter of swamp larch. Swamp larch, of course, grows near rivers, and all he had to do was follow the water to likely breeding grounds for larch and cedar. In escaping through the Black Forest and Alsace, he was able to estimate his probable distance from the town of Bar l'Aube by the sound of a locomotive whistle.

Tom was an antihero in the classic mold of Huckleberry Finn. Unlike the Stratemeyer Syndicate's sleek, well-brushed boy heroes, he was clumsy, unkempt, and ungrammatical. In the beginning he was a hoodlum, "the best all-around hoodlum in town" according to the good citizens of Bridgeboro, New Jersey. His "wonderful reformation" in the early books of the series was due to the scouts and to philanthropist John Temple who had turned his Catskills estate into Temple Camp for boy scouts. Tom the ex-hoodlum became the best scout of them all.

He had a "square, dull face with a big mouth and the suggestion of a frown," and his "shock of hair was always rebellious."

> It was a curious thing about Tom Slade and a matter of much amusement to his friends, that however brave or noble or heroic his acts might be, he was pretty sure to get his necktie halfway around his neck and a dirty face in the bargain.
>
> (*Tom Slade on a Transport, p. 18*)

Tom lived with his drunken, lazy father (a carbon copy of Huck Finn's "Pap") and his ne'er-do-well brother in Barrel Alley, Bridgeboro's skid row. The family was evicted, Mr. Slade died, and the brother wandered out West ("to Arizona or someplace") only to turn up later as a German spy. Tom moved to Temple Camp as permanent charge-of-quarters. When the war came he was too young to enlist, and got a job on a steamer carrying munitions to the Allies, where he helped apprehend a spy, got torpedoed, spent two days in an open boat and was finally rescued with his chum Archibald Archer, a Catskill farm boy. He then signed on aboard the *Montauk*, a troop ship where another spy was signaling secret information to a German submarine by flashing Morse code with a polished tin plate. Trapping the traitor, Tom discovered it was none other than his own brother. After some soul-searching, he turned his relative in to the authorities.

> ". . . I was thinking about Uncle Sam—" He gulped and hesitated, then went on, "and—and—that's what made me think about Uncle Sam being a relation too—kind of—and I got to decide between my brother and my uncle—like." He gulped again and shook his head with a kind of des-

perate resolution. "There—there it is." [indicating the mess plate]

Trying desperately to master his feeling he broke down and big tears rolled down his cheeks. "I couldn't help it," he said to his brother. "It ain't cause I don't remember— but—I had to decide and I got to stand by Uncle Sam!"

(Tom Slade on a Transport, p. 94)

Soon after this incident Tom was to be torpedoed again, picked up by a German U-boat, and sent to a prison camp behind enemy lines where, once again, he discovered his pal Archibald Archer. The boys escaped using scout lore (coating the barbed wire with sal ammoniac to make it brittle) and returned to the Allied lines where they enlisted as dispatch carriers in the Motorcycle Corps until Tom was able to make his way into the Flying Corps. As Archie explained to a French Mam'zelle:

"The Prussians aren't so smart," said Archie. "They're good at some things, but when it comes to tracking and trailing and all that, they're no good. You never heard of any famous German scouts. They're clumsy. They couldn't stalk a mud turtle."

"You are not afraid of zem?"

"Sure we ain't. Didn't we just put one over on 'em?"

"We looped our trail," explained Tom to the puzzled girl. "If they're after us at all they probably went north on a blind trail. We monkeyed the trees all the way through the woods near here."

"He means we didn't touch the ground," explained Archer.

"We made seven footprints getting across the road to the fence and then we washed them away by chucking sticks. And anyway, we crossed the road backwards so they'd think we were going the other way. There ain't much danger. Not tonight anyway."

"You are wonderful," she said simply. "We shall win ze war now."

(Tom Slade With the Boys Over There, p. 15)

During their daring escape, the boys brought with them important documents relating to an impending German attack, which the Allies were able to frustrate in the nick of time. Stratemeyer heroes would have been showered with honors, medals, international publicity, and perhaps a financial bonus too, but not Fitzhugh's scouts. Tom and Archie never got more than a hearty handshake, unlike the Boy Allies who were decorated with the Victoria Cross by King George V himself. One small notice in the London *Times* was all the kudos the lads received, and that got their names wrong.

> Administration officials say that the arrival of two boys, fugitives from Germany, has been officially reported by the military authorities in France, and that they brought with them a letter taken from a dead German soldier which contained references to the impending German assault near Arracourt, thus enabling our men to anticipate and confound the Hun plans. Both of the boys, whose names are given as Archibald Slade and Thomas Archer, are now in training behind the American lines. A *Thomas* Slade is reported to have been in the steward's department of the transport *Montauk* which was struck by a submarine last spring. (Confirmed by Reuters)

(op. cit., p. 204)

A true patriot, Tom never minded being overlooked. In spite of Barrel Alley and his unprepossessing family, he was proud of his heritage.

". . . So I got to be proud of it, anyway," he said in

his honest, blunt fashion. "Maybe you won't understand but one thing makes me like to go away from Bridgeboro, kind of, is the way people say things about my folks. They don't do it on purpose—mostly. But anyway, all the fathers of the fellows I know, they call them Mr. Blakely, Mr. Harris, and like that. But they always called my father Bill Slade. I didn't ever hear anybody call him mister. But anyway he was born in the United States—that's one sure thing. And so was my grandfather and my grandmother too. Once my father licked me because I forgot to hang out the flag on Decoration Day. That shows he was patriotic, doesn't it? The other day I was going to tell you about my uncle but I forgot to. He was in the Civil War—he got his arm shot off. So I got a lot to be proud about anyway. Just because my father didn't get a job most—most of the time—"

"Ah!" vociferated Frenchy, clapping him on the shoulder, "You are ze—how you say—*one* fine boy!"

(op. cit., p. 66)

There was no girl back home for Tom, but nevertheless he had heart and gallantry, and girls went for him, big mouth, unruly hair and all. He knew how to talk to a lady, as we can see in his brief dialogue in occupied Alsace with a *jeune fille de bonne famille* who concealed him and Archie in an abandoned wine cellar during their escape.

"I feel sorry for you," Tom blurted out with simple honesty, "and I got to thank you. Both of us have—that's one sure thing. You're worse off than we are and it makes me feel mean, like. But maybe it won't be so bad. And, gee, I'll look forward to seeing you tomorrow night too."

"I will bring ze sings, *surely*," she said earnestly.

"It isn't—it isn't only for that," he mumbled. "It's because I'll kind of look forward to seeing you anyway."

For another moment she lingered and in the stillness of night and the thickly roofed arbor he could hear her breath coming short and quick as she tried to stifle her emotion.

He stood looking after her as she hurried away under the ramshackle trellis until her slender figure was lost in the darkness.

"It'll make me fight harder, anyway," he said to himself, "it'll help me get to France 'cause—'cause I *got* to, and if you *got* to do a thing . . . you can . . ."

(Tom Slade With the Boys Over There, p. 30)

Tom was to keep Florette Leteur (for that was her name) panting for most of a book. Pressed into service in a German hard labor camp for singing the *Marseillaise*, Florette was making little ones out of big ones with a pickax when Tom suddenly appeared in a captured German uniform and spirited her off over the Swiss border to safety. There were some hair-raising moments in the woods when Florette's morale sagged to the breaking point, and her feet hurt.

"Don't try to talk," he said huskily. "Over in America we have girl scouts—kind of. They call 'em Camp Fire Girls. Some people make fun of 'em, but they can climb and they don't scream when they get into a boat, and they ain't afraid of the woods, and they don't care if it rains, and they ain't a-scared of noises and all like that. You got to be one of them tonight. You got to be just like a feller—kind of. Even if you're tired you got to stick it out —just like France is doing."

"I am ze daughter of France," she said proudly, catching his meaning, "and you have come like America. Before . . . I was afraid. No more am I afraid. I will be zis fiery camp girl—So!"

"Not fiery camp girl," said Tom dully, "Camp Fire Girl."

"So! I will be zat!"

"And tomorrow we'll be in Switzerland."

(op. cit., p. 201)

Thanks to his scout training and a natural aptitude for mechanics, Tom breezed through flying school and won his silver wings, somehow achieving this without gaining any kind of military rank. After a few daredevil missions, he was observed in a dogfight with a swinish German ace and both combatants were reported down in flames. For once the local papers got his name right.

JERSEY BOY'S DRAMATIC END

THOMAS SLADE OF THE FLYING CORPS PLUNGED THREE THOUSAND FEET TO DEATH WHILE PURSUING BOCHE PLANE

HEROIC TRIUMPH PRECEDES HIS TRAGIC END

WREAKS VENGEANCE IN THE CLOUDS BEFORE HE FALLS. VOW TO KILL HUN WHO BOMBED AMERICAN HOSPITAL KEPT IN THRILLING VICTORY IN THE SKIES.

(Tom Slade With the Flying Corps, p. 2)

Tom's flaming end was, of course, all a mistake, compounded by the fact that his wallet was found containing incriminating documents he had captured from the German flyer. Everyone believed that Tom was not only dead but a German agent too, but he was to be found alive (suffering from amnesia) and cleared by a device undreamed of before and after the Slade series, even by Edward Stratemeyer. Fitzhugh wrote *himself* in as a *deus ex machina!* As author of the series he was a writer, and what better place for a writer in 1919 than at the front as a war correspondent? He not only followed Tom to Germany, using the first person all the way, but drummed up a bit of sympathy by getting himself gassed, carried to a field hospital, and undergoing a slow recovery with none other than Archie Archer in the next cot.

Fitzhugh's dispatches from the front kept the home folks informed for the duration.

> For a few seconds I beheld a scene which struck horror to my very heart. They say over here that every American soldier fights with a wrath and desperation born of some particular discovery or experience of Hun brutality. One goes forth with the thought of a maimed and tortured comrade to give him strength; another with the memory of some violated truce or false and murderous cry of *kamerad!* Well, here was the sight to arouse in me the hatred of those beasts which I had not sufficiently felt before.
>
> They had left their own people, *their own sick and wounded,* to suffer the agonizing death of those deadly gas fumes. If there are any degrees of loathesomeness, it seemed to me that this was more unspeakable than was the bombing of an enemy hospital.
>
> (*op. cit., p. 58*)

The Armistice brought Tom back to Temple Camp and Archie home to his Catskill farm, and mercifully got Fitzhugh out of the books so that the scouts could carry on and cope with the 1920s and winning the peace as best they could.

While Fitzhugh was slouching about in his trenchcoat, Edgar Rice Burroughs was not sitting idly in California. Tarzan was, after all, an Englishman and a Peer of the Realm, and there was blood to be let in Africa. Burroughs devoted only one book to the war, *Tarzan the Untamed,* which appeared in 1920, but that one had gore, derring-do and atrocities enough for a whole series. At the outset of the action a German patrol was silently enfilading the grasslands that surrounded the Greystoke estate in East Africa.

"We are in luck," said Schneider to his companions. "Do you see it?"

The lieutenant, who was also gazing through his own glasses, finally brought them to rest upon the same spot that had held the attention of his superior.

"Yes," he said, "an English farm. It must be Greystoke's, for there is none other in this part of British East Africa. God is with us, Herr Captain."

"We have come upon the English swinehund long before he can have learned that his country is at war with ours," replied Schneider. "Let him be the first to feel the iron hand of Germany."

(Tarzan the Untamed, p. 3–4)

The naïve Huns obviously were ignorant of the fact that *nobody* sneaks up on the Lord of the Jungle unawares. Tarzan was not at home, being off on an expedition in search of Wappi the antelope and Horta the boar. When he did arrive at the farm some days later, his sixth sense warned him that something was very, very wrong.

Silent and deserted was the vine-covered cottage. Smoldering embers marked the site of his great barns. Gone were the thatched huts of his sturdy retainers, empty the fields, the pastures and corrals. Here and there vultures rose and circled above the carcasses of men and beasts.

It was with a feeling as nearly akin to terror as he had ever experienced that the ape man finally forced himself to enter his home. The first sight that met his eyes set the red haze of hate and bloodlust across his vision, for there, crucified against the wall of the living room was Wasimbu,

giant son of the faithful Muviro and for over a year the
personal bodyguard of Lady Jane.

The overturned and shattered furniture of the room,
the brown pools of dried blood upon the floor, and prints
of bloody hands on walls and woodwork evidenced something of the frightfulness of the battle that had been
waged within the narrow confines of the apartment. Across
the baby grand piano lay the corpse of another black warrior, while before the door of Lady Jane's boudoir were
the dead bodies of three more of the faithful Greystoke
servants.

The door of this room was closed. With drooping
shoulders and dull eyes Tarzan stood gazing dumbly at
the insensate panel which hid from him what horrid secret he dared not even guess.

Slowly, with leaden feet he moved toward the door.
Gropingly his hand reached for the knob. Thus he stood
for another long minute and then with a sudden gesture
he straightened his giant frame, threw back his mighty
shoulders, and with fearless head held high swung back
the door and stepped across the threshold into the room
which held for him the dearest memories and associations
of his life. No change of expression crossed his grim and
stern-set features as he strode across the room and stood
beside the little couch and the inanimate form which lay
face downward upon it; the still, silent thing that had
pulsed with life and youth and love.

No tear dimmed the eye of the ape man; but the God
who made him alone could know the thoughts that passed
through that still half-savage brain. For a long time he
stood there just looking down upon the dead body,
charred beyond recognition, and then he stooped and
lifted it in his arms. As he turned the body over and saw
how horribly death had been meted he plumbed in that
instant the uttermost depths of grief and horror and
hatred.

(op. cit., p. 8)

Tarzan spent the next hour burying Jane and the other assorted cadavers in the rose garden. The Germans had not come off entirely unscathed, and there were enough deceased enlisted men left behind in uniform to allow the ape man to memorize company and regimental insignia. That was all he needed. With a snarl he was off into the trees in hot pursuit. German Army, watch out!

Needless to say, the charred corpse was not Jane's, but Tarzan was not to find this out until the very last page. In the meantime:

. . . It was Hate—and it brought to him a measure of solace and comfort, for it was a sublime hate that ennobled him as it has ennobled countless thousands since —hatred for Germany and Germans. It centered about the slayer of his mate, of course; but it included everything German, animate or inanimate. As the thought took firm hold on him he paused and raising his face to Goro, the moon, cursed with upraised hands the authors of the hideous crime that had been perpetrated in that once peaceful bungalow behind him; he cursed their progenitors, their progeny, and all their kind the while he took silent oath to war upon them relentlessly until death overtook him.

(*op. cit.*, *p. 11*)

Lucky thing the Kaiser had the Mediterranean, the Alps and most of the Sahara Desert between him and that Hate or he might never have chopped that kindling wood in Amsterdam. The ape man was a tough baby to fool with, as Captain Schneider was to find out. Tarzan trapped a ravenous man-eating lion in a small blind gulch, and dropped the German officer in with him. When last seen, Schneider was sitting in a little tree gibbering while Numa attempted to drag him down. It was only a matter of days, perhaps hours.

The ape man raised his face to Kudu, the sun, and from his mighty chest rose the savage victory cry of the bull ape.

(op. cit., p. 40)

Having done away with Schneider, the ape man was free to wage total war on the Germans. The hungry lion gimmick was an efficient one, and Tarzan kept alternately starving the beast and turning it loose in German trenches and *revêtements*. In this way he turned the tide of battle, and the previously retreating British troops turned to the attack.

The German offensive had been broken and the Huns were now slowly and doggedly retreating along the railway to Tanga. The break in the German lines had followed the clearing of a section of their left flank trenches of native soldiers by Tarzan and Numa, the lion.

(op. cit., p. 77)

With things going well for our side, Tarzan relaxed and devoted himself to observing hostilities from places of concealment in the trees, and Burroughs was able to spend some time in one of his favorite pursuits, undressing his characters. Pretty Bertha Kircher, age nineteen, very self-possessed for her age and why shouldn't she be? She was the pearl of German Intelligence, and had enslaved more than one young British subaltern. Lost in the jungle like every Burroughs character ever created, she came face to face with Numa.

Numa suddenly looked up from the girl's face at the thing beyond her. His growls increased to roars as he drew back, ripping the front of the girl's waist almost from her body with his long talons, exposing her white bosom, which through some miracle of chance the great claws did not touch.

(loc. cit.)

The thing beyond her was Tarzan, determined not to rescue her because she was a German, but it was no good. The gentleman in him came to the fore, and with a cry of "Go Numa! I am Tarzan of the Apes!" he whisked Bertha off into the foliage. She was later to be revealed as a British agent *pretending* to be a German agent, to the great relief of wealthy young Lieutenant Harold Percy Smith-Oldwick who had fallen in love with her while both were marooned in the jungle.

After a number of adventures, during which Tarzan found out that he had killed the wrong Schneider and had to kill another one; and during which Bertha was artfully unbloused several times and almost ravished by a lost tribe of maniacal throwbacks, everything straightened itself out and Tarzan led the young lovers through hostile Warambo country back to British GHQ. The captured diary of Hauptmann Fritz Schneider (the right one) revealed that Jane was still alive.

> "Played a little joke on the English pig. When he comes home he will find the burned body of his wife in her boudoir—but he will only *think* it is his wife. Had von Goss substitute the body of a dead Negress and char it after putting Lady Greystoke's rings on it—Lady G will be of more value to the High Command alive than dead."

(Tarzan the Untamed, p. 200)

Was there no limit to their deviltry? It was off to the rescue, and into *Tarzan the Terrible* and the postwar adventures. The British had won, and Tarzan was needed elsewhere. There were innocents to be marooned and blouses to be torn and virtue to be threatened. Lost tribes, lustful apes, and Arab slave traders were waiting to deflower busty ingenues, and Lord Greystoke's work was cut out for him.

By 1918 young Ralph Fairbanks had left the throttle of the Overland Express and assumed the mantle of Chief Dispatcher of the Great Northern Railroad. He was Mr. Fairbanks now to the boys in the roundhouse. The call of action was too much for him, in spite of his dependent, widowed mother and his essential job, and one fine day he dropped in at the recruiting office to do his bit. But the Stratemeyer Syndicate had decreed otherwise and Ralph was destined never to see the Western Front. During his enlistment physical

> Suddenly the army surgeon halted, stood off from Ralph, and stared him straight in the eye.
>
> "Have you been examined before, young man?" he asked. Ralph nodded. "What did the physician tell you?"
>
> "Something that I did not believe," the young fellow said frankly.
>
> "Something you did not want to believe, you mean?" Again Ralph nodded. "You can't get by with it," the surgeon said. "Don't go bothering about enlistment offices. We have a hard and fast rule regarding that trouble, and you cannot possibly get by with it."
>
> "Is—it—?"
>
> "Is it dangerous?" broke in the surgeon. "I could not say. Some people live long lives in much worse shape than you are in. But the danger is there. A sudden exertion—or an overstrain. Half a dozen things might happen which would work serious results because of your condition. Sorry young man. We can't take you. And you're a pretty specimen otherwise."
>
> (*Ralph on the Army Train, p. 46*)

"There goes a fellow who would make a fine soldier," said the doctor as Ralph went his way, "but he's got a rotten heart." Ralph had a "pronounced murmur" making him the first cardiac hero in the history of boys' literature. The murmur never kept him from leaping on and off speeding trains, and the series continued, as always, with Ralph in mufti.

As a finishing touch, a final *coup de grace* to any possible military career for Ralph, Stratemeyer waved his magic wand in East Orange and dimmed the young dispatcher's eyes.

> Ralph was losing flesh, and deep wrinkles were appearing between his eyes—the result of concentration of mind. His eyes had always been good, for a railroad man's eyes must be good. But he began to feel the strain upon his optic nerves, and he had his eyes tested and put on glasses at his desk.
>
> "A stitch in time saves nine—or nineteen, I don't know which it is," he told John Glidden. "But, anyway, maybe I can see better to get some of these extras through on time."
>
> (*op. cit., p. 97*)

A fine hero. No wonder the series petered out soon after. What kid could identify with a bespectacled desk jockey with a heart murmur? It's a wonder he didn't have flat feet.

Ralph wasn't the only one rejected. A number of the railroaders on the Great Northern were sent back for one reason or another.

> . . . Some thought the draft should have included those older than thirty-one years, for it was not yet universally understood that only the most vigorous and perfectly

healthy men could endure the hardships of present-day warfare.

"And they ain't giving us fellows anything to do at all," complained one ardent patriot in Ralph Fairbanks' hearing. "I'm as good as any lad going—only I happen to have been born a year or two too early, and I got that twisted arm down at Kipper Crossing makin' a flyin' switch about five years ago. It don't bother me none, but I can't enlist because of it."

"And all kinds of foreigners are being took when I'm refused. I'm a four-ply American. Say! when I was over to that enlistment station tryin' to get the doc to pass me, you ought to have seen the foreigners they took. My soul! some of 'em didn't know their right hand from their left—in English."

"Listen," continued the excited speaker to his interested hearers. "Here was one feller that had to stand on his tiptoes to reach the measurin' mark, and he was as hairy as a goat."

"The doc was puttin' him through his paces—askin' him questions. He says to the feller: 'Any scars?' and the feller hunts in his pocket and says, 'No, meester, but I got cigarettes.' What do you know about that?"

"Never mind," said Ralph, above the laugh. "Those fellows want to fight for their Uncle Sam."

"Aw, tell us what I can do?" broke in one of a switching crew. "I've got to stick to my job on this little old hump-backed railroad. I ain't so patriotic as a toad catching bugs in the back yard!"

"Sure you can be patriotic," Ralph declared. "Why the very vitals of this war are in our care."

(*op. cit.*, p. *109–110*)

Not all the crew was impressed by Ralph's little pep talk. Sam Leffert, who was both a slacker and a bully, and who was given to grinning sourly, had to put in his oar.

"What are you doin' besides your little eight-hour trick, Fairbanks?" he asked saucily. "You'll be one of these Four-Minute Men I hear talk about—do all your war work with your mouth, eh?"

(*loc. cit.*)

Ralph kept his temper. After all, there was a job to be done, slackers and wise guys or no slackers and wise guys. He kept his glasses on and did his job. There were enemies everywhere to be watched. The yards were full of potential saboteurs and the neighborhood was infiltrated with inimical "German-Americans, Germans and I.W.W.'s."

He was at the front right here in Stanley Junction! Every few days now troop trains and ammunition trains might be expected over his division.

If conspirators had undertaken to stop this particular train they would attempt similar crimes. "Thus far shalt thou go and no farther," King Canute had said to the tide. And what Canute said to the tide these plotters tried to say to the United States Government and the Great Northern Railroad!

"We'll see about that," muttered Ralph Fairbanks. "It's up to every one of us Americans to be on the watch for such rascals."

(*op. cit., p. 73*)

Ralph stayed on his guard, and an easy guard it was, because all German sympathizers on the Great Northern spoke with vaudeville Dutch accents in the style of Sig Rumann in the Marx Brothers' films. There was no difference in Ralph's (or the Stratemeyer Syndicate's) mind between Germans and Americans of German extraction, *Meyer vs Nebraska* notwithstanding.

"Vell de vorst I vish 'em is shplidt rail ven dey run dose troop trains t'roo mit her. That's de worst *I* vish 'em."

"You're crazy in the head, Jake! What good would it do that Keezer of yourn and that Von Hindenburg, or whatever the guy's name is to ditch just one train of dough-boys? The others'll git 'em just the same."

"Ach! You talk mit a foolishness—not me!" gutturally declared the first speaker, and more excitedly. "A hunderd t'ousand—*Nein!—a hunderd million of Yankee soldiers* won't nefer stop de Kaiser. De Germans can lick de vor-r-rldt yet."

"Sure! Lick their boots, Jake," sneered the other.

The heavy face of the man, Jacob, was mottled with anger; his thick chest puffed out like a bellows; his little gray-green eyes snapped.

"You fellers will see yet!" he growled. "Dere'll be trains wrecked. Dere'll be ships sunk. Dere'll be munitions yet blowed up. Dere'll be grain elevators fired. Herds of hosses undt mules vill die mit diseases. Fields of wheat vill be destroydt. You vait—"

"We won't wait for much more of such talk from you!" put in Ralph Fairbanks, his eyes aflame, pushing his way into the midst of the group of railroad employees.

(loc. cit., p. 3, 4)

Never was a train so encircled with dangers as that first troop train on the Great Northern. Parcels of dyna-mite were left under bridges, switches were left open, brakes were tampered with, engineers and firemen were suborned or abducted, but Ralph was determined to get it through on time, with the help of the railroad's detec-tive Mr. Bob Adair and his comical assistant Zeph. Their work was made no easier by the fact that the local arm of the law, Sheriff Greber, was a German-American ("I knows mein duty undt I do it"). After a thrilling ride on a handcar, his heart murmuring all the way, Ralph found

that the troop train's engineer had been bushwhacked
and hospitalized. Where to find a replacement in time?

"I believe you," agreed the train dispatcher. "Carraway
hasn't the experience."

"That's so, but where—"

"Right here, if you can't find a better man," Ralph said
briskly.

"You, Mr. Fairbanks? You mean that you'll take the first
troop train through?" cried the boss.

"Exactly. If you'll let me. I have studied that machine
of Jenks a little. I think Carraway and I will make out."

"By George!" shouted the engine master, "I wouldn't
ask for a better man. Go to it, sir! If anybody can get that
train over the division and in safety, it is you who can do
it, Ralph Fairbanks!"

(op. cit.)

And Ralph brought the troop train through and hurtled
himself on through Armistice Day and into *Ralph on the
Midnight Flyer, Ralph and the Missing Mail Pouch* and
early retirement with a gold watch and a railroad pass.
The dastardly German-Americans and I.W.W.'s were
foiled and the Yanks won the war.

Another notable non-combatant was Tom Swift, but
not for medical reasons. Tom was as strong as an oak tree
and athletic too. The government had no interest in the
young inventor's physique, however. It was his brain they
wanted, for Tom was a boffin of the best kind, a little too
early for nuclear fission perhaps, but of tremendous value
to Uncle Sam none the less. In the pre-war days the government had shown no little interest in his electric rifle,
and, after the messy business at Sarajevo, Tom produced
in quick succession his great searchlight, his giant cannon, his photo telephone, his aerial warship and his war

tank. Small wonder he wasn't wasted carrying a rifle in
the front lines. The laboratory was the place for him,
and, as he remarked to his chum Ned Newton:

> "I have told the government officials they can have
> anything I've got, and you know they wouldn't let me
> enlist when I was working on the war tank."
> "Yes, I remember that," said Ned. "You're no slacker!
> I wanted to shoulder a rifle too, but they keep me at this
> Liberty Loan work. Well, Uncle Sam ought to know."
> "That's what I say," agreed Tom, "and that's why I
> haven't gone to the front myself."

> *(Tom Swift and His Air Scout, p. 57)*

Tom's inventions, which brought him international
fame and a number of $100,000 bonuses to say nothing of
patents and stock options, were at the disposal of his
country. He was no profiteer, but he wasn't above having
his little joke with the federal procurement officers. When
the government came to negotiate for his silent airplane
engine, he could not resist.

> "The United States hasn't enough money to buy my
> patent of a noiseless motor," he said.
> "Wha—what!" faltered Mr. Terrell. "Why I understood
> —You don't mean—They told me you were rather patriotic,
> and—"
> "I hope I am patriotic!" interrupted Tom with a smile,
> "and when I say that the United States hasn't money
> enough to buy my latest invention, I mean just that."
> "My Air Scout is not for sale!"
> "You mean," faltered the government agent, "You
> say—"
> "I mean," went on Tom, "that Silent Sam is for Uncle
> Sam without one cent of cost!"

> *(op. cit., p. 216)*

Noble Tom, and noble Ned too, who worked with the Red Cross as well as negotiating the Liberty Loan. But enough about gallantry back home. Let's have a look at those who served on active duty.

The Henry Altemus Company, a Philadelphia publisher and competitor of Grosset & Dunlap in the juvenile line, came out with a number of war lovers. There were the Submarine Boys, the Battleship Boys, the Boys of the Army (who gained a stripe with each book, ending up as lieutenants) and two dashing cadets, Dick Prescott of West Point and Dave Darrin at Annapolis. The two last consisted of four books apiece, one for each year at the academy, after which Dick was discontinued but Dave went on to sea duty as an officer in six more books of a new series.

The Submarine Boys served under Captain Jack Benson, aged sixteen, who had become a "world-known expert in the handling of submarine torpedo boats" in spite of his tender years. Although he was too young for a Navy commission, Jack held the titular rank of captain, and commanded the *Benson,* the Pollard Submarine Company's newest and most secret undersea raider. Jack was accompanied by two other sixteen-year-olds, Hal Hastings and Eph Somers. It was 1910, and the powder keg of Europe was fulminating and sputtering in such a way as to thoroughly confuse the good Philadelphia publishers. They had no idea who the enemy was or would be, and the Submarine Boys were beset by every conceivable nationality of spy. There was a mysterious and beautiful Russian enchantress; a British agent; Kamanako, Japanese steward and houseboy who was really a naval officer; and even Miss Pedderson, a Swedish espionage agent. In the background was the evil Lemaire, a professional who worked for the highest bidder, and Gaston Goubeau of the Deuxième Bureau. There didn't seem to be any Germans or Austrians, but fashionable Spruce Beach, Florida, was so crowded with spies that anything could have happened.

The boys had no trouble foiling the plans of these foreign agents and keeping them from penetrating below decks of the *Benson*, at first, but who can reckon the depths to which a foreign agent will stoop to gain his ends? Lemaire was not above using the oldest weapon of all.

"Ah, good evening, Mademoiselle Nadiboff," murmured M. Lemaire, as he bent low before the handsome young woman. "I am charmed."

Then he murmured in a low tone swiftly:

"Yonder are the two boys. Jack Benson is the one you will interest. You, Sara, know the art of conversation well enough. Make him your slave, until he is willing to tell all that we want to know. Invite him to drive with you in your auto car tomorrow. But bah! You will know how to make him talk!"

(*The Submarine Boys and the Spies, p. 41*)

And indeed she did, but she reckoned without the devotion to duty of a teen-age fictional hero. She would have reduced me or any member of my gang to smoldering cinders but not Jack Benson. Beautiful Russian lady spies were nothing to him.

. . . scarlet spots glowed in her cheeks. In either eye a tear of anger glistened behind the lash.

"Are you satisfied?" murmured M. Lemaire in a low voice.

"I fear I shall have to teach the young cub a lesson or two in the art of showing devotion to a woman's wishes," Mlle. Nadiboff answered tremulously.

(*op. cit., p. 50*)

Mlle. Nadiboff was not a girl to take rejection kindly, and she was determined to get into that conning tower and sketch those secret instruments. Luring Jack into her auto car, she drove off with him into the scenic country-side, alone.

"Have you noticed how I seem to please most men?"

"I saw that several were very anxious to dance with you last evening, and that whenever you were seated, men flocked about your chair."

"Why do you suppose they did that?" challenged Mlle. Nadiboff.

"Because you are a very handsome woman, and the men admired you," Benson answered plainly.

"Ah! Then you think I am handsome?"

"I haven't a doubt of it," Jack answered.

"Do you admire me?"

The challenge came plain and direct. Mlle. Nadiboff now gazed searchingly into the submarine boy's eyes.

"I—I think you a very handsome woman to look at," Captain Jack admitted readily.

"Is that all you have to say?"

"I—I am afraid I do not understand you, Mademoiselle."

"You have no desire to be especially gallant to me? It would cause you no jealousy if you saw that I preferred the company of other men?"

Jack Benson returned her glance, almost in bewilder-ment for a moment. Then he leaned back, trying to stifle the impulse to laugh, but he did not wholly succeed.

"You are amused?" cried the young Russian half angrily.

"Amused—yes, at the idea of my falling in love, if that was what you meant to suggest," replied Jack, again speak-ing very candidly.

"And why should that amuse you, Captain?"

"Why, do you know how old I am, Mlle. Nadiboff? Or rather how young? I am only sixteen. At my age, if I formed any notion of being in love, it would be sensible to have me spanked and put on a short diet for a few days."

He laughed merrily, now, and Mlle. Nadiboff turned away her head to conceal the tears of vexation that started to her eyes.

(*op. cit., p. 98*)

Mlle. Nadiboff, who was twenty-nine, was a little mature for me too, but she was beautiful, if short-tempered. Many were the young officers who had succumbed to the witchery of her eyes, but the submarine boy was too tough a nut to crack.

"I was wrong to think Jack Benson a fool," she said to herself angrily. "He is far more clever than the men I have met. I must turn him over to Lemaire—to see if that prince of spies, as he is called, can find the flaw in this submarine boy's armor."

(*op. cit., p. 101*)

He couldn't. The "prince of spies" made the cardinal error of offering a boy hero money, probably the only item more loathesome to the genre than a woman's charms. Ten thousand dollars was offered, and

. . . for a few seconds Jack Benson did not dare trust himself to utter a word. When he did speak, it was to ask, calmly:

"M. Lemaire, who is your master?"

"My master?" repeated the Frenchman. "I do not understand you."

"Every dog, even a dirty one," thundered Captain Jack Benson, "has a master! Who is yours?"

(*op. cit., p. 115*)

As any young reader knows, a refused bribe is followed instantly by rough stuff, and M. Lemaire assisted by Mlle. Nadiboff with her riding whip and the chauffeur with a tire iron soon subdued our hero and tied him up. Perhaps torture would succeed where love and bribery had failed. Of course it did not, and after a wild chase there was a split-second rescue and Jack's life was saved by a chastened Mlle. Nadiboff, who was so impressed by the boy captain's honesty and courage that she promised to reform, and never to insult her womanhood by spying again. The *Benson* sailed off to new adventures and eventual assimilation into the U. S. Navy to fight the Boches on the high seas. It is to be hoped that love finally did find its way into young Captain Jack's heart, but the readers were never to know. The series ended too soon, with its heroes still in their teens.

A. L. Burt, another Grosset & Dunlap competitor, was not slow to get into the lucrative war series. Unlike the Philadelphia outfit, Burt had dabbled in war themes earlier, with the Boy Spies and the Navy Boys. These militant teen-agers were firmly implanted in 1776, however, helping George Washington beat the redcoats. With the commencement of hostilities in Europe, the flintlock and three-cornered hat set lost popular interest. Boys wanted action centered around the latest equipment in the newspapers. Burt complied with a dashing pair called "Our Young Airplane Scouts" who fought in France, Belgium, Turkey, Russia, England, Italy, and the Balkans, with specific stopovers at Verdun and the Marne.

Our Young Airplane Scouts was probably the worst-written boys' series in juvenile literary history. The author, "Horace Porter," was so bad he was almost good. His prose was surrealistic, Joycean in tone. Every paragraph was a single sentence.

To get a "lead-line" on the Hun crowd before they bunched too closely about the defiant "ace" creating proximity that would make a scattering downfire alike dangerous to friend and foe, Billy and Henri, drawing together, swooped, as one, and with machine guns trained in deadly accuracy proceeded to accomplish the "cutting-off" process in as quick a minute as possible.

The decimating operation was working, as the Barry boy would say, "like a house afire," in spite of the counter demonstration of the at first surprised but now aroused infantrymen, blazing away with their rifles at the young war eagles darting about overhead, when all at once the attacking aviators realized from a source higher up that there were others getting into the thrilling game at the topside.

While this new diversion was momentarily agitating the flying twins and stirring their mettle to fight for the best way out, and while, also, the survivors on foot of the boys' lightning-like onslaught were raising a shout of triumph, the "bone of contention," one René Lecompte, went through the thin, gray line in front of him, as a bullet through cheese, and sprinted, a veritable streak of blue, over a hundred-yard course, toward the goal spot that centered the combat plane, out of which the gallant rider had recently hopped to effect an enemy capture.

(*Our Young Airplane Scouts at the Marne*, p. 18)

Any kid who could penetrate the smoke screen of dangling clauses and ragged appositives would find himself in a puzzling morass of unrealistic combat, in which the teen-age aces, Henri Trouville of an old French family and Billy Barry of Bangor, Maine, shot down dozens of Huns a day, attacking as many as twelve of the enemy (as Billy did in *Our Young Airplane Scouts at the Marne: or, Harrying the Huns from Allied Battleplanes*) although he had a damaged engine and one jammed machine gun.

He shot them all down too. By 1919 the smashing of the Hindenburg Line smashed the Our Young Airplane Scouts series too, and Horace Porter dropped into well-deserved obscurity, or, perhaps, moved to Paris to help write the Dada Manifesto.

Although we dabbled with these lesser series because we were willing to read anything at all provided it had to do with the war, and although we had a healthy respect for Percy Keese Fitzhugh and his front-line boy scouts, we were ripe for a couple of extra-special blood-and-gore war series, and we got them. Edward Stratemeyer had not forgotten us, in spite of his keeping Tom Swift away from the front. No sooner had the Great Unwashed invaded plucky little Belgium than a new stream of molten lava issued forth in the form of the Moving Picture Boys series, the creation of our old friend "Victor Appleton" (Tom Swift, the Motion Picture Chums, Don Sturdy).

Simultaneously, A. L. Burt came out with the series that, for some reason, stood head and shoulders above the rest in our estimation. It was the Boy Allies, divided into two completely different sets of teen-age heroes, both of which were called the Boy Allies. One group, written by "Ensign Robert L. Drake" served with the Navy, and the others, the handiwork of "Clair W. Hayes," were with any allied army that would have them including the Czar's Cossacks, until the U.S. moved in and absorbed them.

In spite of competing derring-do and the mastery of the Stratemeyer Syndicate, we fought the war from Liège to Vimy Ridge with the Boy Allies. They were the best-beloved, although their prose was almost as bad as that of the Young Airplane Scouts. It can be noted that Stratemeyer didn't compete too hard. He seemed to think that the war was in questionable taste. He had nothing

against blood and mayhem, but for the most part his
heroes were unwilling or accidental combatants, photographers, inventors, and so on. The Boy Allies, on the other
hand, were in the thick of it. No sooner had they suffered
the deadly twelve days of the Marne, than they were off
to the Carpathians with the Cossacks, back to the Aisne,
and then seconded to the Italian Army for the Alpine
campaign. After that it was the Somme, Verdun, and
detached service with the Canadians at Vimy Ridge. A
stint on General Pershing's staff was broken when they
went over the top at Château-Thierry, and they finished
the war in style as aides to Marshal Foch.

The Navy lads performed similar feats at Jutland and
in the North Sea and the Baltic, serving with every allied
fleet in pursuit of the German Navy. Both sets of Boy
Allies hobnobbed on a basis of mutual personal esteem
with the great men of the war, Haig, Pershing, Winston
Churchill, and all the crowned heads in addition to Foch
and Clemenceau, and they won every possible honor and
decoration.

Since the Boy Allies were the only series heroes to
concentrate seriously on the naval aspects of the Great
War, let's have a look at the seafaring pair. Frank Chadwick was an American lad of seventeen, stranded in Italy
when his father unaccountably vanished immediately
after the outbreak of hostilities. Searching for his parent
in the back streets of Naples, he was shanghaied aboard
an Italian schooner, where the usual mutiny promptly
occurred, leaving Frank a prisoner in irons with one other
unfortunate, a British Secret Service man.

The schooner put in at a small African seaport for supplies, planning to steal them from the trading post run by
orphaned Jack Templeton, eighteen and English. Jack
pursued the mutineers, boarding the schooner just as the

anchor was going up, and by "resourcefulness, strategy, and good hard fighting" subdued the Italians and gained the upper hand. He quickly released Frank and the two boys became instant chums. The British agent was also released, and revealed that his mission was to "play a leading role in the diplomatic coup that was to keep Italy from going to the aid of her partners in the Triple Alliance, Germany and Austria." Would the boys volunteer to help? You bet they would, and of course the coup was brought to a successful conclusion. As a reward, the boys (who had unaccountably become twenty and twenty-one somehow by the second book) were commissioned midshipmen in the Royal Navy by King George V himself.

It was off to Heligoland in the *Boy Allies on the North Sea Patrol*, where they were personally responsible for blockading the German Fleet and sinking four ships. For this feat they were promoted to the rank of lieutenant. In the course of events the boys became involved with Lord Hastings, a naval officer and a distant relative of the King, who took a liking to them and kept them with him for the whole series. Together they pursued the German cruiser *Emden* (*The Boy Allies With the Terror of the Sea*) and destroyed a German squadron off the Falkland Islands. They fought in the Dardanelles, sinking three Turkish cruisers, and with the Japanese at Tsingchau. They served on detached duty with the French fleet in the Adriatic and with the Russians in the Baltic. Of course things did not always go smoothly and they were sunk again and again, and captured on numerous occasions, but they always escaped, wreaking havoc on the enemy as they went.

It was usually Jack who rescued Frank. Although the American boy was sturdy and strong, he was no match

for his husky British chum. Frank was also the more hot-
headed of the pair, and often took foolish chances, but
Jack's British calm always saved them.

> Jack was what Frank called a "real fighter" and had
> proved his mettle more than once since the two had been
> together. Strong as an ox, he was a bad customer to tackle
> in a rough and tumble, and he was exceedingly proficient
> in the use of his fists. Also he was a fair swordsman and
> a fair shot.
> It was in the latter that Frank excelled. He was a dead
> shot with either rifle or revolver, as he had proved in sev-
> eral tight situations . . .
> Fortunately both lads spoke German and French as
> well as English, and under Lord Hastings' tutoring had
> picked up a smattering of Italian, Russian and Hungarian.

> (*The Boy Allies With the Flying Squadron, p. 10*)

With the entree accorded them by their close relationship with Lord Hastings, the lads sauntered in and
out of royal residences with the cool aplomb of Frank
Sinatra strolling into Jilly's. During their Baltic tour, which
allowed them a layover in Petrograd, they overheard a
plot cooked up by the Chief of the Russian Secret Police,
and hurried over to Tsarskoie Seloe to inform the Czar.
The Autocrat of All the Russias was delighted to see them.

> He extended a hand to each, and both lads flushed.
> Jack, the subject of a monarch himself, dropped to one
> knee, but Frank, who recognized no monarch, bowed low,
> and remained on his feet. The Czar signalled Jack to rise
> and then turned to Lord Hastings.
> "Am I to consider this just a friendly call or have you
> anything to impart to me?" he asked.
> "Both, your Majesty," replied Lord Hastings gravely.
> "I may as well come to the point of my mission at once."

"Do," said the Czar briefly.

"Very well. What I have to say is this: In your service —and in high standing and authority—is a man who is a traitor—a man who has sold out to our common foe, the Germans."

"So?" said the Czar, apparently no whit surprised. "His name, if you please."

"His name," said Lord Hastings with a faint smile, "will surprise you. I fear you will find it hard to believe; and had I not the proof of the man's duplicity, I should not have the courage to mention the man."

Evidently Lord Hastings' words made an impression on the Czar. He stirred uneasily.

"Come, come," he said. "The man's name. Out with it, my Lord."

"His name," said Lord Hastings very gravely, "is Count Stephan Blowinski!"

"What!" roared the Czar, leaping from his seat. "Count Blowinski! The chief of the Russian secret police! Impossible, Lord Hastings. I would stake my life and throne upon his integrity, my Lord."

"Then you would lose both, sire," said Lord Hastings, gravely.

(op. cit., p. 73)

It was with some trouble that Jack, Frank, and Lord Hastings convinced Nicholas II that his police chief was sending secrets off to the Germans, but at last the Czar bowed to the weight of their evidence. But what to do about it? In boys books no one ever just gets arrested. It was necessary to outwit the evil count, and any habitual reader of series books could guess what would happen. The Czar and Lord Hastings devised a clever stratagem to send an agent to ingratiate himself with Count Blowinski and learn his plans.

"A clever idea," declared the Czar, after consideration, "if I could but lay hands on such a man. He must be one who speaks German like a native German, and one whom the count could never, by any chance, have seen before. If I could only find a man equal to such a task!"

"Or men or boys, sire," said Frank boldly.

The Czar and Lord Hastings both whirled upon him.

"What is that?" demanded the Czar.

"I mean, sire," said Frank, flushing slightly, "that my chum here and I would be only too glad to undertake such a mission. I am sure that we come up to requirements."

(op. cit., p. 77)

Of course they were employed on the spot, and in short order they had become bosom companions of Count Blowinski. The scheme was very nearly compromised by this close relationship, for Blowinski, a bon vivant of the old Russian school, demanded that the boys join him in a glass of wine, a horrifying suggestion, since neither of the young heroes would ever sully his lips with alcohol. Again quick wit and resourcefulness saved the day.

As the count threw back his head and drained the glass, each lad was able to dispose of his wine in a jardinière which stood nearby.

(op. cit., p. 96)

In the course of the adventure the boys got themselves chased, captured, and sent to a penal colony in Siberia, from which they escaped, discomfited a rebellious Russian general (Frank defeated him in a duel) and returned triumphantly to Petrograd to officiate at the wine-bibbing traitor's downfall. For this success His Imperial Majesty commissioned them honorary lieutenants in the Russian Army.

And so it was back to sea duty again, this time in the latest model submarine, a startlingly revolutionary craft, technically far advanced beyond other U-boat prototypes. The British Navy's D-17 was

. . . as unlike other under-water craft as day is from night.

In the first place she was able to remain under water indefinitely. It was not necessary for her to return to the surface every so often to replenish her air tanks, for she carried no tanks. The D-17 generated her air supply from the water, by means of a secret process known only to high officials of the British Admiralty. She had a speed of more than thirty knots when submerged, could move along even faster upon the surface of the water, and her bow, a solid piece of substantial glass in which reposed a huge searchlight, made it possible for her to pick her course under the water—something that no other submarine craft was able to do. For this latter reason she could venture places where no other vessel would dare.

(*op. cit.*, *p. 7*)

The author had forgotten that in a previous book he had foolishly revealed the secret of D-17's air system. It was *gills*, just like a fish, extracting oxygen and breathing out carbon dioxide. The D-17 was nothing compared to the D-32, on which the boys served much later after the United States had entered the war.

It was a time for versatility in junior officers. Specialized training and restricted career fields had not yet come into fashion, and Jack and Frank were ready and able to handle any kind of equipment, no matter how sophisticated. If it wasn't surface or undersea, it was air, and they were allowed to participate in the Royal Navy's first seaplane raid on Cuxhaven, indiscriminately bombing women and children.

Straight on over the outer fortifications the British air fleet flew, to the very extremity of the German town, dropping bomb after bomb as they progressed.

Below, the people were in a panic. As great bombs fell and burst in the street, plowing them up, killing and maiming those in their way, people cried out in fear and fled toward the interior.

Buildings, wrecked by the projectiles from the air, toppled over on them and buried them. Fires broke out in several parts of the town almost simultaneously.

And still the hail of death from above continued.

In vain did the German guns on the forts strive to drive off the enemy. The British air fleet, darting hither and thither, was untouched.

For an hour they continued to rain explosives upon the fortifications and the city below. The havoc was terrible, and the streets below presented a pitiful aspect.

But it was war.

(*The Boy Allies in the Baltic, p. 137*)

Indeed it was, and the maimed were, after all, only Germans, an expendable group according to the literature of the day. Having softened up Cuxhaven, the boys dressed up in German uniforms and entered Hamburg on an intelligence mission, and then shifted to motorboat duty, where they sank a German cruiser with a single grenade loaded with melinite, a new superexplosive.

Active duty for the Boy Allies was always punctuated with shore leave in a royal palace, and the Hamburg-Cuxhaven capers brought them a spell in London and an invitation to a ball at Buckingham Palace. You know and I know that a large dressy gathering of nobs in fancy clothes always leads to one thing. Spies. Sure enough, the boys spotted a foreign-looking man with a marked German accent, exchanging secret maps behind a potted palm with George Stille, secretary to a high Admiralty official. Inquiry revealed that the man was "Count Bernthol, a Bulgarian noble who has for years been something of a mystery." That did it. It was off to Lord Hastings to report, and that grave nobleman did not hesitate to call a council of war.

The boys followed their commander to the far end of the palace where they were left alone. Fifteen minutes later, however, Lord Hastings returned, and with him some of the highest military and naval officials of Great Britain, among them Winston Churchill, first Lord of the Admiralty, Chancellor of the Exchequer Lloyd George, and Earl Grey, the British Premier. To these men, not without some confusion, the lads repeated their story.

"Stille!" exclaimed Mr. Churchill.

"Well, why not Stille as well as another?" asked Earl Grey.

"Immediate action must be taken," said Lloyd George briefly. "The traitor and the spy must be arrested at once!"

"But," said Lord Hastings, "we must have more evidence. It is not probable that the unsupported word of these two boys would be taken against theirs."

"True," said Mr. Churchill. "What would you suggest, Lord Hastings?"

"My plan," was the quick reply, "would be to have additional maps prepared at once. Then when Stille is making a copy of them we can all watch. Let the arrest be made as he hands them to Count Bernthol."

"A good plan," said Lloyd George, "but Bernthol must be prevented from forwarding the maps he has to Germany."

Jack stepped forward.

"If you will allow us, sir," he said. "My friend and I will follow the spy, and we will guarantee that the maps do not leave his hand!"

(*op. cit., p.* 80)

The plan went off like clockwork, and a chase ensued through wartime London, with the miscreants in a taxi and the boys, Lord Hastings and Churchill in an Admiralty limousine. The spies went to ground in what was "probably the most fashionable restaurant in London and at the same time probably the most notorious," and a gunfight ensued in which Jack saved the First Lord's life.

> The bullet missed Mr. Churchill by a hair's breadth; but before the Count could fire again, or before the First Lord of the British Admiralty could take any action to defend himself, a second revolver cracked and Bernthol went tumbling to the floor.
>
> Jack, perceiving Mr. Churchill's danger, had fired over the latter's shoulder.
>
> *(op. cit., p. 104)*

Foiled again. What course might history have steered in the next three decades, but for Jack's brave act?

Back at Buckingham Palace again, the King greeted Lord Hastings and the boys with a hearty "What's new?" and was so impressed by Lord Hastings's recital of the boys' most recent exploits that he whispered a few words into the ear of an aide-de-camp who left for a few moments and returned with a small leather box.

> King George V advanced quickly toward the two lads, and with a sudden movement pinned to the breast of each a little medal; then stepped as quickly back again.
>
> Frank and Jack glanced at the insignias, and then, in spite of the presence of the King, who smiled at them good-naturedly, uttered exclamations of astonishment.
>
> For pinned to the breast of each by the King's own hand was a Victoria Cross!
>
> Their bravery and daring had brought their reward.
>
> Both lads fell on their knees before the King.

"Your Majesty—" began Frank, but the King interrupted him.

"Thanks are unnecessary," he said quietly. "You deserve them."

(op. cit., p. 248)

And so they did, as any kid reading the series at the time would have agreed. Uncle Sam was soon to enter the war and the boys would carry on their good work until the last shot was fired, having less trouble finding jobs after demobilization than some of us did, I have no doubt. After all, connections count.

The Boy Allies shook the Stratemeyer Syndicate's complacency, and Edward Stratemeyer, in spite of his avoidance of active participation in the war, resorted to counterstrategy. Victor Appleton's Moving Picture Boys were removed from their customary activity of photographing grizzly bears, floods and cattle rustlers, and sent to the front.

The Moving Picture Boys were not to be confused with Appleton's other cinematographic series, the Motion Picture Chums, who owned a chain of theaters and were in the business and production side. The Moving Picture Boys were photographers, and they always beat everyone else to the action and got it down on celluloid, in spite of shot and shell. When they weren't squarely in the middle of no-man's-land, cranking away at their cameras, they were back at the canteen, skylarking with pretty movie starlets Nellie Shay and Birdie Lee, cheering the troops on a YMCA sponsored show tour.

Blake Stewart and Joe Duncan were bright, stalwart American youths working down on the farm until they came into contact with a motion picture company filming some bucolic scenes in the neighborhood. Mr. Hadley, the company manager, took the boys under his wing, and it was good-bye to barns and silos and off to New York for *The Moving Picture Boys; Or, Perils of a Great City Depicted.* They covered disasters of all kinds until

> . . . while they had been having these experiences the United States had been goaded into war with Germany because of the intolerable outrages on her citizens. Blake and Joe were ardent patriots and they eagerly accepted a proposition to visit the battlefront in France and take pictures of American warlike activities for the benefit of the government.

> (*The Moving Picture Boys on French Battlefields, p. 20*)

After the usual submarine disaster, sparked by the usual German spy (all neatly filmed), the boys got to France with their assistant "Mac," and immediately headed over the top.

Appleton-Stratemeyer pulled no punches and the Huns were nastier than ever. There was plenty of blood, and atrocities blossomed in every chapter. As Blake said:

> "I don't want them to quit too soon. That would make it too easy for them. I'd like to see the war pushed on German soil. I want them to taste a little of what they've given to France and Belgium. I want them to hear the roar of cannon and the screaming of shells in their own cities and villages. I want to see their roads choked with refugees fleeing for their lives. Of course, we wouldn't do to them what they've done to the French and Belgians. We simply couldn't. It isn't in our nature. We couldn't stand up old men and little boys and shoot them down. We couldn't kill helpless women and babies, but I would like to see some of their cities go up in flames and their villages turned into piles of rubbish."

> (*op. cit., p. 35*)

Blake's bloodthirsty prophesy was to come true, not once but twice in the coming decades, but his job as a teen-age correspondent was to take pictures (although the boys stopped periodically and hefted Enfield rifles for an occasional bit of Boche blood-letting, legality be damned).

The girls were not sitting idly by, while the boy heroes were soaking up shrapnel at Paaschendaele. Barred by age and sex from enlistment, the Camp Fire Girls were in a pet.

"I wish I were a man," [Sahwah] exclaimed impatiently. "Then I could go to war and fight for my country and— and go over the top. The boys have all the glory and ex- citement of war and the girls have nothing to do but the stupid, commonplace things. It isn't fair!"

"But women *are* doing glorious things in the war," Mig- wan interrupted quickly. "They're going as nurses in the hospitals right at the front; they're working in the can- teens and doing lots of other things right in the thick of the excitement."

"Oh yes, *women* are," replied Sahwah, "but *girls* aren't. Long ago I used to think if there ever *would* be a war the Camp Fire Girls would surely do something great and glorious, but here we are, and the only thing we can do is knit, knit, knit, and fold bandages, and the babies in the kindergarten are doing *that*. We're too *young* to do anything big or splendid. We're just schoolgirls and no- body takes us seriously. We can't go as nurses without three years of training—we can't do *anything*. There might as well not *be* any war, for all I'm doing to help it. Boys seventeen years old can enlist, even sixteen-year-old ones, and go right to the front, but a girl sixteen years old isn't any better off than if she were sixteen months. I'm nearly nineteen, and I wanted to go as a stenographer, but they wouldn't consider me for a minute. Said I was too young."

(*The Camp Fire Girls Do Their Bit, p. 15*)

And a good thing too. Stratemeyer would have had her blown out of a submarine, captured, decorated and typing in a dugout in no-man's-land. Percy Keese Fitzhugh would have dictated his endless dispatches from the front. The Boy Allies would have had her taking down *aides-memoires* from Clemenceau and wearing the Palme Academique. Edgar Rice Burroughs would have unbloused her in a jiffy.

Sahwah might have added that the war sold books too, to the misfortune of girls' series (although top-seller Nancy Drew ignored World War II for four years without any problem.) Hildegarde G. Frey, the Camp Fire Girls' creator, did not keep Sahwah knitting very long. The Camp Fire Girl had a tender, romantic love affair with a dashing young aviation officer, contributing to his morale indescribably by giving him a locket with her picture in it. She also trapped a German spy, masquerading as an American officer.

Even that wet smack the Little Colonel pitched in, in her own unbearable way, by donating her beloved doggie, Hero, to the Red Cross for special training. But Hero, returning to a stateside army camp from a mission in the woods, was accidentally shot by a nervous sentry.

"Think how it must have hurt poor Hero's feelin's," Lloyd was saying, "to go back to their camp so trustin' so happy, thinkin' the men would be so glad to see him, and that he was doin' his duty, and then have one of them stand up and send a bullet through his deah, lovin' old heart. Oh I can't *beah* it," she screamed. "Oh I can't! I can't! It seems as if it would kill me to think of him lyin' ovah there all cold and stiff with the blood on his lovely white and yellow curls, and know that he'll nevah, nevah again jump up to lick my hands and put his paws on my shouldahs. He'll nevah come to meet me any moah wag-

gin' his tail and lookin' up into my face with his deah,
lovin' eyes . . ."

(*The Little Colonel's Hero, p. 130*)

The whole camp turned out to blow taps for Hero and
he was placed in a little grave marked by a white stone
with a brave red cross on it, right under Lloyd's very own
little old window. What wouldn't Edgar Rice Burroughs
have done to *her!*

With a head full of Hitler and Mussolini and a heart
full of Tom Slade and the Boy Allies, I went off to the
wars and found them somewhat different than I had been
led to expect. Older, wiser, and less enthusiastic, I returned home with a box full of souvenirs to delight my
own kid someday, but nobody seemed very interested
in service medals and canvas musette bags any more.
Times had changed and a genre had died. The Boy Allies
and their colleagues were red with rust, their muskets
molding in their hands. If we're lucky, they'll stay that
way.

CHAPTER SEVEN

JUST KIDS LIKE YOU AND ME

("*Whoops! hurrah! Zip, boom, ah! Rockets!*"

"*For gracious' sake Tom, what's all the racket about? I thought we had all the noise we wanted last night, when we broke up camp.*"

"*It's news, Dick, glorious news,*" *returned Tom Rover, and he began to dance a jig on the tent flooring.* "*It's the best ever.*"

"*It won't be glorious news if you bring this tent down on our heads,*" *answered Dick Rover.* "*Have you discovered a gold mine?*"

"*Better than that, Dick. I've discovered what we are going to do with ourselves this summer.*" . . .

"*But where do you propose to go to, Tom?*"

"*For a trip on the broad and glorious Ohio River.*")

(*The Rover Boys on the River, p. 1*)

Just kids, like you and me, so said the authors from the heights of their middle-aged and pre-income tax splendor. But the kids in the series books were not like any kids I ever knew, any more than Andy Hardy, my own contemporary, was any parallel to my high school career.

An ordinary kid, according to the literature of my boyhood, was a cheerful, well-beloved, well-behaved ragamuffin, a little mentally retarded and unable to reason logically. He was invariably honorable, incapable of falsehood, cheating, or double-dealing of any kind. Because he had right on his side, and refused to knuckle down, he could flatten bullies considerably above his weight class. This never worked for me, right or wrong. He either detested girls or reluctantly shared supervised picnics and parties with them, admiring a special girl in a comradely, asexual way. He never thought about them in a context of "disgusting filth" (my pals and I adored them and thought of nothing else).

He hated baths, (I loved them) ate like a horse (I was finicky about meals) and had unlimited freedom (my parents kept a close check on my activities). He lived in a roomy old house with attics and lawns in a pleasant small town (we lived in an apartment in the city).

He was an habitual loser, stumbling into pitfalls at sixteen that any sensible six-year-old would have detected and avoided with ease. He remained in some insoluble pickle until the very last chapter, in which everything came out all right.

As he mellowed into full puberty and progressed into his later teens, his ragamuffin quality gave way to simple, well-brushed good looks. Day-to-day life brought amazing adventures of all kinds, but nothing fazed him. He was totally fearless. His earlier relations with girls developed into an easy camaraderie in which he always had the upper hand, and was much respected and even feared, though certainly admired by the opposite sex. He was Popular. He was Attractive. But it didn't go to his head. He didn't use his attraction to steal kisses or fondle shirtwaists. He saved himself for Miss Right and his eventual and inevitable wedding day.

They were, all of them from Penrod to the Rover Boys, as unlike us as any contrast can possibly be. My gang had more of the sulky violence of Tarzan than they had of the middle-aged crankiness of Penrod or the obtuse priggishness of Tom Rover, yet we identified with those boy heroes through every waking hour. We read them and we loved them, and we would have imitated them if we had known how, but things always happened to them automatically, fortuitously, out of nowhere, in simple school situations. Nothing ever happened to us. We didn't know how fortunate we were. Things would start happening to us soon enough.

The formula for a book about kids, unless the protagonists were specialists like Tarzan, the Hardy Boys, or Baseball Joe, was a simple one. A series always centered around a small town; except that at least once in each

series a boy had to transfer his activities out West, once
to somewhere full of ice and snow, once to a jungle full
of animals and unregenerate natives, and once aboard
ship. The rest of the time he could lounge around the
house or one of the boarding schools that seemed to exist
everywhere at that period. The hero had a small group of
cronies who accompanied him everywhere. There was
always a fat boy, an athletic boy, and a rib-tickling joker.
There was also a bully, accompanied by two or three
toadies, who moved heaven and earth to irritate our
heroes. The bullies, oddly enough, appeared wherever
the protagonists happened to be, even if it were the head-
waters of the Amazon. Just push back a handful of lush,
tropical foliage and there was the grinning face of Dan
Snodgrass or whoever it might be at the moment.

Of course the boys achieved whatever Bluebird of Happiness they had been pursuing, and the bullies were either
shelved for the next book or reformed by contagious exposure to honor, goodness, and truth.

The trips abroad were in the minority in this genre of
boys series, although they were an important part. Most
of the action centered around school or home. Parents
were kidnaped or wiped out by dishonest stockbrokers,
and they and their fortunes had to be reclaimed. Dire
plots were laid (by the bullies and their associates) to
frame the heroes as thieves, cheats, or scoundrels so that
they would be expelled and sent home in disgrace, or
even jailed. Girls had to be defended against nameless
horrors. There was always something to do in those
Riverdales and Grovers Cornerses. In our neighborhood
nothing out of the ordinary had happened since the ex-
tension of the Eighth Avenue Subway into Queens. The
girls I knew never needed defending. They could take
care of themselves. Nobody ever tried to kidnap my parents. As for double-dealing stockbrokers, they would have

had a bad time of it impoverishing my father, who was having his troubles with the Depression. He remembered 1929, and every penny he had was in a small savings account at the Corn Exchange Bank, or in government bonds. A swindling bucket shop proprietor would have been laughed out of our house.

For home town excitement I had to depend on books, at least until I was older and the panzer divisions rolled into Poland. Edward Stratemeyer, Percy Keese Fitzhugh, Leo Edwards, and the rest never let me down. I accepted the fact that there never would be an outbreak of *thuggee* in Kew Gardens, and retreated into the misty, unstable realm of Jerry Todd, Trigger Berg, Tom Slade, Poppy Ott, the Rover Boys, and all their young contemporaries. I resigned myself to the role of a Mycroft Holmes, and slumped in my armchair night after night peering through what my English teacher always referred to as the "magic casements" that looked out on a more interesting world.

A good many of my favorites had originated in the late 1920s and early 1930s in an attempt to keep up with the thinking of modern youth, but there were some sturdy reprints from the turn of the century and the war years. Notable among these was the Rover Boys Series for Young Americans, the work of "Arthur M. Winfield" who was, in reality, none other than Edward Stratemeyer. Stratemeyer wrote the Rovers series himself, and it was his favorite among the boys' books turned out by his syndicate. His enthusiasm was reflected in the sales charts, over six million copies before modern times put the final quietus on the adventures of Dick, Tom, and Sam and their chums. They were to be succeeded by their own sons for a while, and eventually by the Hardy Boys who were very like the Rovers except for their professional specialization.

The first of the series (*The Rover Boys at School*) was written in 1899, at a time when the big sellers in the field were the moralistic works of Horatio Alger. Stratemeyer had written a few of the genre under the names of Horatio Alger, Jr. and Oliver Optic, and the Rover Boys books contained a good deal of the fancy prose and polysyllabic frills of the earlier style. He also inaugurated a new wrinkle, actual communication with his flock in the form of a pastoral letter to his young readers at the beginning of each volume. Sometimes the letters were signed Arthur M. Winfield, but with increasing success he scuttled that idea and began to sign his own name in spite of the fact that Winfield still appeared on the cover as author. Here is a typical letter, from *The Rover Boys on the River*, written in 1905:

My Dear Boys:

"The Rover Boys on the River" is a complete story in itself, but forms the ninth volume of "The Rover Boys Series for Young Americans."

Nine volumes! What a great number of tales to write about one set of characters! When I started the series I had in mind, as I have mentioned before, to write three or possibly four books. But the gratifying reception given to "The Rover Boys at School" soon made the publishers call for the second, third, and fourth volumes, and then came the others, and still the boys and girls do not seem to be satisfied. I am told there is a constant cry for "more! more!" and so I present this new Rover Boys story which tells of the doings of Dick, Tom, and Sam and their friends during an outing on one of our great rivers—an outing full of excitement and fun and with a touch of rather unusual mystery. During the course of the tale some of the old enemies of the Rover Boys turn up, but our heroes know, as of old, how to take care of themselves; and all ends well.

In placing this book into the hands of my young readers I wish once more to thank them for the cordial reception given the previous volumes. Many have written to me personally about them and I have perused the letters with much satisfaction. I sincerely trust the present volume fulfills their every expectation.

Affectionately and Sincerely yours,

Edward Stratemeyer

(*The Rover Boys on the River, p. iii*)

By 1914, success had imparted a new effervescence to Stratemeyer's letters to his readers, and he was thanking their parents as well as the kids themselves.

. . . The publishers assure me that by the end of the present year the total of sales on this series of books will have reached *one million and a half copies!* This is, to me, truly amazing, and I cannot help but feel profoundly grateful to all the boys and girls and their parents who have taken such an interest in my stories. I trust with all my heart that the reading of the books will do the young folks good.

Another innovation put into effect by Stratemeyer, was the first series merger in the history of boys' books. Saving himself the trouble of thinking up an entirely new locale and a fresh group of chums and background characters, Stratemeyer sent the Rovers to Putnam Hall, a fictional military academy, which had appeared for some years in another Stratemeyer series about the adventures of the school's cadets. The crowd at Putnam Hall had been through the *Putnam Hall Mystery,* the *Putnam Hall Encampment,* the *Putnam Hall Rebellion,* and a number of other mysteries, football games, and adventures; and the Rover brothers fit in very well.

The cadets are lively, flesh-and-blood fellows, bound to make friends from the start. There are some keen rivalries, in school and out, and something is told of a remarkable midnight feast and a hazing that had an unlooked for ending.

(*The Putnam Hall Cadets, jacket blurb*)

A perfect milieu for the boys, and soon they were hazing and feasting with the rest.

Dick was the eldest Rover. He was sober, industrious, hard-working and the leader of the group. A year younger was Tom Rover, the fun-loving brother, and the perpetrator of some of the heaviest-handed practical jokes ever conceived. After Tom came Sam, the youngest, a sturdy lad who had little or no reason for being included. He filled in as a kind of understudy for Dick, but had few lines of his own. When the Hardy Boys were created some years later, Stratemeyer switched to the much more maneuverable two-brother team. The three Rovers, strangely enough, were all in the same class at Putnam Hall, and later at Brill College. Puzzled young readers must have written inquiring about this, because Stratemeyer-"Winfield" felt motivated to explain.

It may be mentioned here that Sam, Tom, and Dick were now in the same grade. This may be wondered at, but the fact of the matter was that Sam, by hard work the term previous, had caught up to Tom, while Dick, because of being away on some business for his father at various times, had dropped a little behind.

(*The Rover Boys on the Plains, p. 41*)

The boys lived with their father, former mineowner and businessman Anderson Rover, and their uncle and aunt Randolph and Martha Rover, on a beautiful farm in the Hudson Valley. There was a hired man, Jack Ness, and an egregious and good-natured Uncle Tom named Alexander Pop who was a former Putnam Hall employee and had accompanied the boys to Africa (*The Rover Boys in the Jungle*) yuk-yukking and rolling his eyeballs all the way.

Years before, while their father was prospecting in Africa for the foundations of the Rover fortune, the three boys had been sent to Putnam Hall by their uncle. Captain Putnam, the Hall's founder, was an old friend of the family, and indeed the boys never attended any institution of learning that was not administered by a parental crony.

At Putnam Hall the boys were to make a number of lifelong friends, among whom were John A. ("Songbird") Powell, so-called because of his tendency to make up doggerel poetry at the drop of a hat, and William Philander Tubbs, variously called "the aristocratic chum" or "the dudish chum." Tubbs's interest in his own sartorial elegance was a source of never-ending laughter to the Rovers, and the long-suffering dude had to put up with the lion's share of Tom's practical jokery.

There was also Hans Mueller, a low-comedy German-accented cadet who was the boys' foil up to graduation, at which time Tubbs and Songbird accompanied them to Brill College, but Hans did not ("Hans is not fit for college yet," explained Dick). He was replaced by a dignified German student named Max, who spoke much better English. The year was 1913, and in the following books Max suddenly vanished without explanation.

The Rover Boys at School was followed by a trip to the jungles of Africa, in search of Anderson Rover, who had disappeared. Back in the States, they took a trip to the Far West on their vacation, and then another to the Great Lakes. This was followed by a sojourn in the mountains, and a return to Putnam Hall to go into camp with their fellow cadets.

Their next adventure (*The Rover Boys on Land and Sea*) took them on a long trip to a mysterious island in the Pacific where they had to play Robinson Crusoe. Home again, they sailed down the Ohio and Mississippi Rivers in a houseboat, went on an outing on the plains, and sailed down to the Gulf of Mexico to solve the mystery of a deserted steam yacht.

While they were at Putnam Hall, the boys had become acquainted with three delightful young ladies, who became their steadies for the whole series. Dora Stanhope, the only daughter of the widowed Mrs. Stanhope, was Dick's girl; while the Laning sisters, Nellie and Grace, were the choices of Tom and Sam respectively.

The boys made almost as many enemies as they did friends, and Putnam Hall (and later Brill College) had more than its share of bullies. Dan Baxter was the first and worst of them, and later the boys were to run afoul of Tad Sobber, Dudd Flockley, and many others. A teacher named Josiah Crabtree turned out to be an arch-criminal on the style of Professor Moriarty, and dogged the boys through a number of adventures. He had hypnotic power over Mrs. Stanhope and tried to force her into marriage so that he could gain control of Dora's considerable trust fund, but the boys defeated him every time. Eventually he was forced to leave Putnam Hall, and was sentenced to a jail term, but was released and tried to wreak his vengeance on the Rovers. Again he was defeated. Escaping out a second-story window he broke his leg, and was doomed to spend the rest of his life as a cripple.

The Stanhope fortune, incidentally, was established by the discovery (by the Rovers) of a treasure, hidden on an island in the West Indies. The Rovers got to it just ahead of a number of other treasure-hunters, and made themselves a whole new set of enemies.

After Putnam Hall the boys went on to Brill College, a "fine institution of learning in the Middle West." Brill was chosen in some part because of its proximity to Hope Seminary, where Dora, Nellie, and Grace were studying. (The headmistress of Hope was instructed that the girls were to be allowed to go out, unchaperoned, with the Rover Boys "any time they pleased.")

Just before arriving for their freshman year at Brill, the boys acquired the *Dartaway*, a "modern, up-to-date biplane" and became increasingly mobile. They could fly over to Hope Seminary for their dates, and it was in the *Dartaway* that Dick was to place a diamond engagement ring on Dora's finger, just before she was abducted by Josiah Crabtree and Tad Sobber.

The *Dartaway* didn't last very long (it was smashed by a railroad train, and the boys received a handsome insurance settlement). The boys went on a trip to Alaska in pursuit of Tom, who was suffering a temporary bout of amnesia, and then went to New York City, where Wall Street high-binders were trying to get the best of Anderson Rover. By this time popular interest had run down, and the original fans of the series had grown up. Stratemeyer had moved on to other, more modern series, but he could not bear just to drop his beloved Rovers. At least he could write them a happy ending, and so he gave them splendid weddings with lots of presents, lucrative business careers, and numerous progeny of both sexes, born in their lower teens so that they could be slipped easily into series of their own. "The Second Rover Boys Series for Young Americans" started with the new generation of male Rovers, but it was not a great success and soon died out.

There are few physical descriptions of the Rovers, except for generalities, such as that they were athletic and well-muscled. Dick was the activist of the family, as well as the natural leader. When bullies got out of hand, it was usually Dick who leaped in ahead of the others to administer corrective action. The incidents in which he did so are startlingly similar, and dealt with attempts by one bully or another to terrorize a helpless girl.

As they looked into the [candy store] they saw Tad Sobber reach over the counter and catch the girl clerk by her curls. He held fast, grinning into her face, while she tried to pull away from him.

"The mean wretch!" cried Dick. "He tries to make himself as obnoxious as he can to everybody he meets."

"Oh please let go!" came in the girl's voice through the open doorway. "You hurt me!"

"Don't worry, I won't hurt you," replied Sobber, still grinning.

"But I—I don't want my curls pulled," pleaded the frightened girl. "Oh, please let go, won't you?"

"I want you—" began the bully, but did not finish, for at that moment he felt Dick's hand on his ear. Then he received a yank that pained him exceedingly.

"Ouch!" he yelled, and dropped his hold of the girl. "Oh my ear! Dick Rover what did you do that for?"

"I did it to make you behave yourself," answered Dick sternly.

(*The Rover Boys on the Farm, p. 109*)

Dick's ear-grabbing was to be repeated periodically. In the boys' freshman year at Brill, they stopped at a neighboring farm, only to find two of their less savory classmates up to the usual skullduggery

"But you must go now, you really must!" said the girl.

"We'll go if you'll say good-bye in the right kind of way, eh, Dudd?" said the person called Jerry Koswell.

"Yes, Minnie, but we won't go until you do that," answered the young man named Dudd Flockley.

"Wha—what do you mean?" faltered the girl. And now, looking through the sitting-room window and through a doorway leading to the kitchen, the Rover boys saw a pretty damsel of sixteen standing by a pantry door, facing two dudish young men of eighteen or twenty. The young men wore checkered suits and sported heavy watch fobs and diamond rings and scarf pins.

"Why you'll give us each a nice kiss, won't you?" said Dudd Flockley with a smile that was meant to be alluring.

"Of course Minnie will give us a kiss," said Jerry Koswell. "Next Saturday I'm coming over to give you a carriage ride."

"I don't want any carriage ride," answered the girl coldly. Her face had gone white at the mention of kisses.

"Well, let's have the kisses anyway!" cried Dudd Flockley, and stepping forward he caught the girl by one hand, while Jerry Koswell grabbed her by the other.

"Oh, please let me go!" cried the girl. "Please do! Oh, Mr. Flockley! Mr. Koswell! don't—don't—please!"

"Now be nice about it," growled Dudd Flockley.

"It won't hurt you a bit," added Jerry Koswell.

"I want you to let me go!" cried the girl.

"I will as soon as—" began Dudd Flockley and then gave a sudden roar of pain as he found himself caught by the ear . . .

(*The Rover Boys at College, p. 22*)

Dick, as the eldest, was the natural heir to Mr. Anderson Rover's wide business interests, although there was plenty for all three boys. Mr. Rover proved, like all fathers in all boys' series since the beginning of time, to be in failing health, and was quite happy to retire to the farm permanently, leaving the hurly-burly of Wall Street to the boys when the time came. As early as 1913, it was obvious that Dick was on the way out. There were hints of his departure from college. When the *Dartaway* was run over by a train and reduced to matchwood, he showed foreshadowings of his legal and business talents, flim-flamming the railroad lawyer.

> "We might accept three hundred dollars for the shaking up we got, although we don't know if our nerves are all right or not. Sometimes these things turn out worse than at first anticipated. But the railroad has got to pay for the airplane it smashed."
>
> "Never!"
>
> "I think it will."
>
> "You got in the way of the train—it was your own fault."
>
> "Your track isn't fenced in—I have a right to cross it where I please. If I had a wagon and it broke down, you would have no right to run into it. The law might not hold you criminally liable, but it would hold you liable for the worth of the wagon and its contents."
>
> "Say, are you a lawyer?" queried Belright Fogg, curiously.
>
> "No, but I know my rights," returned Dick promptly.
>
> (*The Rover Boys in New York, p. 54*)

The lawyer and the railroad had to capitulate in the face of Dick's shrewd argument, and the boys received their money.

> "Got out of that better than I expected," whispered Sam to his big brother.
>
> "It pays to put on a front, Sam," was the answer. "If I had been weak-kneed about it that fellow wouldn't have done a thing."
>
> "Oh you've got a head for business, Dick—I can see that," said the youngest Rover, admiringly.

"I hope so, Sam—for I think I'll need it soon."

"You mean for helping Dad?"

"Yes."

"It's too bad he has these weak spells, isn't it?"

"Yes, what he needs, I think, is a good long rest."

(op. cit., p. 71)

At the time there were only a few more books to go in the series, and the skids were being prepared for everyone, although we readers could not have known it. Dick not only had a head for business, he was to become the first boy hero in any series to kiss a girl without being married to her, although Stratemeyer made it very plain to one and all that they were engaged and marriage was only a short distance away. He was also to be the last (except for his brother Tom) Stratemeyer hero to get an unsanctified kiss. The Hardy Boys never touched Callie and Iola, nor did Nancy Drew ever allow her lips to touch those of faithful Ned Nickerson. But Dick Rover in 1910 was a child of a lustier era.

Under the trees Dick allowed his horse to drop to a walk and managed to drive with one hand while the other found Dora's waist and held it.

"Dick, somebody might see you!" she half whispered.

"Well, I can't help it, Dora," he answered. "It's been such a long time since we met."

"Yes, it seems like years and years, doesn't it?"

"And to think we've got to go through college before —before we can—"

"Yes, but Dick, isn't it splendid that we are going to be so close to each other? Why we'll be able to meet lots of times!"

"If the seminary authorities will let you. I understand they are very strict."

"Oh, we'll meet anyhow, won't we?"

"If you say so, dear."

"Why, yes, dear—that is—Oh now see what you've done!
—knocked my hat right down on my ear! Now you mustn't
—one is enough! Just suppose another carriage should
come up—with somebody in it from the seminary?"

"I've got my eye open," answered Dick. "But just one
more—and then you can fix your hat. They've got to make
some allowance for folks that are engaged," he added
softly as he pressed her cheek close to his own.

"Are we engaged, Dick?" she asked as she adjusted
her hat.

(*The Rover Boys at College, p. 126*)

Tom, the "fun-loving Rover," was more of a bully than
all the Dudd Flockleys, Tad Sobbers, and Dan Baxters in
the series. He displayed a whole textbook full of paranoid
and manic depressive symptoms, and tortured everyone
he came near, but his doting chums and siblings always
chuckled and described his atrocities as practical jokes.
The usual butt of Tom's humor was William Philander
Tubbs, the dude, but no one was immune, even his sweetheart Nellie, who was the first heroine in series history to
receive a ringing blow over the ear from her chosen
fiancé.

"The best of friends must part, as the hook said to the
eye!" sang out Tom merrily.

"I believe you are anxious to leave us!" returned Nellie,
teasingly.

"Sure thing," he retorted promptly. "I planned to get
away an hour before I came." And then she playfully
boxed his ear, at which he chased her around the biplane
and gave her a hearty smack just below her own pretty
ear.

"Tom Rover!" she gasped. But somehow she looked
pleased, nevertheless.

"All in the family!" sang out the fun-loving Rover coolly, "as the lady said when she kissed her cow."

(*The Rover Boys in New York, p. 35*)

Whoever was within reach, male or female, friend or enemy, would feel the sting of Tom's weird sense of humor sooner or later. And Heaven help those who offended him in any way, or who he thought had snubbed or slighted him. To walk past the Rovers without saying hello meant harassment for weeks. A local merchant, the proprietor of an ice-cream parlor, summarily ordered the Rovers out after a short fracas with a pair of bullies had taken place on his premises. Tom slipped a sign into his window reading *FREE BOUQUETS OF ROSES TO ALL YOUNG LADIES BUYING ICE CREAM HERE TODAY. COME IN!* Of course crowds of ladies poured in and ordered ice cream. When the proprietor denied any knowledge of free roses, they left without paying, bringing him to the verge of bankruptcy.

Even the beloved family retainers were not immune. Jack Ness, the hired man at the farm, was a frequent butt.

"Hi! Hi! Wow!" spluttered Jack Ness straightening up and brushing his shoulders. "Say, what did you put that snow down my back for?"

"Just to keep you from sweating too much, Jack," answered Tom with a grin.

(*Rover Boys at College, p. 219*)

Tom was never above plaguing his schoolmates with tortures of every kind in the spirit of good clean fun. Poor Hans Mueller was a favorite target when William Philander Tubbs was not around.

"Hans, they tell me you feel cold and want your blood shook up," said Tom to Hans Mueller, the German cadet.

"Coldt is it?" queried Hans. "Vot you dinks I vas cold mid der borometer apout two hundred by der shade, ain't it? I vas so hot like I lif in Africa alretty!"

"Oh Hans must be cold!" cried Sam. "Let us shake him up, boys!"

"All right!" came from half a dozen. "Get a blanket, somebody!"

"No you ton't, not by my life alretty!" sang out Hans, who had been tossed up before. "I stay py the groundt mine feets on!" and he started to run away.

Several went after him, and he was caught in the middle of an adjoining cornfield, where a rough-and-tumble scuffle ensued, with poor Hans at the bottom of the heap.

"Hi, git off, kvick!" he gasped. "Dis don't bin no football game nohow! Git off, somebody, und dake dot knee mine mouth out of!"

"Are you warm now, Hansy!" asked Tom.

"Chust you wait, Tom Rofer," answered the German cadet, and shook his fist at his tormentor. "I git square somedimes, or mine name ain't . . ."

"Sauerkraut!" finished another cadet, and a roar went up.

(*Rover Boys on the River*, p. *15*)

William Philander Tubbs, the school (and later the college) dude was Tom's favorite target. The foppish cadet had an inexhaustible supply of high collars, spats, and silk ties, and Tom never lost an opportunity to splatter mud on them or to embarrass Tubbs in front of the young ladies who were constantly inviting him to tea. Burrs in his bed were commonplace. On one occasion Tom blackened Tubbs's face while he slept, and then woke him and told him the headmaster wanted to see him at once. Tubbs scurried off, and reported to Captain Putnam who did a number of double-takes, thinking that a Negro cadet (unheard of) had somehow matriculated at Putnam Hall without his knowledge. Good clean fun!

It poured through the books like the Colorado River rapids.

Here is Tom at his best (worst?) stimulated by the fact that Tubbs was off to take tea with a stuck-up girl who had made the mistake of snubbing the Rovers. Tubbs had bought her a box of candy, and this triggered the perverse in brilliant Tom.

All looked around and presently found the box of candy on a dresser. It was tied up with a blue ribbon, but this Tom slipped off with ease. Inside the box were chocolates and bonbons and some candied fruit.

"Hold the box, Sam," said Tom, whipping out his knife. "We've got to move mighty quick!"

On the instant he was at work with his pocket knife, cutting the floor wax into various shapes to resemble candy. He took out some of the candied fruit and substituted the wax. Then he felt in his pocket.

"This will help," he said, bringing forth a soapstone slate pencil, which he cracked into tiny lengths. "The candy that lasts!" he cried softly, as he dropped the bits into the box.

"Rather rough on the girl," declared Dick.

"Not at all, Dick," said Sam. "I was introduced to her last week and the very next day she passed me on the street with a stare as if she had never seen me."

"And Stanley says she is stuck up to the last degree," added Tom. "Maybe this will take her down a peg—at least I hope so."

(*The Rover Boys in New York, p. 79*)

The boys continued to doctor the candy, with Sam in his usual role of toady to his brother Tom outdoing the rest. Dried beans, rubber bands, and similar items followed the wax and the slate pencil into Tubbs's candy

box. When they had finished and put the ribbon back in
its place, Tubbs appeared on cue.

> The stylish student was faultlessly attired in light trou-
> sers, dark Prince Albert coat, white vest, spats and a silk
> hat. In one hand he carried a cane and in the other the
> box of candy.
>
> (*loc. cit.*)

Unable to miss the cream of the jest, the whole gang
followed him, and gathered under the young lady's parlor
window to see the fun.

> They saw William Philander sitting in a chair the box
> of candy on his lap. Presently Clarabel Ruggles came in,
> attired in an elaborate evening gown. Tubbs at once arose
> to his feet and, bowing very low, accepted her hand, which
> was held on high. Then the dudish student said some-
> thing and offered the box of candy.
> "Oh, is this really for me!" those outside heard the
> young lady cry, the words coming through the partly open
> window.
> "No, he bought it for the cat!" murmured Tom, and at
> this the others had to snicker.
>
> (*loc. cit.*)

In the ensuing hilarity William Philander was to break
a tooth and incur the wrath of the young lady and her
aunt-cum-chaperone, who promptly threw him out on his
ear. Talk about fun!

Tom was no less a terror outside of school, especially
when his burly brothers were along to back him up. Almost any fancied slight would evoke a diatribe that
would wither an unsuspecting stranger in his tracks.
During a trip out West the boys stopped for dinner at a

small-town hotel, and a local resident happened to remark on their excellent appetites.

The long ride had made all of the boys hungry, and
when they had procured supper at the hotel, they cleaned
up nearly everything that was set before them.

"Nothing the matter with your appetites," observed a
sour-looking individual who sat next to Tom at the table.

"Nothing at all, sir," answered the fun-loving youth,
"what made you think there was?"

"Eh?"

"What made you think there was something wrong
with our internal machinery, whereby we might be wanting in a proper regard for victuals?"

The man stared at Tom, and while a few at the table
snickered, the man himself looked more sour than ever.

"See here, don't you poke fun at me!" he cried.

"Never dreamed of it, my dear sir," said Tom, unruffled.
"By the way, how's your heart?"

"Why—er—my heart's all right."

"Glad to hear it. Yesterday I heard of a donkey who
had his heart on the wrong side of his body. Odd case,
wasn't it?"

"See here, you young imp, do you mean to call me a—
er—a donkey?" and the man grew red in the face.

"A donkey? Why, no, sir! What put such a notion in
your head?"

"You said—"

"So I did. Go on."

"You said—"

"So you said before."

"You said—"

"You said that before. You said, I said, and I said so
I did. It's perfectly clear as the strainer said to the tea."

By this time, all sitting at the table were on a broad
grin. As a matter of fact, the sour-looking individual was
not liked in that locality, and the boarders were glad to
see somebody "take him down."

"I won't put up with your foolishness!" stormed the man. "I am not a donkey and I want you to know it."

"Well, I'm glad you mentioned it," said Tom calmly. "Now there won't be the least occasion for a mistake."

"Don't insult me!"

"No sir, I am not looking for work."

"Eh?"

"I said I wasn't looking for work."

"What do you mean by that?"

"That, sir, is a mystery puzzle, and there is a reward of one herring bone for the correct solution. Answers must be sent in on one side of the paper only and have a certificate added that the sender has not got cold feet."

At this quaint humor, some at the table laughed outright. The sour-looking individual looked thoroughly enraged.

"I—I'll settle with you another time, young man!" he roared, and dashed from the room.

(The Rover Boys on the Plains, p. 66)

This kind of activity never failed to confuse me and my gang. My father was not sparing in the use of such terms as "wise guy" and "smart aleck," two categories which, he made it plain, I ought to steer clear of. My mother, when faced with a boy who acted as Tom had done with a strange adult in a restaurant, would have summed him up as "fresh." Dan Baxter, Lew Flapp, or Dudd Flockley would have had his ear firmly tweaked by the nearest non-bully available, but Tom got away with it. Moreover, we were aware that we were supposed to find the scene funny. Most of us didn't, especially in such instances as Tubbs's broken tooth (we knew about dentists' bills) but we also knew that there were some things we were "too young to understand" (God knows we'd been told so often enough). If Arthur M. Winfield meant Tom to be funny, he obviously knew more about it than we did. We chuckled nervously and read on. Nor did we let our lack of sophistication keep us from enjoying the books. Someday we would learn about humor. We already knew about bullies and jungles and football. It was a year or two later that I unexpectedly came upon Stephen Leacock and Robert Benchley, but by that time Tom Rover was a million miles behind me.

Tom's ability to get away with enormities that would have earned me a vigorous clout over the ear is further illustrated in the incident of the circus clown, owner of a small, poverty-stricken traveling tent show. This poor devil made the mistake of colliding accidentally with the Rovers' buggy, and bawling them out for reckless driving. That was enough to galvanize the brothers, led by Tom, into vengeful action. The boys and some of their cronies took seats for the performance, and the following example of public harassment, reminiscent of the "mohocks" of the eighteenth century or of Brown-Shirted bully-boys letting off steam after a successful pogrom, took place in the presence of the assembled townfolk.

"How are you tomorrow?" sang out the clown. And after doing a flip-flop, he continued: "Mr. Ringmaster, what's the difference between your knife and me?"

"I know!" shouted Tom. "His knife is a jack-knife while you are a jack-of-all-trades!"

At this sally there was a loud laugh.

"What is the difference between my knife and you?" queried the ringmaster as soon as he could make himself heard.

"That's it."

"I don't know."

"I told you!" shouted Tom.

"The difference between your knife and me," answered Frozzler, "is that you can shut your knife up but you can't shut me up," and then he made a face and did another tumble.

"His knife is sharper than you too," cried Sam. A roar followed, which made Frozzler so angry he shook his fist at the youngest Rover.

"Why is that boy like a fish?" cried Frozzler.

"Because he's too slippery for a clown to catch," put in Fred loudly, and this created such a laugh that Frozzler's answer was completely lost on the crowd. Again he shook his fist at our friends, but they merely laughed at him.

"I had a funny dream last night," went on the clown. "What do you think I dreamed?"

"That you had paid all your bills," called out Dick.

This brought forth another laugh at Frozzler's expense, in which even some of the circus hands joined.

"Say, those boys are sharp," said [a] clown who had been discharged. "I shouldn't care to run up against them."

"Three of them are the Rover Boys," answered a man sitting near. "Nobody can get the best of them."

(Rover Boys on the River, p. 124)

Perhaps Stratemeyer himself began to tire of the fun-loving Rover, who certainly had all the qualifications of a vicious and dangerous bore. Toward the end of the series, in 1914 (*The Rover Boys in Alaska*), Tom was beaned by a stool, hurled from a second-story window by a felon named Pelter, an associate of the evil Josiah Crabtree. The result was a head wound and some months of mental weakness and blinding headaches. Then one day, Tom snapped like a dry twig. His good-natured grin gave way to a maniacal leer, and his practical jokes became murderous.

Sam was the last to enter, coming directly behind his brother and he saw Tom suddenly put his hand to the back of his head and stop.

"Does it hurt again, Tom?" he whispered kindly.

"Just a—a spasm!" gasped Tom, and then he drew a long

breath. "There, it's gone now," he added, and walked on. Sam sighed and shook his head. What was this queer condition of Tom going to lead to? It made him shiver to think of it.

There was but little to see in the old mill. It was a damp, unwholesome place, and the boys soon came out again. Not far away was a well hole, rather deep and partly filled with water.

Tom was the first to notice this hole, which was partly covered with rotted boards. Of a sudden he commenced to grin, as if he scented a huge joke. He ran up and rearranged the rotted boards, so they completely covered the hole. Then in the center he placed the bright colored cap he had been wearing, and hurried along to the path leading beside the dam.

"Hi, Stanley!" he called out, as the others came from the mill. "Get my cap, will you? The wind blew it off. It's back there somewhere."

"I see it!" shouted Stanley.

"I see it, too," came from Spud, who was close by. "I'll race you for it, Stan."

"Done!" was the reply, and side by side the two collegians raced for the cap.

"An apple for the fellow who wins!" shouted Sam, who saw nothing wrong in what was going on.

"Leg it, both of you!" added Songbird.

Side by side, Stanley and Spud sped over the uneven ground in the direction of the cap. Then both made a plunge forward in true football style. In a heap they landed on the rotted boards, each catching hold of the coveted headgear. Then came an ominous crash, and both boys disappeared headlong into the well hole!

"Look! Look what has happened!" shrieked Sam in dismay.

"They are in the old well!" gasped Songbird.

"Ha! ha! ha! ho! ho!" came from Tom, and he shook with laughter. "Isn't that the dandy joke?"

(Rover Boys in Alaska, p. 28)

Quick action by Sam and the others kept the "joke" from becoming a tragedy, but it was obvious that Tom was due for a doctor's care. Before he could be treated he disappeared and was later to be discovered in Alaska, suffering from amnesia. Dick had to be recalled from his honeymoon and his many business activities for this adventure, and Tom was given a rest cure, medication, and eventual complete recovery.

The supporting players were pretty much the same as any group of fictional chums, although it wasn't until the sons of the Rovers started their own series that the traditional fat-boy appeared. Hans Mueller was known for his stupidity and his comical accent, Larry Colby and Stanley were athletic American lads, Fred Garrison was the same, and Spud was so called because of his love for potatoes. William Philander Tubbs with his spats and cane was at once effeminate and girl crazy, constantly attending "pink teas" and courting stuck-up society girls. Songbird Powell wrote poetry which he considered to have tremendous literary value, which made him a perfect foil for Tom's petty cruelties.

> Hark to the silence all around!
> The well-trained ear doth hear no sound.
> The birds are silent in their nest.
> All tired nature is at rest.
> The brook in silence finds its way
> From shadows deep to perfect day.
> The wind is dead, there is no breeze—
> "To make a fellow cough and sneeze!" murmured Tom,
> and gave a loud ker-chow! that set the girls to laughing.

> (*Rover Boys at College*, p. 200)

Alexander "Aleck" Pop, family retainer at the Rover farm, was the standard gibbering darkie of the period. Of course, like all his counterparts, he was a superb cook and slavishly loyal. On one occasion he had produced a dainty gourmet repast for the Rovers and their lady guests (breast of lamb, green peas, apple cobbler) and Dora Stanhope saw fit to compliment him.

"Why, Aleck, this is a surprise," said Dora. "Some day they will want you to become the chef in a big hotel." And this compliment tickled the colored man greatly.

"T'ank you, Miss Dora," he answered. "But I don't want to be no chef in a hotel. All I wants is to stay wid de Rober boys so long as I lib."

(*Rover Boys on the River, p. 147*)

With such an ante-bellum attitude, small wonder he was a favorite objective of Tom's pranks. He suffered them with masochistic joy, delighting in his own discomfiture.

"My! My! But dis am like old times at Putnam Hall," said the colored man, grinning, from ear to ear when Tom hit him on the head with a snowball. "Hab yo' fun while you' am young, Massa Tom."

"That's my motto, Aleck," answered Tom. "Have another." And he landed a snowball on the colored man's shoulder.

(*Rover Boys at College, p. 223*)

When the boys headed for the circus, Aleck revealed a desire to accompany them. This Tom was unable to resist.

"Say, I'd like to see dat show, Tom," said Aleck Pop, when he got the chance. "Ain't seen no circuses since I was a little boy."

"Then you must go by all means, Aleck, but don't you get too close to the monkey cage."

"Why not, Tom?"

"They might take you for a long-lost brother."

"Yah! Yah! Dat's one on me!" Aleck showed his ivories in a broad grin. "Maybe da will take yo' for a long-lost brudder too—yo' is full of monkey-shines," and then Tom had to laugh at the sally.

(*Rover Boys on the River*, p. 117)

Not bad for Aleck, knowing his adversary and what the fun-loving Rover was capable of. It was, perhaps, the only note of black rebellion in any Stratemeyer book.

As always, the bullies were the best written and most interesting characters. They were brutal, villainous, cowardly, and sniveling. The Rovers handled them easily, knocking them about, twisting their ears, or just simply staring them down. It was reform or terrible restitution in the Rover series, and nearly all of the bullies served jail sentences. Josiah Crabtree ended up a permanent cripple after his second kidnaping (he served a short sentence for the first one). Tad Sobber, who sent the Rovers a box with a live poisonous snake in it, went to jail as did Lew Flapp, who had robbed a jewelry store and concealed his ill-gotten gains in the Rovers' dormitory to make it appear as though they were the thieves. Lew was "tall and lanky with a sour look on his face and several scars which made him particularly repulsive." He teamed up with Dan Baxter, the Rovers' first Putnam Hall enemy, to kidnap Dora, Grace, and Nellie in *The Rover Boys on the River*, but got his comeuppance after a thrilling chase in motorboats down the broad Ohio River.

"The game is up! Here comes a tug with the Rovers and a lot of other people on board."

"The Rovers!" faltered Lew Flapp, and for the instant he shivered from head to foot.

"Oh good! good!" cried Nellie. "Help! Help us! This way!"

"We are coming!" came back in Dick's voice, and a moment later the steam tug crashed into the side of the houseboat, and the Rovers and several others leaped aboard.

"Stand where you are, Lew Flapp!" cried Tom, and rushed for the bully of Putnam Hall. "Stand, I say!" and then he hit Flapp a stunning blow in the ear which bowled the rascal over and over. In the meantime Dan Baxter took to his heels and made for the front of the houseboat. From this point he jumped into the branches of a tree and disappeared from view . . .

"Follow me at your peril!" he sang out, and then they heard him crashing through the bushes. Gradually the sounds grew fainter and fainter.

(*Rover Boys on the River,* p. 250)

Dan would be back, of course, for more villainy. He was a second-generation bully. His father, Arnold Baxter, had plagued the Rovers and their father in the early books, and it wasn't until 1906 that he, "after suffering for his crimes by various terms of imprisonment, was now very sick and inclined to turn over a new leaf and become a better man." His boy Dan went on with his malefactions, however, for a number of additional books, scoffing at his father's weakness. Then one day it occurred to Stratemeyer that there might be more mileage in one sinner that repenteth than in ninety and nine who are pure. Dan saw the light. On his promise to get a job and abjure his former life of misdemeanor, the Rovers lent him a hundred dollars and he vanished, to turn up from time to time much improved.

"Dan Baxter was our worst enemy in that school, and he is going to reform, Sam."

"Perhaps. I won't feel sure of it until I really see it," answered the youngest Rover.

"By the way, I got a postal from Dan today," said Dick. "He is in Philadelphia, and working for a carpet manufacturer."

"Well, if he's gone to work, that's a good sign," said Tom.

(*Rover Boys on the Farm, p. 6*)

The postal card was followed by a long correspondence, in which Dan kept our heroes informed of his progress.

The next few days flew quickly by. During that time Dick received a letter from Dan Baxter, the former bully of Putnam Hall, which interested him not a little. This letter ran, in part, as follows:

"I am glad to say that I am now doing fairly well. I tried several positions and am now a traveling salesman for a large carpet house. I get fifteen dollars a week, all my expenses, and a commission on sales, so I consider myself lucky.

"When I look back on what I once was, Dick, I can scarcely realize what a change has come. But I feel happier than I ever was, and I am in hopes that I shall live to make a man of myself yet. I am trying to give up all my bad habits, and I haven't smoked or drank a glass of liquor since I left you in the South."

"That's the kind of letter I like to get," said Dick, as he let his brothers peruse the communication. "It does a fellow's heart good, doesn't it?"

"I'm glad we let him have that $100," said Sam.

(*op. cit., p. 62*)

The new Dan Baxter was to rise rapidly, and a few books later we find him out of carpets and in the wholesale jewelry line.

"Maybe you'll be a member of the firm some day," added Sam with a smile.

"I don't know about that. I'm willing to work, and the traveling suits me first-rate. They pay me a good salary too—thirty dollars a week and all expenses."

"Good enough!" cried Dick.

(Rover Boys at College, p. 111)

Dan was to appear from time to time, usually to help the Rovers trap miscreants and turn them over to the police. He did become a member of the jewelry firm, and an affluent citizen of New York, where he married and settled, producing a son, hot-tempered, scrappy Walter Baxter ("willing to fight almost any time") a classmate of the second generation Rovers at Colby Hall. Walter was no bully, and so, the sins of his father and grandfather forgotten, he was able to become something his forbears had never been, a chum.

Dudd Flockley, poltroon and molester of pretty girls, was another who escaped the arm of the law by repenting. Faced with expulsion from Brill College because of his nefarious activities, Dudd swallowed his pride and sought the Rovers' intercession.

"What do you want?" asked Sam, abruptly.

"I want—I want—" commenced Flockley brokenly. Then he stepped into the room and confronted Dick. "Oh, Rover!" he cried. "Won't you—won't you please, please, get Dr. Wallingford to let me stay at Brill? Please don't let him send me home! I'll do anything—apologize, get down on my knees if you like—but please help me to stay here!"

Flockley caught Dick by the arm and continued to plead, and then he entreated Sam, Tom and Stanley, also. It was a truly affecting scene. They all commenced to speak. He had been so mean, wicked, so unlike a decent college fellow, how could they forgive him?

And then came a pause, and during that pause a distant church bell sounded out, full and clear, across the hills surrounding Brill. Dick listened and so did his brothers and Stanley, and the anger in their faces died down.

(Rover Boys at College, p. 288)

The Lord in His infinite mercy softened their hearts to the extent that they were moved to help him stay in college and become a better man.

No description of the Rovers would be complete without a glimpse of Dick's wedding. Stratemeyer was nothing if not lavish with his favorites, and Tom and Sam were to have their day too, with less description, of course. Dick's was the first boy hero's wedding, and we reacted to it sadly because it meant that shocking trauma, the end of a series. Where would we go from the Rovers? Were there other books to read? Indeed there were, as we were to learn, but our reaction to Dick's nuptials was not in the same joyous vein as the reactions of his happy wedding guests.

"The day of days, Dick!"

"Right you are, Sam! And what a perfect day it is!"

"Oh, I had this weather made to order," came from Tom Rover with a grin . . .

Dora had left Hope as soon as it was settled that she and Dick should be married, and she and her mother and the others had been busy for some time getting ready for the wedding. Nellie and Grace were also home, and were as much excited as Dora herself, for they were both to be bridesmaids. The girls had spent several days in New York shopping, and a dressmaker from the city had been called in to dress the young ladies as befitted the occasion.

Tom was to be Dick's best man, while Sam was to head the ushers at the church—the other ushers being Songbird,

Stanley, Fred Garrison, Larry Colby, and Bart Connors. A delegation of students from Brill—including William Philander Tubbs—had also come up and were quartered at the Cedarville Hotel.

The wedding was to take place at the Cedarville Union Church, a quaint little stone edifice covered with ivy, which the Stanhopes, and the Lanings both attended and which the Rover boys had often visited while they were cadets at Putnam Hall. The interior of the church was a mass of palms, sent up on the boat from Ithaca.

Following the sending out of the invitations to the wedding, presents had come in thick and fast to the Stanhope home. From Dick's father came an elegant silver service and from his brothers a beautifully-decorated dinner set; while Uncle Randolph and Aunt Martha contributed a fine set of the latest encyclopedias, and a specially-bound volume of the uncle's book on scientific farming! Mr. Anderson Rover also contributed a bank book with an amount written therein that nearly took away Dora's breath.

"Oh, Dick, just look at the sum!" she cried.

"It sure is a tidy nest egg," smiled the husband-to-be. "I knew Dad would come down handsomely. He's the best dad ever was!"

"Yes, Dick, and I know I am going to love him just as if I was his own daughter," answered Dora.

Mrs. Stanhope gave her daughter much of the family silver and jewelry, and also a full supply of table and other linen. From Captain Putnam came a handsome morris chair, and Songbird sent in a beautifully-bound volume of household poetry, with a poem of his own on the flyleaf. The students of Brill sent in a fine oil painting in a gold frame, and the girls at Hope contributed an inlaid workbox with a complete sewing outfit. From Dan Baxter, who had been invited along with the young lady to whom he was engaged, came two gold napkin rings, each suitably engraved. Dan had written to Dick saying he would come to the wedding if he had to take a week off to get there, he being in Washington on a business trip.

The wedding was to take place at high noon, and long before that time many guests began to assemble at the church. Among the first to arrive was Captain Putnam, in military uniform, and attended by about a dozen of the Hall cadets. George Strong, the head teacher, was also present, for he and Dick had always been good friends. Then came the students from Brill, all in full dress, and led by William Philander Tubbs, bedecked as only that dudish student would think of bedecking himself.

The Lanings and Mrs. Stanhope came together and the Rovers followed closely. Soon the little church was packed, and many stood outside, unable to get in. The organ was playing softly.

Suddenly the bell in the tower struck twelve. As the last stroke died away the organ peeled [sic] forth in the grand notes of the wedding march. Then came the wedding party up the middle aisle, a little flower girl preceding them. Dora was on her uncle's arm, and wore white satin, daintily embroidered, and carried a bouquet of bridal roses. Around her neck was a string of pearls Dick had given her. The bridesmaids were in pink and also carried bouquets.

Dick was already at the altar to meet his bride, and then began the solemn ceremony that made the pair one for life. It was simple and short, and at the conclusion Dick kissed Dora tenderly.

The organ peeled out once more, and the happy couple marched from the church, everybody gazing after them in admiration.

(Rover Boys in New York, p. 291)

And so it was all over, except for Mrs. Stanhope's tears and a few reminiscences from Captain Putnam. Stratemeyer must have mingled his own tears with Dora's mother's. It was the end of an era, and he had permitted himself a surge of sentiment. Silver services and descriptions of Dora's satin embroidered gown indeed! And the bridesmaids in pink! What kind of a boy's book was that? We wanted to follow the happy couple to Ithaca, where Dick ostensibly rained burning kisses on Dora's upturned face while his heart fluttered like a captive bird, but we were diverted to Alaska instead, to follow Tom through his bout of amnesia.

In the last two books the other Rovers married too, and all three went into their father's business (*The Rover Boys in Business*) which seems to have been a conglomerate covering various lines of endeavor. The Rover Company was organized with offices on Wall Street in New York City, where the boys occupied a whole floor and supervised a staff of twenty. The company dealt mainly in stocks, bonds, investments, and real estate. Dick, of course, was president, Tom was secretary, and Sam treasurer.

At first all of them lived in cosy New York apartments, but after two years the brothers bought a plot of land on Riverside Drive and built three adjoining houses (Dick's was the middle one). Soon all three were blessed with children, Dick's Dora giving birth to Martha and Jack, Grace giving Sam Fred and Mary, and Tom and Nellie producing the twins, Andy and Randy. The girls were packed off to remote boarding schools at once, and the boys were the nucleus of a new series (*The Second Rover Boys Series for Young Americans*).

Stratemeyer decided that Putnam Hall had served its purpose, and burnt it to the ground, netting the aging Captain Putnam enough insurance money to retire. Larry Colby, the boys' old school chum, had gone into the Army and come out a short while later a full colonel. He opened Colby Hall, a carbon copy military boarding school of the good old Putnam Hall class. After a bad start in a fancy private school in New York ("That school is altogether too fashionable" had been Dick Rover's comment. "They make regular dudes of the pupils and they think more of high collars and neckties and patent-leather shoes than they do of reading, writing and arithmetic.") the kids were sent off to Colby Hall where they could receive a fine education and a little discipline too.

A ready-made set of chums was waiting, mostly sons of old Putnam grads and the boys were off, camping out (*The Rover Boys Under Canvas*), out West (*At Big Horn Ranch, On Sunset Trail*), shipwrecked, treasure-hunting and many more adventures, exactly like their dads'. They were never to achieve the same success. The war had come, Tom Swift had appeared, the Hardy Boys were waiting in the wings. The generation that had loved the Rover Boys moved on to new things. Did the Crash wipe out the Rover Company? Did their Riverside Drive houses succumb to high taxes and urban blight? We never found out.

Jaded and fickle, like all book-buyers since the beginning of time, we turned our backs on the Rovers and found new heroes to worship. Grosset & Dunlap had come out with a series about kids of our own generation. A new star was creeping over the horizon, one "Leo Edwards," author of the books about Jerry Todd, Poppy Ott, Trigger Berg, and Andy Blake. We could really identify with these kids. They were postwar. Automobiles, telephones, and radios were commonplace to them. Their adventures, fanciful though they might have been, all happened at home. They scoffed at jungles, cowboys, and trips up the Amazon. That was storybook stuff (so said Jerry Todd) written for babies. Those things never happened to *real* kids. Didn't we know it though! We were ready to move from the romantics to the pragmatic philosophers, and "Leo Edwards" was there to capitalize on the transition.

Edwards was in reality a gentleman named Edward Edson Lee, who wrote his books at "Hi-Lee Cottage" on Lake Ripley near Cambridge, Wisconsin. When the books caught on and the royalty checks started rolling in, he switched his operations to St. Petersburg, Florida, spending only the summers at Lake Ripley, mailing his copy in from those seasonal fleshpots. Lee-Edwards had even more *chutzpah* than Stratemeyer and Percy Keese Fitzhugh about injecting himself into his books, writing long chatty prologues and epilogues to his readers. Sometimes these were in the first person, and sometimes they were written by "real live boys" like sixteen-year-old Eddie Blimke of Elmhurst, Illinois.

> "Well, as you can imagine, we hang around Mr. Lee's cottage quite a lot when we're at the lake. He's jolly and always ready for fun. He likes kids. Whenever he finishes a new book, he sends word to us, up and down the lake shore, and that night we crowd around him on his front porch while he reads the book to us. Only it isn't a book then, it's what he calls a manuscript."
>
> (*Jerry Todd and the Purring Egg, p. 183*)

Flushed with the success of his books, Lee borrowed Stratemeyer's device of beginning each volume with a personal letter to his young readers. Kids were encouraged to reply, on the promise that their letters would be published (although, oddly enough, most of those selected were written in a style very similar to the author's own, and read for all the world like jacket blurbs). They could also submit poems, jokes, and other material (none were printed in the books I was able to find). A free book was sent to the lucky selectees.

With some help from Grosset & Dunlap, Lee also created a boys' club, the Secret and Mysterious Order of the Freckled Goldfish, with a membership card, a button, and an initiation ritual. There were no dues. Kids had only to send two two-cent stamps. Girls could join too.

Here is an example of a "Leo Edwards" letter to his readers (the letters were in the form of a column entitled "Our Chatter-Box"):

> The geezer who started the report that boys don't like to write letters and won't write letters is all wet. For my hefty mail (this is Leo Edwards speaking) proves that boys *do* like to write letters—to a pal! Which is the way many thousands of young readers regard me. And do I like it? Oh baby! My boy pals, scattered all over the country, are dearer than gold to me. We call these young readers Jerry Todd fans. I write chummy letters to them, and they write chummy letters to me.
>
> (*Jerry Todd and the Purring Egg, p. iv*)

A few years later we find the "Chatter-Box" getting so long that the publishers had to use smaller print. Edwards's style became more ebullient with financial success.

> Here in Cambridge where I live the postmaster frequently says to me: "Mr. Edwards, you get a *lot* of letters," and I think my face shines like a big red prune (if there is such a thing) when I tell him, with pride, that the big bulk of these letters are from the young readers of my books.
>
> (*Jerry Todd, Pirate, p. viii*)

With the advent of the Freckled Goldfish Club, a kind of junior-grade edition of the Elks, Edwards was jubilant.

And the response was wonderful! I never realized before how many thousands of loyal pals Jerry and Poppy had. The letters simply poured in. Letters from big boys, small boys, freckled boys, good-looking boys, pug-nosed boys, skinny boys, fat boys, sawed-offs and bean-poles. Girls even wrote. Not bean-poles, of course, for we never would call any little girl a bean-pole. But the girls wrote, just the same. Which, of course, was all right . . .

(loc. cit.)

Warming to his subject, Edwards could wax jovial and sincere at the same time.

As a matter of fact, there is nothing in this world, including wealth, swell automobiles, gingersnaps and everything else, that I prize as highly as the friendship and companionship of boys. I read every letter that I receive. And every letter is answered. Of course, I don't write personal letters to all of the boys joining our lodge. We have a special printed letter for that. But when a boy asks me a question, that question is answered, with a pen, on the margin of the printed letter. And in some cases I write separate personal letters. I don't *dictate* these letters: I pound them out with my own "mitts." I mention this, for I want you to realize fully how much I value the friendship that your bully good letters have made possible.

(op. cit., p. ix)

In 1929, when Edwards had moved his winter palace to St. Petersburg, things were bad everywhere. Perhaps he had overextended a bit with his two vacation homes, or perhaps he had delved too deeply into the mysteries of the stock market, but the "Chatter-Box" became less joyous, and a wee bit plaintive.

I wish I had a dozen hands! (so says Leo Edwards). Then by operating six typewriters at once, I probably could answer all of the letters that I get from boys. Alas, though, I have but two hands.

The fun I have, though, reading these bully good letters. And how they inspire me. So keep up the good work, fellows. I need your letters.

(Jerry Todd and the Bob-Tailed Elephant, p. vii)

In all probability he did need them, badly. The Depression had come, and the competition was keen. There was no further mention of personal replies to letters (Grosset & Dunlap staff cuts?), and the latest book was dedicated to the "Boy Scouts of St. Petersburg, hoping that before I leave here in the Spring . . . I will have become better acquainted with them."

Perhaps he did, but there was no cutting in on the lucrative scout monopoly enjoyed by Percy Keese Fitzhugh. The Boy Scouts of America did not take the bait, and soon the "Chatter-Box" vanished altogether.

Much as we enjoyed the books, my crowd was strangely reluctant to join the "lodge." Although we were inveterate senders-in (Orphan Annie Shake-Up Mugs, Buck Rogers rings, plaster statuettes of Tarzan) we were not seduced by the ritual and the membership card and button. I never knew a single kid in our school or neighborhood who sported a Freckled Goldfish membership. We always skipped the "Chatter-Box," which was mainly about kids in impossible places like Idaho and Michigan, and plunged right into the story.

Our defection did not stop Edwards, and he religiously printed letters from "readers," each containing a blatant sales pitch.

"Gosh!" writes Hugh Gilman, Waterville, Maine, "you certainly can write boy stories. I bet you're a regular feller. Because nobody but a regular feller can write boy stories and make the characters act and talk like real boys. A boy can't stop reading your books, they are so natural. And, oh, what fun when the Stricker gang gets chased by Jerry's gang."

I hope I'm a "regular feller," Hugh. I try to be. I'm older than you, by many years. But I'm just as much of a kid at heart as I ever was. Have you read the "Tittering Totem" book? There's a "battle" in the book, between Poppy's and Bid's rival gangs, that will give you a thrill. As Jerry says in the book, "Rotten tomatoes dropped from Zulutown trees and telephone wires for a month." Which is, of course, an exaggeration. But the point is that it was *some* battle. And who won? Sh-h-h-h! Read the book, Hugh.

(Jerry Todd and the Bob-Tailed Elephant, p. vii)

New markets appeared from nowhere. Richard Wilcox of Hartford, Connecticut, wrote to ask if his father could join the Freckled Goldfish. "Sure thing, Bob [sic]—if he's a Jerry Todd fan. That's the main requirement." Jack Read of Niagara Falls wrote in to say his mother enjoyed the books too. Lots of moms ought to read them.

The books were written in the first person, ostensibly by Jerry Todd himself. He was the writer of the gang and often asked the advice of the "regular feller" out in Wisconsin. Jerry also wrote the Poppy Ott series, which began in one of the early Jerry Todd volumes. Although he was sixteen, he wrote like a boy of ten, in short, almost imbecilically simple sentences. He was gullible and foolish (a kid dressed as a ghost in a white sheet could scare the dickens out of him) but straight as a string, God-fearing, polite, and honorable.

All the moms and dads in the books were wonderful people, much respected by the kids, even the bullies.

There was no violence, mayhem or arson, unlike the Stratemeyer series. On one occasion when Jerry was captured by the bullying Stricker gang after he had fallen into the lake, the tough kids wrapped him carefully in a blanket before tying him up, so that he wouldn't catch cold. What a contrast to the Hardy Boys or even Nancy Drew! No wonder parents wanted to join the Freckled Goldfish.

There was one thing Jerry and his pals did that no other series heroes did before or after, and that was sharing beds. It was a time when most grown-ups had never heard of homosexuality, and certainly kids had not and wouldn't have believed it if they had. The nervous generation was yet to come. There were no psychiatrists (who could afford them in the Depression?). Such things were luxuries for the very rich. You were sane, or you were crazy and they put you in an asylum, and there were no shades of gray in between. There were "fairies" and there were "queers" but they were, to our minds and the minds of our parents, merely overfastidious "dudes" like William Philander Tubbs. They were effeminate (we knew about "sissies") but we never really believed they did anything about it.

Very few people had guest rooms then. A kid had his own room, and the greatest fun in the world was "sleeping over," either in a double bed inherited from some forgotten relative or a studio couch that opened up. Lights out, door closed, parental injunctions to "keep quiet" delivered, you could both (sometimes three of you) whisper and giggle half the night through. Secrets were told, confidences exchanged, information about forbidden subjects discussed and wondered at. Jerry Todd and his pals were the only ones who enjoyed that happiness. We warmed to them for it.

Jerry and his gang did something else that was considered rather daring in the modest 1930s too. It was nude swimming. There was never a bathing suit in the crowd, and the boys were always stripping down for a cooling dip in the lake. Stratemeyer and Percy Keese Fitzhugh kids always wore bathing suits (so did my gang) and skinny-dipping was a throwback to the days of Tom Sawyer and Huck Finn, when bathing suits were an effete luxury. Of course Jerry and his crowd were never accompanied by girls, as were the Rovers and the Hardys, but we city kids of the 1930s always felt a pleasurable thrill of foreboding when Jerry and his chums peeled for a swim. What if somebody should come along! What if a *girl* should see them. Of course none ever did.

Jerry's gang lived in Tutter, Illinois, a typical Middle-Western American small town, and every volume had a detailed map on its end papers, showing Main Street, Jerry's house, and all the other points of interest. Tutter was

> . . . a small town. It is one of the smallest towns in La Salle County. And instead of murdering each other, as is frequently done in the big cities, if one is to believe the newspapers, the people, for the most part, go to church and lodge, and otherwise behave themselves—which is all right, of course, and proper, but it's hard on the man who has to publish a daily newspaper.
>
> (*Jerry Todd and the Purring Egg, p. 82*)

Including Jerry, the gang numbered four. Although he was the narrator, Jerry was not the leader. That post was reserved to Scoop Ellery, a smart kid whose father owned the Tutter grocery, which had a candy and ice-cream counter. The other members were Red Meyer whose dad owned the Tutter movie theater, and Peg Shaw. Red was small and fiery-tempered, with a gargantuan appetite for pie. He was as gabby as they come, and, as his nickname implied, had bright red hair and numerous freckles. Peg was big, with "cast-iron muscles," the Porthos of the group. His father was a painter-plasterer. Peg was the oldest and calmest, and avoided fights where possible in spite of his size.

On the other side were the bullies, residents of "Zulutown" as the good burghers of Tutter called the tough section of town. Leader of the Zulutown contingent was Bid Stricker, parochial roughneck, followed by his cousin Jimmy Stricker, Hib and Chet Milden, and Jum Prater (who had the "loudest mouth in Tutter"). The two gangs fought at least one pitched battle per book, with our side losing steadily until the end, when they always outwitted Bid and his boys. The battles were fought with harmless ammunition like mud, rotten tomatoes, and rotten eggs, never with anything dangerous like rocks (although the Strickers did let loose with acorn-bearing sling-shots on one occasion. Jerry and his friends stood well back. After all, a fellow can lose an eye that way).

A strong characteristic of Leo Edwards's heroes, in addition to reverence, truth, and a compulsion to do good deeds, was their intense respect for their parents. Jerry's dad owned the Tutter brickyard, a lucrative enterprise that shipped building materials nationwide. And wasn't he the swellest dad you ever heard of! Jerry thought so.

While I was washing my face and hands in the kitchen sink Dad came into the room, whistling and jiggling his feet in time to the music. In hugging Mother he reached behind and untied her apron strings. Then he gave me a swat on the head with the evening newspaper. When it comes to being lively and full of fun I'll put my dad up against any other man in La Salle County. He's great!

(*Jerry Todd and the Purring Egg, p. 9*)

As Jerry says, he was a humorist, and always up to something, even on an out-of-town business trip.

As I say, Dad is forever up to some kind of nonsense or other. And what do you know if he didn't send me a Christmas card! In the middle of summer! That's Dad for you. I bet he hunted for an hour to find that particular card, for, as you know, Christmas cards aren't usually on sale in July. He wrote under the Christmas tree that the snow was seventeen feet deep in Indianapolis and it was a big inconvenience for him not to have his overcoat along. He was coming home Sunday, he said, if the train could buck the snow-drifts.

(*op. cit., p. 83*)

Life was not all one-liners for the senior Todd, however. He could wax serious, like a real-life father on occasion.

He slapped me on the knee where I've got the fishhook scar.

"It keeps me so blamed busy making and shipping bricks that I haven't any chance to get out and fool around with the best little pal in the world."

He meant me. You can see how he appreciates me.

"Are you still chumming with the Ellery boy?" he inquired after a moment.

I nodded.

"I chum with Peg and Red too," I said.

"Um—They're all pretty good kids I think."

"We have lots of fun," I told him.

"I imagine so. And it's right that you should. For a boy is a boy only once in his life. But stick to the kind of fun that is wholly clean and manly. Mother and I expect it of you, Jerry."

(*op. cit., p. 51*)

In analyzing Jerry's relationship with his dad, it should be remembered that he was the same age as Joe Hardy or of any of the Boy Allies. Yet he was not averse, at sixteen, to crawling up on his father's lap and cuddling, a move which indicated to me that Leo Edwards really didn't know kids as well as a "regular feller" should have —perhaps had never been as close as he pretended to any teen-agers. I stopped sitting on my father's lap at the age of seven, although my daughter, woman-like, still sat on mine until she was eleven or twelve. But a male of sixteen? Never.

As I told Dad that night when we got home from Zulutown it was more fun to be just myself and know that I was on the square with him and my chums than it was to be a young millionaire with a troubled conscience. Anyway, riches are a bad thing for a boy. I found that out.

In our talk I told Dad how sorry I was for what I had done. And I further told him how it had troubled me to think that I had gone back on him for money. He said he understood. And big as I am—and I have a long-pants suit, I want you to know—he took me on his lap and held me tight and rubbed my head with his nose. That's a chummy trick of his. He said I was all right. As for the million dollars, we didn't need the money, he said, for we already had one millionaire in the family. He meant himself. "I've got you, Jerry," is the way he bragged on me, "and you're worth a million dollars to me any day in the week."

I tell you I've got a swell dad. I guess I won't ever go back on him again for *anything*. No, sir-*ee!*

(*op. cit., p. 178*)

Oddly enough, that sort of thing didn't put us fans off very much. If it had been his *mother*—well, that would have been a different story.

A typical Jerry Todd (or Poppy Ott) book began with the basic gang of four kids, plus one new kid, usually a poverty-stricken young ragamuffin the boys take into their gang who either gets adopted by a millionaire or finds a buried treasure by the last chapter. The boys then get into some kind of "mystery," a mummy in the local museum that whispers, a five-hundred-dollar rose-colored cat, a waltzing hen, a large object that could be a fertile dinosaur egg, a talking bird (and later a talking frog). There is a lot of camping out, and a great deal of activity on the lake on a converted clay scow from Mr. Todd's brickyard which the boys turned into a showboat and later a battleship for their wars with the Strickers. The prose is joyous, if overly simple (Edwards's idea of how kids talk) in every book.

> Circling to the top of a wooded knoll we got our first return view of the wide waters. And there in the middle of the big lake, as we sometimes called the wide waters, was our island. *Our* island, mind you. Oh gee! I can't begin to describe the happy feeling that stole over me. It was, in fact, something more than mere happiness—a sort of reverent thankfulness, I guess. God gives boys life and health, which is proof of His great love for them. But just think of all the extra things that had been given to us—an island, thirteen cats, seven dogs and a boiled ham. Yes, we sure were lucky.
>
> (*Jerry Todd, Pirate,* p. 27)

That surge of joy was something we could understand. We could just see that island and those dogs and cats!

About halfway through the series Poppy Ott appeared out of nowhere. Apparently Edwards (or his editor) felt the need of new blood. The three members of Jerry's gang lacked individuality enough for the late 1920s and early 1930s. They were too much like Jerry. A foil was wanted, a Huck Finn for his white-collar Tom Sawyer. The Jerry Todd series kept right on going, paralleled by the Poppy Ott books which were supposedly written by Jerry too. In one swoop, Edwards had revamped his cast and doubled his output.

Poppy (real name: Nicholas Carter Sherlock Holmes Ott, his father was a would-be private detective and a mystery story fan) entered in *Poppy Ott and the Stuttering Parrot*, in 1926. His appearance was duly recorded by Jerry Todd.

Red and I ran into a couple of tramps this morning on our way to the swimming hole. One was a man, a quite oldish man, and the other was a boy our age. Say, I wish you could have seen the outfit they had! It was a sort of ramshackle bungalow built on a rickety four-wheeled wagon. The house had side windows, all of different shapes and sizes. There was a back door and a little back porch with a rickety railing. Up in front a stovepipe poked its rusted snout through the roof. Like everything else in the outfit, the stovepipe was wabbly and ready to fall to pieces. It was some tacky outfit, all right. The wonder to me was that it didn't fall to pieces in travelling the country roads . . .

A tousle-headed kid came into sight on the bungalow's back porch. And at the sight of him Red pushed my hand and giggled.

"Lookit, Jerry," says he, pointing, "Huckleberry Finn has come to town."

The kid was a dead-ringer for Huckleberry Finn all right. His shirt was ripped at the neck and his pants were three sizes too big for him. They hung on him like Charley Chaplin's pants. And did a kid ever have dirtier feet! Good night! I wondered what his bed sheets looked like.

(*Poppy Ott and the Stuttering Parrot, p. 4*)

Poppy moved right in and became leader because his first adventure had to do with freeing his lazy, ne'er-do-well, tramp father who had been falsely jailed on circumstantial evidence. When that had been cleared up, the senior Ott decided he liked Tutter, and Mr. Todd gave him a job at the brickyard. Poppy enrolled in school and the complacent Scoop Ellery allowed Poppy to keep the leadership of the gang. "That's the way for a boy to be, I think," philosophized Jerry. "The leadership 'hog' doesn't register with me at all. A fellow has got to give and take in this world. He can't be the drum major and head of the profession *all* the time."

The "regular feller" stopped writing in the 1930s, after giving us Trigger Berg and Andy Blake as well as Poppy and Jerry. We were too busy to mourn him. There were too many other series to read. Don Sturdy, Bomba, Baseball Joe, we had no time for the past. New worlds were opening for us all the time. Leo Edwards had no dynasty to carry on for him as Edward Stratemeyer did. I like to think of him there in St. Petersburg, basking in the sunshine and in the adulation of the kids he made happy everywhere.

CHAPTER EIGHT

THE SATURDAY HEROES

> "I don't know w'y it is, but jes' bein' wid youse makes me want ter do der square t'ing."
>
> (Frank Merriwell at Yale)

We called it sport in those days, and sport is what it was —the endless pursuit of leather spheroids and whatever transient glory they could bring us. Sportsmanship was very much in evidence. Although we might hotly contest an umpire's decision, we never cheated. A dirty player was ostracized immediately and forever. Reputation was a precious commodity, even at twelve. The empty lots of Kew Gardens rivaled the playing fields of Eton when it came to building moral fibre.

This gentlemanly attitude came from the books we read. It was important to win the big game, but only on a fair-and-square basis, our heroes taught us, as they chalked up win after win for their happy, fun-filled boarding schools, and later for Yale and Harvard. In *Baseball Joe in the Big Leagues* the manager of the Chicago Cubs telephoned the manager of the St. Louis Cardinals to tell him that a sneak had offered to sell him the Cardinals' pitching signals. There was no question of buying them. The game—America's favorite game—must be kept clean. In *Dick Merriwell's Choice*, Frank's younger brother suggested that there were loftier purposes than making money, and that in the drive for success honor must take precedence over ambition. In *The Spirit of the School* Hansel Dana refused to play in the big game because his beloved Beechcroft Academy had a football scholarship halfback on the team.

Another myth? Perhaps. Harvard and Yale were possible if improbable with scholarships and hard work in those Depression years, but New England prep schools were out of the question for my crowd. It was a tuition-free city or state college for us if we were lucky, and a vocational high school if we were not. We dreamed of fun in the dorm and hazing and midnight feasts and moonlight singing on the quadrangle as we hurried off to school on the subway.

A pudgy little *samurai* named Tojo saved the day for some by ordering the Japanese Navy to wipe out Pearl Harbor. Bolstered by the GI Bill of Rights, some of us made it to the Ivy League, only to find that Edward Stratemeyer, Ralph Henry Barbour, and Gilbert Patten had swindled us again. The real thing wasn't like the books at all. Football was big business, and the First Eleven was usually made up of beefy semi-professional ringers purchased at great expense from Middle-Western high schools. The gallant chums who had really gone to New England prep schools were more interested in debutante parties than they were in sports. After graduation they turned into red-faced, martini-swilling stockbrokers who cheated on their income tax, mulcted their clients and stayed up nights conspiring to keep Jews and Negroes out of their clubs and neighborhoods.

It wasn't a complete swindle. To swindle someone you have to take something away from him that he values. We hadn't really lost anything. The Spirit of the School was in our own middle class hearts, firmly planted there by Baseball Joe, Garry Grayson, the boys of Beechcroft,

Yardley, Ferry Hill, and all the other schools, and the Merriwell Brothers. Those of us who read them and loved them would keep the spirit forever, perhaps a trifle bent and discolored, but stuck in there nevertheless. We were capable of dishonor and I suppose we always will be, but we knew what it felt like to be mightily ashamed of ourselves.

When we were not discussing girls and conjecturing about their silken mysteries, we always talked about sports in those days. Fortified with massive collections of data gleaned from Dixie Cup lids and bubble gum cards, we knew every batting average from the Babe himself to the juniormost rookie in the Three I League. We idolized the college football stars, groomed and beautified in the magnificent drawings of Burris A. Jenkins, Jr., in the New York *Journal*. Best of all, the genuine article was only minutes away. For fifty-five cents you could buy a bleacher seat on Olympus, and watch the immortals go by. The great George Herman Ruth was there, and Lou Gehrig, Joe DiMaggio, Lefty Gomez, Bill Dickey, and Red Ruffing. Over at the Polo Grounds were Mel Ott (who had joined the big leagues at fifteen!), Carl Hubbell, and Bill Terry. Brooklyn had the Dodgers, and the visiting teams were just as exciting—Dizzy Dean, Jimmy Foxx, Hank Greenberg!

You could sit out there in the sun all day in a state of pure euphoria, smelling the indescribable perfume of peanuts and hot dogs blended with springtime, and bellow encouragement at your idols until you thought your heart would leap right out of your mouth and over the Gillette Razor Blades sign into left field. They *wanted* you to make noise! Who can forget the gasping thrill that went with the hearty thwack of a solid base hit—heard a fraction of a second after you saw the bat meet the ball, because the bleachers were so far away.

With the first chill of autumn, and the World Series safely tucked away in baseball history, we turned to football—not professional football but the college kind. We knew the names of the pro stars because many of them had been our heroes when they were varsity players in earlier years, but our real idols were juniors and sophomores whose gridiron exploits were trumpeted in the sports pages every fall. The movies turned our enthusiasm into frenzy with dozens of features about ivy-covered universities and the Big Game, with Ronald Reagan, Richard Arlen, Jack Oakie, and bouncy June Preisser as the eternal cheerleader.

How many hundreds of kids of my generation built their futures on education chosen because of the football rather than the academic reputation of a college? Given a choice, any kid in my gang would have turned down Yale or Harvard in favor of Carlisle, because Jim Thorpe went there. My mother suggested that I might consider Johns Hopkins and medical school. Was she kidding? Who ever heard of *that* team?

In the wintertime came basketball, which was all right for girls, but not very exciting to play. Somehow basketball lacked the quality that legend is made of. It was thoroughly ignored by Stratemeyer, Barbour and the rest, probably because no one ever thought of buying a basketball book. It is significant to note that when winter came at Brill College, the Rover Boys pointedly elected to take P.T. instead of basketball. For the most part Ralph Henry Barbour's prep schoolers played ice hockey on nearby lakes and rivers (there were none in my neighborhood). We played basketball and swam at the YMCA, but only to fill the time until spring came again.

Five minutes after school was out we were chasing a ball. In the street, in the park, on any parcel of vacant real estate, we held endless contests that were really all the same contest. The goal, of course, was that boyhood paradise known as "making the team." If you were big enough and strong enough and resilient enough, you might win a place on the school nine or eleven, where an inept "coach" who doubled in Latin or history wielded the power of life and death over boyish egos. Making the team meant you were Somebody at school (and didn't the girls know it!). To prove your manhood you were authorized to wear your varsity letter on the sweater your mother had knitted for you, an accolade roughly equivalent to sporting the golden spurs of knighthood or the Victoria Cross.

A berth on a team, regardless of what kind of ball was involved, had sexual undertones. The whole school turned out for games, and that included the girls in their polo coats, pink-cheeked, saddle-shod and Tangee lipsticked, glowing in the March or October winds. They were the real prizes. A touchdown or a homer would melt the iciest female heart, just as silver Air Corps wings would do a few years later. The price of kisses was then as always measurable in blood and splinters of bone.

The grandest spur, the major contributor to this national state of mind in the twelve-to-fourteen world was the literature of the day. If there was money in major sports, there was also money in books about them. Edward Stratemeyer was warming up his first team in the bullpen, and he came up with a winner, Baseball Joe, written by "Lester Chadwick" in fourteen action-packed volumes. Joe moved inexorably up the Stratemeyer ladder from sand-lot ball to the New York Giants and on to immortality breaking every extant record on the way. We worshiped him. Every kid who knew what Stratemeyer meant by "the smell of crushed grass, dust, leather and hot sunshine" bought and read the whole series.

Joe Matson, later to be called Baseball Joe by an adoring

world, lived in the town of Riverside, "located on the Appleby River in one of our New England states." Borrowing a leaf from Barbour's book, Stratemeyer made him a newcomer to Riverside. Sports heroes were always new boys in town or at school, despised until they suddenly showed what they were capable of on the diamond or the gridiron. Other boy heroes belonged to third and fourth generation families, but never an athletic star. It would have spoiled the surprise that was so essential to every plot.

Joe was a "tall, well-built lad, with dark hair and brown eyes, and a way of walking and swinging his arms that showed he had some athletic training." At the outset he was a high school junior, although unlike most Stratemeyer heroes he would age appreciably during the saga, achieving full maturity and getting married before the series was halfway completed. We forgave him that, although it would have finished the Hardys or Don Sturdy. We didn't care as long as he played baseball.

He had come to Riverside from Bentville, a hundred miles away, with his father and mother, and his pretty sister, Clara (who in later years, at the height of Joe's success, would marry his closest chum, the Giants' number two pitcher Jim Barclay). He had played a little ball at Bentville, and by the time the family migrated to their new and permanent home he knew that he would never want to do anything else as long as he lived.

Joe's dad was the classic Stratemeyer *schlemiel*-father figure, sickly, improvident, and always in trouble. If it wasn't stolen patents it was bad investments or surgery. Tom Swift's dad had nothing on him for being a burden to his only son. Matson, senior, was an inventor who had worked in a machine works at Bentville and had "invented several useful appliances." Aware of the financial value of the old man's inventions, scheming Mr. Isaac Benjamin, manager of the Royal Harvester Works, had lured the family to Riverside to facilitate his plot to steal the patents. In every one of his father's tribulations, Joe came to the rescue in the nick of time, but only *after* the game. Fathers were important, but baseball came first.

"I've been served with a summons from the court," said Mr. Matson slowly. "It's a move on the part of Benjamin and Holdney. The court has taken my patent models and documents away from me, and I may lose everything. It's hard just as I was about to succeed—very hard."

"And you may lose everything, Dad?" asked Joe, huskily.

"Yes—everything, son—I may have to start all over again. I'm out of the harvester works now."

For a moment one disappointing thought came to Joe. He would not be able to go to a boarding school as he had hoped. Then the look of trouble on his father's face drove all other thoughts from his mind.

"Don't you care, Dad!" he exclaimed stepping close to him. "You can beat those fellows yet. We whipped the Blues today and I'm the regular pitcher for the Stars!"

(Baseball Joe of the Silver Stars, p. 220)

Two years later Joe was following his destiny in the Central League, a minor aggregation from which the major leagues drafted their rookie players. A few minutes before game time, a telegram arrived from home.

YOUR FATHER HURT IN EXPLOSION. NO
DANGER OF DEATH, BUT MAY LOSE EYE-
SIGHT. IF YOU CAN COME HOME DO SO.
                    MOTHER

(Baseball Joe in the Central League, p. 119)

His team colleagues were properly sympathetic, and the manager offered Joe an immediate emergency furlough.

"Awfully sorry, old man," [the manager] went on. "Come back to us when you can. You'll find us waiting."

Joe made his mind up quickly. It was characteristic of him to do this, and it was one of the traits that made him, in after years, such a phenomenal pitcher.

"I—I'm not going home," said Joe quietly . . . "At least not until after the game."

(loc. cit.)

Joe's mother conformed to the pattern that Mrs. Fenton Hardy would later exemplify by disapproving heartily of her son's career choice. She had him programmed for the ministry, and failing that for what Stratemeyer snidely called "one of the so-called learned professions." Our hero did make it to prep school (Excelsior Hall) and on to delight his mother by matriculating at Yale, but he never got his degree. A bid from Pittston of the Central League put the kibosh on that, and Joe became the first boy hero-dropout.

"Of course we just love to have you home, Joe—"

"There now, Mother, I know what you're going to say!" he interrupted with good-natured raillery. "You rather wish I'd stuck on there at Yale, turning into a fossil, or something like that, and—"

"Oh, Joe! Of course I didn't want you to turn into a fossil," objected his mother, in shocked tones. "But I did hope that you might—"

"Become a sky-pilot! Is that it, Momsey?" and he put his arm about her slender waist.

"Joe Matson! What a way to talk about a minister!" she cried. "The idea!"

"Well, Mother, I meant no disrespect. A sky-pilot is an ancient and honorable calling, but not for me. So here I am. Yale will have to worry along without yours truly, and I guess she'll make out fairly well. But how is everything? Seen any of the fellows lately? How's father? How's the business?"

The last question seemed to open a painful subject, for mother and daughter looked at one another as though each one was saying:

"You tell him!"

(*Baseball Joe in the Central League, p. 2*)

It was bad investments again. In 1914 with a rising market, the old man had bought another lemming. "Momsey" and Clara had not written to Joe about it because they thought it might affect his performance in the Yale-Princeton game.

Mrs. Matson was surprised to find out that ball players make more money than ministers, and when Joe impressed that fact on her, her disapproval vanished like magic. The Pittstons were paying him $1500 a year ("Why, that's more than $100 a month!") and he pointed out that it was more than his father had made when they were married. That did it.

"Well, of course, Joe—O! I *did* want you to be a minister, or a lawyer, or a doctor; but since you feel you can't, —well, perhaps it's all for the best, Joe," and she sighed softly. "Maybe it's for the best."

(*op. cit., p. 10*)

Women. Money made the mare go, even in those days. Would my mother react in the same way when I told her I wanted to reject the "so-called learned professions" and go to West Point to be a soldier? A silly question, but then I was only twelve and Joe was making $1500 a year.

If Mrs. Matson straightened up and became Joe's staunchest fan after the World Series bonuses started rolling in, Mr. Matson stayed a loser to the end.

> For a moment Tom stood there a bit embarrassed, for he saw that something unusual had happened.
>
> "I—I hope I'm not intruding," he stammered. "I didn't think—I came right in as I always do. Has anything—"
>
> "It's all right!" exclaimed Joe quickly. "We just got word that Dad has lost his patent case."
>
> "Gee! That's too bad!" exclaimed Tom, who knew something of the affair. "What are you going to do?"
>
> "I'm going to pitch against the Resolutes, the first thing I do!" cried Joe. "After that I'll decide what's next . . . Come on, Tom, we mustn't be late. We're going to wallop them—just as you said."
>
> "I hope you do!" burst out Clara.
>
> "Play a good game and—and don't worry," whispered Mrs. Matson to her son as he kissed her good-bye.
>
> (*Baseball Joe of the Silver Stars, p. 233*)

Like the rest of the genre, Baseball Joe books kept to a simple formula. In every step of his career Joe was beset by conspirators who moved heaven and earth to keep him from pitching. In the early books of the series it was rival pitchers, already installed on the teams Joe was to join. These lads, quite understandably, were not anxious to lose their places to the newcomer. They resorted to skullduggery of every kind to cripple him so that he would be unable to pitch. In later years, when he was the brightest star to grace the Golden Age of Baseball, it was gamblers, but Joe's pitching arm was in constant danger. And never did a human limb absorb so much punishment! In his whole baseball life Joe rarely pitched a game with-

out mastering excruciating pain from wrist to shoulder,
but he always won out in the end.

> The muscles ached very much in spite of all Tom could
> do with rubbing in the liniment, but Joe gritted his teeth
> and kept his place in the pitcher's box . . .
> "Fine, old man! Can you keep it up?"
> "I—I'm going to!" burst out Joe, though he had to grit
> his teeth to keep back an expression of pain when he
> moved his pitching arm.
>
> (*Baseball Joe of the Silver Stars, p. 190*)

On one occasion he wrenched the arm half out of its
socket saving a boy from a runaway streetcar. On another,
a sorehead deposed pitcher bribed a thug to twist it in
a crowd. On yet a third, after Joe had joined the Giants
and was rooming with Jim Barclay in the Westmere
Arms near the Polo Grounds, gamblers hired a crooked
inventor to move in across the street and weaken the arm
with a mysterious electrical ray. But the old soup-bone
never let him down—not permanently, that is. It did put
him out for a season (after effects of the ray). Undaunted,
he bought the Riverside semi-pro club and coached it
through a triumphant summer before returning to the
Giants and new glories.

After establishing Mr. Matson's troubles and the in-
destructability of Joe's arm, and introducing a few double-
dyed anti-baseball villains, each book became a chronicle
of baseball games. There were anywhere from five to
eight games a book. A few were lost, to give a cliff-hanger
touch to the story, and to make it less obvious that Joe's
team would win the Blue Banner or the cup or the
pennant or the World Series. The team (and Joe too)
always went into a slump halfway through, but pulled
out in time to rake in the money. In the final pages, Joe

always won the Big Game, with brilliant pitching and superior batting. "Chadwick" never failed to inform his readers that it wasn't Joe *alone* who won the games, it was the whole team, working in harmony. We knew better. A star was a star, and it was obvious to us that without Joe the team was a total loss.

The games were described in minute detail. To understand them, you had to memorize the names of eighteen new minor characters every chapter. "Blackley hit a slow roller to Grant who threw to Rockwell for the out." We didn't mind. If a single inning had been omitted, we would have been disappointed. We were used to painstaking box scores. A kid could re-enact Joe's games on paper, minute by minute right up to the breath-taking climax.

To give the readers a change of pace, a respite from the incessant game chronicles, a number of minor subplots were injected between innings. Joe saved an old woman from a burning house. He was kidnaped and trapped in a burning barn. He fell in love with and married lovely Mabel Varley of North Carolina. He befriended a has-been big-league pitcher, drummed out of baseball because of drink and dubious companions, and put him on the right track again. He captured a pair of Wall Street swindlers trying to fix a Giants game and turned them over to the D.A. (who allowed Joe and Jim to give them a thrashing instead of prosecuting, saving the taxpayers the expense of a trial). There was always something, but the last chapter was reserved for that inevitable Big Game.

As a ball player, Joe had everything. He started as a center fielder on the Riverside Silver Stars (an amateur team made up of boys between fourteen and nineteen) but soon switched to pitcher. The old soup-bone produced a superb fastball, in-shoots, out-shoots, and Joe's world-famous "fadeaway," a ball that seemed to be approaching at terrific speed but dropped off at the instant the batter swung at it. Pitchers, Chadwick reminded us, are notoriously bad hitters, but the readers wouldn't stand for it, and by the time Joe was established on the Giants he was leading the league in batting too. It was impressed on us that Joe's success was due to more than skill. It was hard work that put him on top. Practice and "inside stuff"—knowledge of the weaknesses and idiosyncracies of his opponents through study of their past performance —that made him a star.

In the earlier books Joe also pitched something that Chadwick called a "moist-ball" (in line with the concept of the times that "spit is a horrid word"). It wasn't until the fifth book that he broke down and called a spitball a spitball.

In his final big league year Joe was sitting on top of the baseball world. His pitching average was over .900 and his batting average exceeded the .400 mark. He led National League in both. But it wasn't enough. "What else are you gunning for?" asked his brother-in-law, Jim Barclay.

"Just this. Now don't laugh, old man, or tell me that 'twas through ambition that the angels fell' or any more of those bromides. I want to lead the league in homers. That's number one. I want to lead the league in general batting. That's number two. I want to lead the league in base stealing. That's number three. I want to lead the league in strike-outs. That's number four. I want to lead the league in the percentage of earned runs I allow opponents. That's number five. I want to lead the league in consecutive victories. That's number six. I want, as captain, to have the Giants win more games than they've ever won before in a single season. That's number seven, the lucky number. Let's hope it brings me luck."

Jim was staring at him open-mouthed. "Wow!" he ejaculated. "Is that all?"

(*Baseball Joe, Champion of the League, p. 66*)

Stratemeyer-Chadwick, with his characteristic gener-
osity to dying heroes, let him have them all. There were
to be two more books in the series, but Joe, champion
of champions, was already on the way out.

The fourteen books were segments of Joe's professional
life, starting in Riverside and ending at the Polo Grounds.
Playing on the local amateur Silver Stars, his ambition
was to go to one of those splendid boarding schools that
made Ralph Henry Barbour so much money. Rescuing
his father's patents, Joe left Riverside for Excelsior Hall
and a happy year marred by bullies who tried to keep
him off the team. Fat chance! Joe pitched the school
team to the coveted Blue Banner and went on to Yale.

University life brought our hero good times and good
friends he often regretted in later years when he had put
them behind him to follow a diamond career. Yale also
brought his first national prominence, when he pitched
the Eli team to victory at the Polo Grounds over their
arch-rival Princeton. Professional scouts bombarded him
with offers, but Joe chose Pittston of the Central League,
a respectable outfit where he received much-needed sea-
soning. At the end of his first season, in 1917, Joe was
drafted into the St. Louis Cardinals while other healthy
lads were being drafted into the Army. Characteristically,
Stratemeyer ignored World War I since it had nothing to
do with baseball, and Joe joined the ranks of his non-
combatants, with Tom Swift and Ralph the Railroader.

After a season with the Cards, Joe was purchased by
the Giants, saw them through a World Series, and made a
triumphant world tour, ending up as captain of the team

and champion of the league. After that it was happy retirement to Riverside with Mabel, to join the Chamber of Commerce and Rotary, and "put Riverside on the map" with his snappy semi-pro club.

It sounds a simple and direct itinerary, but villains and enemies blocked him all along the way. These base-ballophobes were always ex-players, put out of the game either by Joe's superior skill or by association with gamblers or criminals. They were dirty players, every one, and the game was the better for their absence. In frustrated rage, they had sworn revenge on Joe, and stopped at nothing—murder, mayhem, arson, kidnaping—to get him. They always failed.

In spite of the pitfalls that beset young athletes, Joe remained pure and unsullied to the end, eschewing groupies and alcohol. The nickname "Broadway Joe" could never have been applied to him.

> The Cardinals were on the move again. They went from city to city, playing the scheduled games, winning some and losing enough to keep them about in fifth place. Joe saw much of life, of the good and bad sides. Many temptations came to him, as they do to all young fellows, whether in the baseball game or other business or pleasure. But Joe "passed them up." Perhaps the memory of a certain girl helped him. Often it does.
>
> (*Baseball Joe in the Big League*, p. 212)

At one point in his career, Joe found it necessary to enter a "low haunt," in this case a boarding house frequented by petty criminals who played cards and plotted mischief there. His purpose in going into such an establishment was the rescue of good old "Pop" Dutton, the ex-drunk he was rehabilitating. He hustled "Pop" out just in time to avoid a police raid. Chadwick found it necessary to halt the action and call time out for an apology and an explanation to his readers.

> I am making this explanation, and portraying this scene in Joe's career, not because it is pleasant to write about, for it is not. I would much rather take you out on the clean diamond where you could hear the "swat" of the ball. But as Joe's efforts to make a new man of the old pitcher took him into this place I can do no less than chronicle the events as they happened. And a little knowledge of the sadder, darker and unhappy side of life may be of value to boys, in deterring them from getting into a position where it would appeal to them—appeal wrongly, it is true, but none the less strongly.
>
> (*Baseball Joe in the Central League*, p. *182*)

Professional baseball was all white in those pre-Jackie Robinson days, and the readers were spared the usual ethnic stereotype. Mr. Matson, senior, was too erratic to afford a grinning, woolly-haired family retainer, and Joe's touring kept him in hotels after he made his pile. But baseball was big business, and a bit of 1920s bigotry crept in anyway, in the person of Moe Russnak. Mind you, some of Joe's best friends were . . . but there are all kinds, good and bad. Russnak wanted to buy the Riversides, and Joe outbid him.

> "He's a Jew that lives in Pentolia. Not that I have anything against him because of his race. Our shortstop, Levy, is a Jew, and he's as fine a fellow as there is on the team. Cracking good ballplayer too. But this Russnak is a low, greasy specimen that makes a decent man feel a crawling in his spine whenever he looks at him . . .
>
> "I'd hate to see the club get into such hands, if he's that kind of fellow," remarked Joe.
>
> (*Baseball Joe, Club Owner*, p. *77*)

And that kind of fellow is precisely what he was.

> He was a fat, oily fellow of medium height, dressed in a suit of loud checks with a diamond pin in a flashy tie and with several rings on pudgy hands that were none too clean. His eyes were small and bead-like with an unpleasant glitter in them. He had a protuberant nose, thick loosely hung lips and flabby cheeks. His face was stamped with meanness and avarice.
>
> (*op. cit., p. 95*)

As a contrast, Levy the shortstop was a good Jew, perhaps not quite good enough for the country club, but he did his job and never got uppity.

> . . . Joe was most delighted with the sparkling work of Ike Levy, a young Jewish lad at short. Here was a man who bore all the marks of a coming star . . .
>
> "Better make the most of him while I have him," mused Joe to himself. "If any big league scout comes along, he'll nab Levy sure."
>
> (*op. cit., p. 122*)

Eventually Russnak showed himself up for the scoundrel that he was, paying thugs to saw through Riverside's grandstand supports, and hiring discharged big league ex-players to cripple Joe's men. Joe was able to gather enough evidence to run him out of organized baseball.

> "You white-livered coward!" Joe's voice was low, but each word came clear-cut and stinging like the lash of a whip. "I've stood about all the sneers and insults from you that I'm going to. My right arm may not be much good at present as far as pitching is concerned, but it's still good enough to put you out of commission for a long time to come."

"You—you rat!" [Russnak] spat at Joe. "You should be afraid to hit a man half your size—"

(*op. cit., p. 150*)

Men like Joe don't soil their hands on that sort of canaille, however, as every boy knows.

"That will do, Mr. Russnak," said Joe sternly, rising. "There is the door. You will find that it closes automatically when you release the knob on the further side."

(*op. cit., p. 115*)

The supporting cast that accompanied Joe to glory was undistinguished. There were no chums to speak of, and the familiar fat boy was missing, since Joe's associates necessarily had to be clean-limbed athletes. A foil always helps, and the nearest thing to a counter-Joe was his brother-in-law, Reggie Varley, a good fellow for a non-ball player, and probably the only dude that Stratemeyer ever allowed to be on the side of the angels.

His chief defect, and after all not a serious one, was his love of clothes. He was always dressed, as he was now, in the very extreme of fashion, fawn-colored gloves, creamy spats, cut-in coat and costly tie, the whole finished off with a cane and a monocle. He was inordinately fond of anything English, and cultivated an accent that he thought would pass current in London and stamp him as one to the manner born.

(*Baseball Joe, Champion of the League, p. 43*)

Joe's other brother-in-law and crony, Jim Barclay, might have been cut with a pair of scissors from one of those self-same bubble gum cards that gave us so much joy.

Mabel, Joe's love and later his wife, was simply described as "pretty." Anything Joe did was fine with her. She was a baseball fan, and during the season she stayed home in Riverside with the folks and left him alone.

Love came to Joe suddenly, out of nowhere, in the fourth book of the series. Out of Yale and in the minors, he had reported in at a North Carolina training camp. Strolling in the country, he observed a runaway carriage containing a young woman. It was impossible for him to stop the plunging, half-crazed horse in mid-gallop with his bare hands. There was only one thing to do. Picking up a rock, our hero let go his famous fast ball, conking the animal between the eyes and stunning it. ("Sorry, old fellow," Joe was to apologize later. "It was the only way.") Mabel, bruised and shaken, but otherwise all right, was profuse in her thanks. It was love at first sight for both. Introductions followed.

> "It's awfully kind of you, Mr.—" she paused suggestively.
>
> "I'm Joe Matson, formerly of Yale," was our hero's answer, and, somehow, he felt not a little proud of that "Yale." After all, his university training, incomplete though it had been, was not to be despised.
>
> "Oh, a Yale man!" her eyes were beginning to sparkle now.
>
> "But I gave it up to enter professional baseball," the young pitcher went on.
>
> (*Baseball Joe in the Central League, p. 63*)

The courtship flourished, blooming like an American Beauty rose. On a moonlit sleigh ride in Riverside:

> "Oh what a glorious night!"
> "Did you ever see such a moon!"

"Looks about as big as a baseball does when you're far from first and the pitcher is heaving it over to tag you out!"

(*Baseball Joe in the Big League, p. 61*)

Presumably, they lived happily ever after and Joe sewed his old man up in an irrevocable trust, bought Momsey a mink coat, and retired to a happy old age of autographing baseball bats and franchising restaurants. "Lester Chadwick" was kept around long enough to do the College Sports series of six books before being permanently benched. Stratemeyer came up with "Graham B. Forbes" and the eight-volume series about the Boys of Columbia High, one of whom (Frank Allen) was graduated into a series of three volumes of his own. He also drafted "Elmer A. Dawson" and "John R. Cooper" who produced, respectively, the Garry Grayson football stories and the Mel Martin Baseball Stories.

Some of the highest quality boys' book prose of the period came from the pen of Ralph Henry Barbour, man of a million prep schools, and one of the few that I would not be afraid to recommend to a twelve-year-old today. I got almost as much fun out of rereading *The Crimson Sweater* as I did on my initial exposure to it thirty years ago. Barbour was no prizewinner, but he certainly stood out above the rest in his day.

Barbour died in 1944 at the age of seventy-three after writing eighty boys' books at the rate of three a year. A native of Massachusetts, he never went to college, completing his education at New Church School in Waltham and Highland Military Academy in Worcester. While he was still in school he discovered that "certain words sounded alike and could be set down on paper in such a manner that certain editors called them verse and paid good money for them." He sold schoolboy doggerel verse and jingles to the papers under the name of "Richard Stillman Powell," earning considerable pocket money.

Instead of college, Barbour chose to go to work as a reporter, serving in that capacity on various newspapers in Boston, Denver, Chicago, and Philadelphia. During this period he wrote a football story, "The Arrival of Jimpson" in which an obscure substitute wins the big game. It was published in *St. Nicholas,* and an alert publisher suggested that he extend it into book length. The result was *The Half-Back* (1899), followed by a second novel, *For the Honor of the School.*

With book-writing out of his system, Barbour returned to journalism as night city editor of the Philadelphia *Times.* Like so many good men before and after him, he was merged out of existence, when the *Times* combined with the Philadelphia *Ledger.* He turned to fiction permanently, to the benefit of generations of sportsminded boys. In the chips at last, he retired to Coral Gables until the final three years of his life, when he settled in Pass Christian, Mississippi. He never lost his interest in games, however, and we find him at the age of seventy writing to the New York *Times* suggesting a radical new football rule, that no one be allowed to kick any kind of goal who had not participated in the last three consecutive plays.

A typical Barbour book dealt with a new boy at a New England prep school. Ordinarily the newcomer came from some outlandish place like Ohio or Kansas, and was welcomed with little enthusiasm by the cliquish group in residence, most of whom had attended the same primary schools. But wait! On arrival the outsider turned out to be a superbly aquiline young WASP with good shoulders and an air of casual insouciance, bristling with honor and the qualities of leadership. He was dependable, cool, unruffleable. He avoided trouble with a good-humored, confident smile although he could take care of himself in a scrap if need be. Best of all, he was a whiz on the athletic field. By the end of his first year, he was the leader of the school. Somewhere in the vicinity was a girl a few years younger—perhaps fourteen (Barbour heroes were usually seventeen), pretty, tomboyish, and athletic, who looked people in the eye when she talked to them. It was obvious at once that our hero had won her heart.

There was no single Barbour hero who commanded a long series, like those published by the Stratemeyer Syndicate. Each hero-cum-school lasted long enough to complete a whole year of seasonal sports, football, baseball, crew, hockey, track; and then gave way to a new school and protagonist. Sometimes this could be accomplished in a single book. Sometimes it took four or five. The hero's rise to glory as captain of this or that sporting aggregation was accelerated by judicious choice of chums. When things looked bad and it looked as though he would be condemned to Unpopularity, he was befriended by a Power, usually a team captain who appreciated his good qualities and helped him along. Sometimes there were bullies and sometimes there were none. They weren't essential. The plot was too strong to have to depend on them. When there were bullies, it was never necessary to thrash them. School spirit made them come around and become good fellows on their own.

The best thing about Barbour's efforts was that they were believable. Romanticized though they might be, the things that happened could have happened to real kids. There was no murder, no mayhem, and no kidnaping. The worst thing a bully could do to get a hero in trouble or put off the team was to hide a live rabbit in the Latin teacher's desk. No one sent an athletic star a rattlesnake in a box, or chained him up in a burning barn.

The schools were identical little New England enclaves, Yardley, Hilton, Erskine, Grafton, North Bank, Wyndham, Cheltham, Hillfields, and the rest. I cannot imagine why he didn't merge them, and center all his action on a single campus. It would have been better organized, but Barbour enjoyed dreaming up new towns and new colors. Every school had a wonderful, warm, teacher; formerly a member of an Ivy League first eleven, who doubled as coach and loved and was loved by the boys. There was also "the Doctor," a remote but splendid headmaster who lived in "the Residence" or "the Cottage." The campus was always bisected by a meandering river that was fine for rowing, canoeing, and ice hockey.

> Maple Ridge School lies a mile and a half from the town of Charlemont, Massachusetts. The campus overlooks a wide valley of farm and meadow pricked out with white homesteads, with the river trailing like a blue ribbon down the center. Southward the smoky haze shows where Springfield lies. Back of the school property rises the steep slope of Maple Ridge. The buildings are five in number; the two dormitories, North and South; the recitation hall, or School Building as it is called; the Residence, abode of the principal, Doctor Benedict—more familiarly known as "Benny"—and the gymnasium . . .

> (*Finkler's Field, p. 5*)

Having given us a zoom lens long shot of the locale, Barbour was ready to introduce his star, and he was never one to spare the chiaroscuro. Remember how Baseball Joe was described simply as a "tall, well-built lad with dark hair and brown eyes who walked as though he had had some athletic training"?

> Hansel Dana was seventeen years old, a tall, clean-cut boy with very little superfluous flesh beneath his neat,

well-fitting grey suit. Despite his height he looked and was heavy. His hair was brown and so were his eyes, and the latter had a way of looking straight at you when he talked that was a little bit disconcerting at first. Harry Folsom, who, being out of the running himself, had a deep liking for good looks, mentally dubbed Dana the handsomest fellow in school. His nose was straight, his mouth firm without being thin, and his chin was square and aggressive. There was a liberal dash of healthy color in each cheek . . . He wore a white negligee shirt, a suit of gray flannel, low tan shoes, and when he had entered had worn a gray cloth cap. The clothes were not expensive but, as Harry ruefully acknowledged to himself, looked better than did his own garments, for which he had paid possibly three times as much.

(*The Spirit of the School, p. 13*)

Here is a typical Barbour girl, sportive but at the same time very feminine, beautiful but simultaneously a "good fellow." Not only was fourteen-year-old "Harry" (for Harriet) Emery all woman, but she beat the star of a rival boys' school in an ice-skating race because there wasn't a boy at Ferry Hill who could touch her on the blades.

Roy decided that she was rather pretty. Her hair was luridly red, but many persons would have called it beautiful. Her eyes were very blue and had a way of looking at you that was almost disconcerting in its frank directness. Her face was brown with sunburn, but there was color in the cheeks. A short, somewhat pugnacious little nose, not guiltless of freckles, went well with the red-lipped mischievous mouth beneath. For the rest, Harry was a wholesome, lovable little minx with the kindest heart that ever beat under a mussy white shirtwaist, and the quickest temper that ever went with red hair.

(*The Crimson Sweater, p. 30*)

She certainly wasn't La, High Priestess of Opar, but she had *my* heart beating under my mussy white shirt-waist. The illustrations showed her straight as an arrow in a Peter Thomson and a ribboned sailor straw. She was the kind of girl my crowd dreamed about, loyal, true-blue, adorable. You could play your heart out and make the winning touchdown for her and she would understand. You could *marry* a girl like Harry some day.

Athletic prowess brought Barbour heroes to the top, but for the most part they were undistinguished in the classroom. A good B-minus would describe them. Grinds were looked down on then, and anyone who had the tuition could get into Yale, but football was something else again.

> A fellow can't make a touchdown in the last thirty seconds of play, and so win the game for his school, without affecting his position. No matter what he was before, after that he's a hero and a saint and a public benefactor all rolled into one. Roy's case was no exception. He woke up Saturday morning a rather unimportant and quite unpopular person. He climbed out of bed Sunday morning to find that, metaphorically, the world was his! As soon as the bell had rung, the difference was apparent. There was no more dressing in silence, no more waiting till the others were through for a chance at the washroom. It was "Morning, Porter! How are you feeling after it?" "Hello, Mr. Quarterback! How'd you sleep?" "Here, Stearns, get out of here and give Porter a show; he's been waiting hours! . . ."
>
> (*The Crimson Sweater, p. 116*)

To keep his readers from becoming too intoxicated with the fumes of glory, Barbour injected plenty of propaganda about honor, spirit, fair play, and the other qualities he felt ought to be foremost in the minds of prep school boys. Before the big game with Fairview, Mr. Ames, Beechcroft Academy's English teacher and beloved coach, had a heart-to-heart chat with a few of the boys. It had come to the attention of the more high-minded clique that Billy Cameron, star halfback, and kingpin of the wished-for victory against Fairview, had a football scholarship. Was this honorable? Did Mr. Ames and the headmaster condone it?

> . . . let me tell you . . . that I don't give a hang who wins. This may sound strange to you but it's a fact nevertheless. I've watched things pretty closely for several years, and I've just about reached the conclusion that the school that wins more than a fair share of athletic contests is in a good way to slide downhill. There is nothing, it seems, so demoralizing to a school or college as a reputation for winning in football year after year. It brings a flood of undesirable material to the school and the *morale* suffers in consequence. Fellows who come here because they want to play football on a winning team are not the fellows we want. They introduce the 'win-at-any-cost' spirit, and it's that spirit, as you fellows know, that causes just the sort of trouble we're experiencing here now. 'Win at any cost' means trickery and dishonesty."

> (*The Spirit of the School, p. 141*)

No analysis of Barbour's books would be complete without at least one example of the grand, heart-stopping moment when someone crashes across the line to make the touchdown that wins the big game. There were similar moments in baseball, hockey and track, but none of them ever seemed to equal a football victory.

> From the sides of the field came a confused, inarticulate roar as the spectators, on their feet, watched with anxious hearts the outcome of the race. Five yards ahead

of the nearest pursuer sped Hansel, running like a flash. Behind him, with outstretched clutching hands, ran the Fairview right end. Back of him friend and foe were strung along the field. Hansel's feet twinkled above the thirty yard line. Beside him, dangerously near, was the white boundary line, but he dared not edge farther toward the middle of the gridiron lest it prove his undoing. Another white line streak passed beneath him, and then a second. The goal line was clearly in view. But he had played through almost seventy minutes of a hard game, and his limbs ached and his breath threatened at every stride to fail him. Once he faltered—that was near the fifteen yard line—and a note of triumph burst into the pandemonium of sound from the watchers. But he struggled on again. The ten-yard line was almost under foot when he felt the shock of the tackle. Grimly he hugged the ball, struggled to advance, did manage to cross the white streak and then stretched his length on the turf, hunched his head out of danger, and had the last breath driven from his body as the foremost of the pursuit hurled themselves upon him. Somewhere, very, very far away it seemed a whistle blew. And then he knew nothing more until the big sponge splashed over his face, and he regained consciousness to find them pumping his arms up and down and kneading his chest . . .

(op. cit., p. 264)

No boy hero ever made that winning touchdown without losing consciousness. It was all part of the mystique. To cross the goal line standing up, in books or in the movies, spoiled the whole thing. In our own sand-lot games, we always flopped on our bellies as we crossed the line. It looked so—well—*gallant!*

Stratemeyer was not one to overlook the gridiron, especially when it had been proven to be such a winning investment by his rivals. In 1926 the Syndicate came out with Garry Grayson. Most of the series was written after Stratemeyer's death, and, alas, it showed the lack of the master's guiding hand. Garry's books were awful. But we didn't care. Literary values were nothing to boys whose favorite light reading was the sports page of the *Daily Mirror*. We wanted football, and we got it, long detailed chronicles like the games in the Baseball Joe series. Plot was unimportant, shoved in to give us a breather between halves. Most of the plots were lifted from other Stratemeyer series. There were frame-ups, missing money, fathers faced with ruin, abduction of stars before the game, and all the tried and true situations of the past three decades. Garry was an athletic male Nancy Drew, perfect and infallible.

Garry and his chums were younger than the Barbour boys. They averaged fourteen years of age, and at the beginning of the series they were eighth-graders at the Hill Street Grammar School. They would later attend Lenox High, in their hometown of Lenox, a thriving settlement of fifteen thousand souls. In the beginning there were no fancy prep schools for Garry and his pals. They attended big, healthy, American public schools, crammed with students, half of whom were football-minded girls who attended every game and most practice sessions. Whenever Garry did anything praiseworthy on the gridiron, they yelled their heads off.

Later, after securing the public high school market, Garry switched to Stanley Prep, a standard boys' fiction boarding school, and went on to Passmore Tech for his college years. The series lasted ten books and took us well into the 1930s before we outgrew it.

Garry was a "frank, likeable boy, straightforward, truthful and courageous. He was a good scholar and stood well in all his classes . . . He was of medium height, strongly built, fleet of foot, and a leader in boyish sports.

He had brown eyes, brown wavy hair, and a straight nose that indicated decision and force of character . . ."

His father was a prominent and well-to-do criminal lawyer, and his two most intimate chums were Nick Danter and Ted Dillingham, whose dads were partners in the town's leading department store; placing our hero, like most Stratemeyer Syndicate protagonists, in the upper middle class. Ted had red hair and a quick, short temper, and Nick was tall, slim, and studious. The chums were joined in later books by "Sloppy" Hume, the familiar fat-boy chum turned beefy right guard, and "Rooster" Long and Bill Sherwood, all football fans and members of the first team.

A prominent figure in the series was Garry's pretty but sharp-tongued twin sister, Ella, who rode him incessantly. She was waspish and hypercritical, but in reality she was proud of her sibling when he fell across that goal line. Or perhaps she was jealous. In any event, the knife was always out for the male twin.

"I suppose you've been having great sport with that new football." [Garry's mother asks]

"Where is it?" asked Ella quickly. "I didn't see you bring it in. It can't be that you've lost it already."

"That's just what I have!" blurted out Garry. "That is, it's been stolen from me . . ."

"Did some big bad man take it away from him, bless his little heart?" asked Ella.

"Keep still, Ella," commanded her mother. "You've done nothing but tease Garry ever since he came in. Now, Garry, tell me all about it."

Garry narrated the incident in all its details, and Mrs. Grayson listened with sympathy for the boy and a growing resentment at the fellow who had made off with the ball.

"It's a burning shame!" she exclaimed . . . "but don't worry about the ball, Garry dear. Dad will get you another one."

"And you'd better tie a string to that," put in the irrepressible Ella. "Then you can yank it back when it wants to go for a ride."

(Garry Grayson's Hill Street Eleven, p. 16)

The enemies who dogged Garry through the series were led by one Sandy Podder, who had a reputation for being "wild." He had a sleek convertible, and "more pocket money than was good for him," to the chagrin of his mother, who saw him get into more and more trouble as the books went by. Sandy's father was a bad one himself, given to sharp business dealings. Sandy was always accompanied by interchangeable toadies, many of whom were ex-football team members, put off the team for unnecessary roughness or illegal play. Their main objective was Garry's reputation, and they did everything they could to make our hero and Hill Street-Lenox-Stanley Prep-Passmore Tech lose. Garry was impatient with them, and handled them with firmness.

"There are those fake heroes spouting again," growled Sandy, in a voice loud enough to reach those for whom it was intended. "To hear them talk you'd think they were the whole cheese."

"Ain't it the truth?" drawled Lent. "Lenox never knew anything about football until they came here."

"Say, listen, Sandy Podder! And you, Lent Stewart!" Garry whirled on his heel and regarded the two contemptuously. "Whenever either of you two fellows makes the Lenox team or does anything worth while for the school, it will be time for you to talk. Until then you'd better sing small. Get me?"

(Garry Grayson's Football Rivals, p. 50)

In spite of Garry's stern warning, the miscreants followed the *Stratemeyer Instruction Manual for Bullies* and kidnaped three members of the team before an important game. It got through to Garry after some analysis that *they wanted their own school to lose!* Words were no longer enough. He trapped all three of them and painted the word "traitor" on their foreheads with yellow paint. They were disgraced before the student body, the cruelest punishment of all.

> "There may be some one else in the school that'll have to be thrown overboard [admitted Garry]. Why can't such fellows be decent? Why should there be such things as traitors?"
>
> "Why should there be such things as skunks and snakes and mosquitoes?" Bill answered. "But there are, just the same. We've just got to grin and bear them."
>
> "Not on your life!" cried Garry, clenching his fists. "We've got to fight them!"
>
> *(op. cit., p. 145)*

The bullies were spurred to greater effort by Garry's continued popularity and gridiron successes. It was not enough to kidnap stars for a single game. Nothing would satisfy them but expulsion and lasting shame for their nemesis. A rumor of wild parties among the high school set was leaked to the Lenox weekly gazette. The principal and the PTA were up in arms. Then, lightning struck.

> In the desks of Garry Grayson, Bill Sherwood and Rooster Long three squat flasks were found, hip flasks, each containing a small amount of liquor! No other desk offered anything incriminating.
>
> The hapless trio were thunder-struck. The other members of their class were utterly bewildered. They could not believe it. Yet there was the evidence, those three evil-

smelling flasks with their wretched contents. The evidence was overwhelming.

"We're done!" groaned Bill, after class had been dismissed and they were awaiting with dread a summons from the office. "We've been framed, all right, and I only wish I could get hold of the fellow who did it."

"We've got to think how to get out of this jam first," said Garry. "Keep still, fellows, and let me think."

(*op. cit., p. 99*)

Of course Garry's nimble wits won out. The boys were reinstated and the bullies thrown out of Lenox High. In every book, when skullduggery was over and miscreants vanquished, it was time for football. Always in mid-book a loss would discourage the team. With morale flagging, a what's-the-use attitude would prevail, but Captain Garry Grayson always came through with a pep talk worthy of the late Knute Rockne extracting one more for the Gipper. When rivals for the championship had put on an unusually good performance against another team, and Lenox was down in the dumps:

"That doesn't mean anything in my young life," declared Garry stoutly. "Comparative scores are nix. I don't deny that Webster Street has a mighty good team. But I didn't see anything today to scare me stiff. It only means we've got to practice like the mischief."

(*Garry Grayson's Hill Street Eleven, p. 185*)

It is interesting to compare Garry's winning touchdown with Hansel Dana's, quoted *supra*, as a good example of Stratemeyer Syndicate style versus Ralph Henry Barbour.

Garry set his lips in a determined line.
"Now or never!" he muttered to himself.

The ball was snapped to him. He made as though to throw to Dick. Then, as the enemy line swayed in that direction, Garry, holding the ball, was off toward the right end with Sloppy and Bill acting as interference in front and Nick and Dick close behind.

Down the field Garry went like a deer, running as if for his life. Bill downed a tackler on one side, Sloppy on the other.

While the sidelines rocked with the stamping and cheers of the Hill Street fans, Garry straight-armed a tackler in his way, writhed out of the near embrace of another, flung himself head-on into a third, bowling him over, and with a last desperate effort flung himself over the goal line for the touchdown that spelled victory . . .

The crowd rushed across the field, a yelling mob.

Garry, covered with mud and grime, was hoisted on the shoulders of his hero-worshipping schoolmates and borne in triumph down the field to an improvised chorus:
"Garry Grayson! Garry Grayson!
Yea, yea, yea!
Garry Grayson! Garry Grayson!
Saved the day!
Yea, Garry! Yea, Garry! Yea, *Garry!*

(*op. cit., p. 212*)

How that Stratemeyer Syndicate could peer into a twelve-year-old heart and then play it like a balalaika. Who cared about prose style and three-syllable words? Yea, *Garry!*

No chapter dealing with sports heroes would be complete without the Merriwells, Frank and Dick, and later Frank's boy Frank, Junior. Strictly speaking, they don't really belong in this book. For one thing, they were earlier than most of our fictional heroes, arriving on the heels of the Horatio Alger-Oliver Optic books, which were antiques when my crowd reached reading age.

They were not easy to come by when I was twelve. Although they were practically contemporaries of the Rovers and Ralph the Train Dispatcher, they were out of print and couldn't be purchased anywhere except in secondhand stores, where we rarely went (you could get a disease in those places). Thus, they had little effect on us compared with, say, Baseball Joe.

A great deal has been written about the Merriwells and their prolific author, Gilbert Patten ("Burt L. Standish"), much more than was ever written about Stratemeyer, Barbour, Rohmer, and the rest. There are dozens of scholarly treatises about the dime novel and its affect on American mass culture. Articles have appeared about Patten and his boys in such prestigious periodicals as *Fortune*, the *Saturday Review*, the New York *Times* and *The Saturday Evening Post*. Among the better ones are Barney Lefferts's "The Return of Frank Merriwell" (*New York Times Magazine*, August 19, 1956); "Gilbert Patten and the Merriwell Saga" (*University of Maine Studies*, Orono, Maine, 1934), by John L. Cutler; and Patten's own "Dime Novel Days" (*Saturday Evening Post*, February 28, 1931). Russel B. Nye has given an excellent short portrait of Patten and Frank in his recent (1970) book, *The Unembarrassed Muse*.

Patten was born in 1866, four years after Stratemeyer, in the small town of Corinna, Maine. His parents were pacifists and religious zealots, and young Gilbert (or George William, as he had originally been christened) was forbidden to play with other boys. The Pattens were a two-book family, and most of his childhood was spent in lonely perusal of *Morgan's Masonry*, an illustrated history of the Civil War, and Joseph Holt Ingraham's novel *The Prince of the House of David*. Enough was enough, and after passing four years at the Corinna Union Academy, Patten ran away from home and got a job in a machine shop in Biddeford.

Independent at last, he tried his hand at fiction, and sold his first two stories to the *Banner Weekly* when he was seventeen. Erastus Beadle of Beadle & Adams, gave him six dollars apiece for them. His next story (*The Diamond Sport*) got him $50, the next one $75, and the one after that $100. It was good-bye to the machine shop, then. Patten was on his way.

He moved to New York in 1891 to write westerns for Beadle & Adams under the pseudonym of William West Wilder ("Wyoming Will") for $150 apiece, and was hired away by Street & Smith in 1895 to write for their magazine *Golden Hours* at $250 per 60,000 word serial.

He wrote the first Frank Merriwell story in 1896, and did weekly stories about Frank for eighteen years. Instead of paying him by the story, Street & Smith put him on the staff at $50 a week, a salary which rose to $150 as the years went by. There were 986 consecutive Merriwell installments, later printed as 208 books and sold to 125,000,000 readers, among whom were Al Smith, Babe Ruth, Jack Dempsey, and President Woodrow Wilson. Frank became a comic strip in 1931, a radio program in 1934, and a Broadway musical in 1971, but he never made it into the movies.

Unlike his contemporaries, the plutocrats of the juvenile fiction field, Edward Stratemeyer, Edgar Rice Burroughs, and the rest, Patten received no royalties. There were no stocks and bonds and vast real estate deals for him. He was an employee, nothing more, which probably accounts for his announcing himself as a Fabian Socialist in the early part of the century. In 1940 Franklin P. Adams, columnist for the New York *Post,* wrote that Patten was in financial trouble and was in danger of losing his home on a mortgage foreclosure. Contributions rolled in from everywhere (Wendell Willkie was one of the first donors) and the publicity resulted in a contract for a new Merriwell book in 1941. Patten died in Vista, California, in 1945.

The Merriwell books were based on the thesis that sports ennoble. A clean mind in a clean body, sang Patten a far cry from the earlier Horatio Alger heroes who were so busy striving that they had little time for games. According to Patten, hard work was not the only short cut to the top. If you were good at athletics, you could be popular, revered, and honored, even at Yale and Harvard. It was only necessary to have a strong sense of honor as well as a good physique, and to "play the game" and the world would beat a path to your door.

Frank was a superb natural athlete, good at any and all sports. A whiz on the gridiron, he also revolutionized the college baseball world with his famous "double-shoot," a pitch that curved twice in different directions on the way to the plate. His brother, Dick, threw a "jump ball" that rose twelve inches as it approached the batter. Both brothers were fullbacks, and both participated in track in the fifty-yard dash, the half mile, the mile, the pole vault, the broad and high jumps and the hammer throw. These extra-curricular activities did not keep them from graduating *cum laude,* or from enjoying vacations dedicated to big game hunting, exploring, and similar esoteric activities.

On graduation from Yale, Frank Merriwell, '03, was faced with the need for a job. What do ex-football stars do for an encore? Frank had no trouble at all. He wrote a hit play, beat the heavyweight boxing champion of Ireland, bought a Derby-winner in England, broke the course record at St. Andrews, and settled a railroad strike.

None of the Merriwells smoked, drank, or swore, not

because of any moral compunction, but because of the effect those vices have on athletic prowess. Thus readers were not subjected to a sermon, but simply to a medical advisory. Dick Merriwell once pointed out that "cigarettes dull the faculties, stunt and retard the physical development, unsettle the mind, and rob the persistent user of will power and the ability to concentrate."

Villains in the series, Chester Arlington and Roll Ditson, were guilty of pride, avarice, hypocrisy, and self-indulgence. Humility was Frank's strong point and he always forgave and befriended his enemies, leaving them better for having known him. In line with Patten's thesis of the athletic field as equalizer, Frank and Dick stood up for the weak and persecuted. Frank once drew the jeers of a crowd for shaking hands with a Negro jockey and complimenting him for having ridden a good race.

My crowd devoured the sporting series with the same appetite we had had for the other boys' series. We had about as much chance of becoming big-league stars or college immortals as we had of becoming millionaires by starting at the bottom and working hard, which was practically none. We didn't care. It was another avenue to the top, and any chance was welcome. How could we know then that a fine, well-coordinated body, good timing and excellent reflexes were a short cut, not to the chairmanship of the First National Bank, but to the combat infantry of the United States Army in the 1940s? The kids who dropped every pop fly and wore glasses and fractured easily went into the Finance Corps or became company clerks or chaplains' assistants. They stayed home to keep the girls company while the athletes were overseas. Oh well, we enjoyed reading about the sports heroes anyway. It was good to have been part of the Golden Age of something, even if it didn't last.

CHAPTER NINE

THE SUPERBOYS

Don helped Uncle Frank out into the open trail, where they could not be touched by those loathsome thrashing coils. There they waited until the older man had recovered some measure of his strength.

Uncle Frank did not utter any words of thanks, but silently held out his hand, which Don grasped. That handclasp, as they looked into each other's eyes, said more than words could. Then they turned and started back toward camp.

(Don Sturdy in the Temple of Fear)

In my twelve-to-fourteen period grown-ups had an irritating habit of cutting me off from all possible avenues of escape and interrogating me about my plans for the future. What did I want to be? In those Depression years the expected answer was centered around security, tenure of office, and the professions. I was supposed to be motivated toward medicine, law, dentistry, or accounting; and having secured my position as a licensee of one of those disciplines, to carry it further into a safe berth in some branch of the civil service. An ambition of this kind would label me as a "smart boy."

I didn't know what I wanted to be, but I certainly knew what I *didn't* want to be, and that was anything my parents categorized as being good for me. How could I tell them that what I really wanted was the chairmanship of a tribe of Great Apes, or a military command fighting Bedouins in the Sahara, or failing that to trap spies, shoot down a German ace, or ship out as mess boy on a tramp steamer? My mother would have said, without batting an eye, "First get your college degree."

As I progressed into my later teens, my "plans for the future" became less strenuous. I saw myself as the raffish younger son of an aristocratic family, subsisting in a warm climate on an annual stipend that would continue as long as I didn't come home and bring scandal on the family name. There were several things wrong with that picture. First, my father couldn't afford the remittance. Second, there was nothing in the world I could do that would embarrass my family. They loved me too much.

The question of what I was going to do with my future was solved very easily one afternoon at Loew's Willard Theatre, when the film was interrupted by the manager who wished to announce that the United States had just declared war on Japan. The world of Stratemeyer, Burroughs, Fitzhugh, and the other propagandists of my boyhood suddenly became very much alive. Adventure and romance! It was with some difficulty that I was able to restrain giving the victory cry of the bull ape as I signed the enlistment papers.

Escapism was what we needed in those pre-war days. We needed something to take our minds off the eternal money worries, the never-ending fear of the future, the need for practicality. We needed wings to soar on.

The last thing in the world we needed was Ragged Dick and his fiscal problems, or any of the other rags-to-riches boys with their dogged concern for the future. Howard R. Garis, a former Stratemeyer assistant famous for creating the "Uncle Wiggly" series, came out in the late twenties with the Dick Hamilton books, a complete reversal of tradition because they dealt with "the handicap of a millionaire's son." The books told of Dick's attempts to make his way without the prestige and influence of his tremendous fortune, and how money can really be a mill-stone around a boy's neck. We weren't impressed, and the books were not an overwhelming success. We needed something even more utopian than millions, and Stratemeyer was there with the goods. He wasn't about to let us down.

In the late 1920s, the Stratemeyer Syndicate brought out three heroes with whom we could fantasize ourselves out of the drabness and into the sunshine. They never went to school, they had unlimited free time, they had either no parents, or complete control of their parents, and they dealt in exotic adventure, travel and danger. They never mentioned (or needed) money. They were possessed of superior physical and mental powers that made them the masters of all grown-ups who dared to cross them. They were superboys in every sense of the word.

Bomba the Jungle Boy was Stratemeyer's answer to Tarzan. He lived in the jungles of the upper Amazon and wrestled pumas with his bare hands. Don Sturdy was a teen-age explorer with riding breeches, cavalry boots and a pith helmet. He could shoot any known firearm with phenomenal accuracy, and he had a store of woodsy lore that shamed even Fitzhugh's boy scouts. The X Bar X Boys were cowboys who were never out of the saddle and spent their afternoons in running gunfights with rustlers and bandits.

Best of all, they were contemporary series. When you had read all fourteen volumes of Baseball Joe there were no more. But Bomba, Don and the X Bar X Boys were being written as we read them. When you finished one you knew another would soon be published. They were up-to-date and we adored them. We could hardly wait for the next of the series.

Don Sturdy was the work of our old pal "Victor Appleton" whom you may remember as the author of the Motion Picture Chums, the Movie Boys, the Moving Picture Boys, and, of course, Tom Swift. There were fifteen in the series, and Stratemeyer wrote the first ten of them before he died. Bomba was written by "Roy Rockwood" who had given us Dave Dashaway, the Great Marvel Series, and the Speedwell Boys. There were twenty, and Stratemeyer wrote ten of them. The X Bar X Boys were the creations of a new Stratemeyer star, "James Cody Ferris," under which pseudonym Stratemeyer wrote ten of the twenty-two. Sixteen Bombas and thirteen X Bar X's were published abroad in a number of foreign languages, and a film option was taken on Bomba, but Don Sturdy was less fortunate and dropped out of sight.

Don and Bomba covered the same locales and the same activities, and "Rockwood" and "Appleton" were not too proud to lift ideas and great lumps of prose from each other. Whatever happened to Don was sure to happen to Bomba a year or two later. Both boys were encircled by boa constrictors, time after time, saving themselves by lopping off the reptiles' heads with machetes. Both were treed by wild peccaries. Both were attacked by alligators. Both (and the X Bar X Boys too) were nearly submerged in quicksand. Both were shipwrecked. Both searched several continents, in spite of deadly danger, in quest of amnesiac fathers. When Bomba was asked to give a display of his prowess with the rifle, he shot the spots out of the nine of clubs ("There are too many clubs," he said) and then shot a circle and a bull's eye into a white card before hitting coins tossed into the air. When Don was asked to demonstrate *his* rifle skill

"Show him, Don," urged Teddy.

Without raising his rifle to his shoulder, Don shot from the hip, and the sharp ring of metal on metal showed that the second bullet had hit the first, already imbedded in the bull's eye.

(*Don Sturdy in the Temple of Fear, p. 51*)

Don then shot the spots out of the nine of clubs, traced "C.A." on a white surface (for "Central America") and hit coins tossed in the air.

Both Don's chum Teddy, and Bomba himself, shared the experience of having a blood-sucking vampire bat with a two-foot wing spread land on their bare feet as they slept, fanning them gently with its wings to lull them into staying asleep. Both Don and Bomba were miraculously rescued from the poisonous bite of the dreaded and bad-tempered cooanaradi.

Bomba was the Stratemeyer Syndicate's answer to Tarzan, and in some of the books "Rockwood" approached the flowery prose style of Burroughs. In the first volume, the Jungle Boy was fourteen, like most of the latter day Syndicate heroes, but over the next twenty books he moved up to eighteen.

> He was nothing more than a boy, fourteen years at most, of a little above the ordinary height at that age, compact and muscular. He had brown eyes and brown wavy hair and the whitest of teeth. His skin was darkly tanned by exposure to the sun.
>
> On his feet were rude, home-made sandals, and around his body was wrapped a small bit of native cloth and a small puma skin—the skin of Geluk, the Puma, who had tried to eat the friendly parrots, Kiki and Woowoo. Bomba had caught him in the attempt and killed him with an arrow.
>
> The skin heightened the resemblance of Bomba to a young panther as, light and supple, the muscles of arms and legs rippling under the bronzed skin, he threaded his way deftly through the underbrush.
>
> (*Bomba the Jungle Boy, p. 6*)

A few books later, we find that

. . . [his features] were undeniably those of a white boy.
They were strongly though finely chiseled, the nose
aquiline, the mouth firm and handsome, the brow broad
and high. Keen intelligence looked through the large
brown eyes. The head was magnificently shaped and
covered with a mass of wavy brown hair.

The boy's muscular development was remarkable, and
the rippling ridges on arms and legs marked the athlete.
Grace showed in every movement.

(*Bomba the Jungle Boy Among the Slaves, p. 2*)

And, undoubtedly, charm showed in every pose. The
Kiki and Woowoo referred to *supra* were Bomba's gaily
colored parrot pals, who with Doto the monkey, made
up Bomba's dearest chums. There was also Polulu the
puma, whom Bomba had rescued from a fallen tree in
exactly the way Tarzan had freed Jad-bal-ja, the Golden
Lion and Sheeta the Panther of *The Beasts of Tarzan.*
To make the comparison even more amazing, Bomba
sported, in addition to his puma skin, a bow and arrows,
and a foot-long, razor-sharp machete (longer than Tarzan's). He could swing through the trees like an ape,
and he made use of the friendly Arao tribe of Indians
in exactly the same way Tarzan ruled his faithful Waziri.

It would have been entirely too obvious to have the
Jungle Boy raised and educated by apes, especially since
the largest apes in Bomba's habitat, the upper Amazon
outback of Brazil, were only a little more than two-feet
high. He had to have an origin and some kind of education, and "Rockwood" made him a foundling living in the
jungle with a half-demented old naturalist-botanist named
Cody Casson. The old man taught Bomba rudimentary
English, and the two existed on hunting and fishing with
the aid of the friendly Araos, who thought Casson was a
magician. Bomba knew nothing of his origin, and Casson

promised to tell him about his mother and father as "soon as he was old enough," but, alas, before that happy age was reached the old naturalist fell ill of a fever that left him totally without memory. The next dozen books (until Stratemeyer's death) dealt with Bomba's search for information about his folks, and did he search! Nobody ever went through so many dangers to find out who he was.

In spite of Casson, and the proximity of the Indians, Bomba became proficient in the ways and languages of the animals. There was no animal he couldn't speak to, or charm, although he was forced to kill hungry jaguars, snakes, and pumas six or seven times per book. The nuances of monkey language, including subjunctives and idioms were an open book to him.

> Bomba drew one red-faced old ape aside. It was the leader of the swarm.
> "Tatuc, ba?" asked Bomba, meaning in monkey language, "Tatuc, what is wrong?"
> In the jabbering monosyllabic chatter, which Bomba from years of intimacy and observation had come to understand sufficiently to get its essential meaning, Tatuc gave the boy the news that his flock had been attacked by a swarm of vultures while trying to defend two of their young that the voracious birds had swooped down upon, with the intention of carrying them off to their retreats, where they could devour them at leisure.

Of course Bomba was glad to help, and from time to time the monkeys helped him. His mysterious powers of communication with beasts were to save the ship *Pamela* from disaster many years later. An elephant, part of a shipment of wild animals en route to the London Zoo, had run amok. The huge beast threatened to smash the cages that held the lions and tigers. Something had to be done to pacify the raging bull and get him back into his cage. What had goaded the great pachyderm into his bad humor?

"He has a wicked toothache," replied Peabody.

"Can't blame him for squealing, then," said Bomba's father. "Is there anything you can do for the poor fellow?"

"That's just the trouble," mourned Peabody. "If I could get near him, I might pull the tooth. I know just which one it is too . . . and I have the forceps that could yank it out," he continued, displaying a formidable-looking device he was carrying. "But he's in such a fearful temper, with the pain and all, that I don't dare go near him, and that's the truth."

"Too bad," murmured Mr. Bartow sympathetically.

"And so I thought," went on Peabody, somewhat shame-facedly, turning to Bomba, "that if you—perhaps—I know it's a lot to ask—that maybe you'd be good enough to make a try at it."

"To pull that mad elephant's tooth?" put in Bomba's father amazedly. "Why, man, it's ridiculous—preposterous. It would be risking his life . . ."

"I'll try it," declared Bomba, taking the forceps from the wild animal dealer's hand and preparing to follow him.

"But, Bomba—" remonstrated Mr. Bartow, greatly disturbed.

"Let my father not fear," replied the jungle boy. "It will go well with Bomba."

(*Bomba the Jungle Boy Trapped by the Cyclone, p. 7*)

Our hero, of course, soothed the animal with a few well chosen epigrams (apparently Brazilian badinage went over well with African animals too) and slipped inside the mighty tusks to extract the offending molar. The ship was saved.

"By Jove, the lad's a wizard!" cried Carson. "Never saw anything like it before in my life."

Andrew Bartow, seated beside him, smiled. "You haven't seen anything yet," he declared . . .

"How proud you must be of such a son, Mr. Bartow!"

"I am," smiled the lad's father, simply.

(op. cit., p. 49)

There was never a Stratemeyer dad, amnesiac, sickly, broke, bankrupt, or under the surgeon's knife, who wasn't proud of his boy. Talk about suspicious moisture dimming the reader's eye!

Bomba's voyage through twenty books in search of his heritage rivals the Odyssey in its imaginative intensity. After the first volume (*Bomba the Jungle Boy*) in which our hero made a lifelong enemy of Nascarora, chief of the head hunters, the quest for Mom and Dad was officially launched. Casson was given to occasional lucid intervals, during which some fragment of information would be revealed, some tenuous and cryptic clue. It was in one of these periods that Bomba learned his parents' names, Andrew and Laura Bartow.

Casson revealed in his maunderings that Jojasta, Medicine Man of the Moving Mountain, knew the facts about Bomba's birth. Although the Medicine Man was feared throughout the jungle for his cruelty and ferocity, the Jungle Boy set out to visit him, launching the second book. It was no go with Jojasta, but Bomba learned that Sobrinini, the witch woman who dwelt beyond the Great Cataract could help. This half-crazed crone had been a brilliant European opera star, but she was now the queen-prophetess of the Island of Snakes. All Bomba got out of her was an inordinate amount of shrill cackling and an old photograph he was sure was Laura Bartow. Sobrinini, not unwilling to go along with a gag, told the jungle lad that Japazy, the half-breed of Jaguar Island, held the key to the mystery of his birth.

Another book was on its way. We breathless readers followed Bomba to Jaguar Island (so-called because it was full of jaguars) where, after many dangers and jungle fights, he was to discover that Japazy was not at home. He had gone to the Abandoned City. Bomba decided to wait, but Japazy's people, thinking to please their chief, decided to sacrifice him to the Sacred Alligators. Bomba held them off manfully and escaped, taking with him the Indian, Gibo, who was to become his lifelong faithful servant (he collected half a dozen of them as the series went on.)

They followed Japazy to the Abandoned City where the cruel half-breed informed Bomba that he had killed the Bartows, and would do the same to the jungle boy after a suitable interval of hideous torture. Bomba escaped, adding to his Bartow lore a torn diary that he had found among Japazy's effects. He was sure it held the answer to the secret of his birth.

What to do now? No more clues, and Bomba could only return to Casson and wait for the next lucid period. En route he met a party of scientists and physicians collecting rare herbs. He saved the life of one of them (another jaguar fight) and the scientist agreed to examine Casson. He prescribed as an almost certain cure a rare plant that grew only in the Swamp of Death, home of the ferocious Arabagoes! There was no time to unpack, and in a trice our hero was off on his way into the next book.

Having secured the plant for Casson, Bomba whiled away the time by involving himself in a slave uprising on the rubber plantation of the sadistic Mendoza, who told the jungle boy that he was the real Andrew Bartow in order to enlist Bomba's aid in getting more work out of his field hands. Mendoza died in the ever-present quicksand, but only after Bomba had found out he had lied.

In the next volume, Bomba was to find his parents at last. His father was a famous painter and his mother an equally famous opera singer. Bomba had been kidnaped as a baby, and the Bartows had spent a fortune trying to find him. They were inordinately rich, and in no time at all had spirited Bomba off to New York and placed him under the finest tutors. He learned fast, but he always missed (and rightly so) his beloved jungle. We readers couldn't wait to get him back there again. We were mightily relieved when Mr. Bartow sailed off to Africa to "paint the gorgeous scenery of that continent" and got himself captured by cannibals. Not only were Bomba and his dusky sidekick Gibo off for the jungle again, they were out of Brazil and on their way to Tarzan country. Bomba could pit his rippling muscles against lions, leopards, crocodiles, and gorillas!

Bomba saved his dad, but the experience left Mr. Bartow in poor health. They reached Mombasa and set sail for New York via London and the Indian Ocean, on the *Pamela*, scene of the elephant toothache drama. They had added Tobo, an East African native and Wafi, a Zulu, to the entourage. The *Pamela* encountered mutiny, collision, cyclones, reefs, and all sorts of other troubles, and our intrepid little band of adventurers was shipwrecked not once but six separate times with interim sojourns aboard a derelict ship, a raft, and a coaster whose crew re-marooned them on the ground that they brought bad luck.

There were to be other books, but only a few of them before the end of the series. Stratemeyer's death and the discovery of Bomba's parents took all the zip out of them. Nevertheless they were reprinted again and again, coming out only a few years ago in a washable plastic forty-nine cent format. The Syndicate still regards them as active properties, but they are not being published now.

Although the grown-up Tarzan spoke like a true English gentleman, and conversed easily in French as well (and Don Sturdy spoke the hearty American of the Rovers or the Hardy Boys) Bomba never grew out of his early gibberish. In spite of all his fine tutors, the Jungle Boy usually referred to himself in the third person like Julius Caesar or Gertrude Stein. Sunk in a quagmire and descending slowly out of sight, he found himself surrounded by hungry pumas, anxious to devour the parts that still showed. Suddenly four of the faithful-unto-death servants whose lives he had saved appeared with spears.

> "Gibo!" cried Bomba. "Lodo! Ashati! Neram! Oh what good friends you are of Bomba!"
>
> "Yes, Master," responded Gibo, his eyes glowing with delight. "The spears of Bomba's friends have found the hearts of the pumas . . ."
>
> Death had come so near the jungle lad that its dark wings had brushed him. But now he was safe and his eyes were full of gratitude as he turned them upon his dusky friends . . .
>
> "Bomba will never forget," said the lad feelingly, "He will remember Gibo and Lodo and Ashati and Neram until the cloud of death comes over his eyes."
>
> "It is but a little thing," asserted Ashati . . .
>
> (*Bomba the Jungle Boy Among the Slaves*, p. 42)

The natives in Bomba's jungle, especially the hostile ones like Nascarora the head hunter and the fierce Arabagoes, spoke suspiciously like Metro-Goldwyn-Mayer Cherokees. They said things like "Ugh" and referred to rifles as "the white man's fire stick."

"Ugh!" The Indian grunted noncommittally, as he scanned Bomba with glowering eyes that had in them nothing of friendliness. "You white boy?"

Bomba nodded.

"The white man bad medicine," said the Indian, his scowl deepening as his hand tightened on his spear.

"He is good medicine," declared Bomba.

"He is a Man of Evil," was the reply. "He bring trouble on my people. Much sickness. Many die. Chief Nascarora very angry. He make talk with big medicine man, and medicine man say there will always be sickness as long as white man stay alive."

A thrill of apprehension ran through Bomba.

(*Bomba the Jungle Boy, p. 51*)

Like Tarzan, Bomba was a firm white chauvinist. He had a fond contempt for the dark-skinned natives, and since he was the mightiest hunter and warrior, he regarded them as inferior in every way. There was nothing he couldn't do better than any native in Brazil (or later East Africa) and the natives accepted him as a born leader. He equated this with color. Time and again in the books Bomba would meet a strange party of explorers, and would pull aside his puma skin to show his untanned chest. "Bomba is white! White!" he would cry.

He also had an appreciation of natural beauty and poetry that had escaped the darker aborigines. This thought Bomba, was a matter of "soul." White people had "soul." Blacks had none.

Why did they feel so differently than he? Was it because they did not have souls? He dismissed this thought as improbable. But perhaps their souls were asleep. Oh, that must be it! They were asleep!

But his was awake. At least it was waking. Perhaps that was because he was white. The thought gave him a thrill.

Now he was sure that he had found the truth. The natives' souls were asleep. The white mens' souls were awake. And he was white!

(*op. cit., p. 147*)

This philosophy ran all through the books, at least until the jungle lad got to civilization and found that all men are vile and only the virgin jungle is pure. By the end of the series he had found out that you can't trust anybody, regardless of color. However, in the early books he rivaled George Wallace and Lester Maddox in the white supremacy field. He even lectured his animals on the subject.

"You are all my friends," he cried. "You helped Bomba when the men with bad hearts came to the cabin. Bomba loves you all. He does not want to leave you, but he must go. He will always think of you, and some day he may come back to you. But Bomba must go! He must find the men who have souls, the souls that are awake. For Bomba has a soul. And he must find the white men. For Bomba is white."

He tore the puma skin aside and displayed his chest.

"Look Woowoo! Look Kiki! Look Doto!" he cried, in an ecstasy of joy and pride. "Look all of you! I will tell Polulu too. I am white! Bomba is white!"

(*op. cit., p. 204*)

There is no record of how Woowoo and Kiki, who were green and yellow, or Doto, who was fuzzy and brown, reacted to this speech. Perhaps with insouciance masking deep, deep hurt, who knows? As the series progressed, less and less was heard of them. They left whitey alone and spent more time with their own kind.

Bomba's white superiority platform was tempered

with benevolent paternalism. During one of his many shipwrecks the lifeboats had gone over the side for disembarking passengers.

"Come on," cried Dondy, addressing himself to Bomba and his father. "We have just room for you two." . . .

"How about these?" asked Bomba, pointing to his servants.

"No," replied Dondy, "We'd all go down. After all, they're only niggers."

"They are my friends," said Bomba gravely.

"Call them what you like," roared Dondy. "Are you coming or aren't you?"

"No," said Bomba, and his father nodded in approval. "Either we all go or we all stay. We live or die together . . ."

"Looks like the end, son," said Andrew Bartow.

"We are still alive," replied the jungle lad, his indomitable spirit refusing to be quelled.

(Bomba the Jungle Boy Trapped by the Cyclone, p. 73)

The Bomba series had a Famous First to its credit. It was the first, and as far as I know the only series, in which a character smoked marijuana. No Stratemeyer hero ever allowed liquor to touch his lips, and those bibulous characters who did were considered to be villainous or pitiable. Marijuana, however, was mildly funny. It was not too long after the end of Prohibition, and the liquor industry had not yet decided that *cannabis sativa* was a dangerous narcotic and passed the information to the politicians. One of Bomba's co-castaways was Brasser, an ill-mannered card cheat. He took shipwreck as a personal insult.

One thing, however, somewhat soothed his disgruntled feelings. He was an inveterate smoker, and his being deprived of tobacco had been one of his special grievances during the time of drifting. While wandering about the camp he had found dried leaves of a plant which, though not tobacco, was very much like it in smell and texture. He had rolled some of the leaves into a crude cigar and tested it. This he found extremely soothing. It eradicated all his troubles.

"Better than any tobacco I ever smoked," he muttered to himself with great satisfaction . . .

(Bomba the Jungle Boy Trapped by the Cyclone, p. 109)

Bomba later discovered that Brasser had disappeared, and followed his tracks into the jungle.

Instead of walking in a straight line, he had staggered along like a drunken man. Bomba knew that the wavering tracks were not caused by liquor, for there had been none available since the collision.

Near the couch were the bits of several home-made cigars Brasser had been smoking the evening before. Bomba picked one of them up and smelled it. It had a queer pungent odor that reminded him of a certain African plant which was greatly in favor with the natives, making them merry and irresponsible . . .

More than likely Brasser's excessive indulgence in cigars made from this queer plant had caused him to become light-headed and he had wandered off into the night.

(Ibid.)

Significantly, Bomba only curled his lip at the fellow's self-indulgence. He didn't try the stuff himself.

Unlike Bomba, Don Sturdy was strictly a civilized boy, a product of the metropolitan suburb of Hillville "about fifty miles from New York City." At fourteen he showed no sign of attending any kind of school. After the success of the first few books, Stratemeyer promoted him, like Bomba, to eighteen.

Don was the son of Mr. Richard Sturdy, an eminent explorer, and his lovely wife, Alice, "a gracious, cultured woman" intensely devoted to her son and his sister Ruth, two years his junior. Mr. Sturdy was a "man of means" and the Sturdys enjoyed a "handsome home surrounded by spacious grounds", in the Stratemeyer upper-middle class tradition. During the early books, when the senior Sturdys and Ruth were missing like Bomba's folks, Don was cared for by the dream guardians of all time, two bachelor uncles. And what uncles! Every kid I knew longed for a life with such a pair. If only you could get rid of your parents first.

Captain Frank Sturdy was a big-game hunter, a superb shot, and a man without fear, internationally known for his exploits. He was a "man of herculean frame with strongly marked features, black hair, and eyes of the same color." His profession was bringing-'em-back-alive for the International Museum and Menagerie Collection Corporation, a live animal and reptile cartel with "branches in America and most of the capitals of Europe."

The other uncle, Professor Amos Regor Bruce was a "famous scientist and archaeologist, whose delight lay in collecting and studying relics of old and dead civilizations." He was "rather frail in appearance, but strong and wiry; and although a man of peace, had always faced dangers undauntedly when they had confronted him."

Get the picture? One of these splendid uncles was always off to the land of lions or tigers. The other was constantly preparing to embark in search of lost cities, tombs of gold, and mysterious caves. And Don went along. Of course there was always an initial cliff-hanger chapter in which they debated whether he was quite ready for such an adventure. Capturing poisonous snakes or digging for an accursed mummy is pretty dangerous for a teen-age boy. There are bandits and cannibals . . . maybe they ought to leave the kid home. It was even worse after his parents were rescued and his mother got to put in her oar, but somehow Don always convinced them, and a good thing too. He saved the lives of both uncles at least twenty times in the series.

The rest of the Sturdy Hillville ménage consisted of a couple-of-all-work, Mr. and Mrs. Dan Roscoe, and a loquacious, gum-chewing maid, Jennie. Our young hero himself was

> a tall, clean-cut, muscular lad, frank, truthful, generous, a leader in all kinds of boyish sports, truly a fine specimen of Young America . . .
>
> (*Don Sturdy in the Temple of Fear, p. 2*)

Of course Don had a best friend and comical sidekick, Teddy Allison, slightly younger than himself and also the son of a prominent explorer. Teddy had an impish grin, and fiery red hair that earned him the nickname of "Brick." On one occasion, in a mysterious lost city in Central America, Teddy's hair saved everyone's life when the natives (among whom, for some reason, red hair was considered sacred) made him a god.

Teddy was good, but not quite as good, as Don at everything. His minor flaws always put him in a position from which Don could rescue him from certain death. It was Teddy's feet, not Don's, that the vampire bat settled on, although Bomba had to deal with *his* bat alone and personally. It was Teddy who fell into the alligator-infested pool. It was Teddy who was attacked by the jaguar. Don always did his stuff and saved his chum.

There was one quality in which Teddy did outdo his superior chum, and that was his sense of humor. Teddy was the joker of the group, and wherever the explorers might be, he was always there with a snapper.

". . . I overheard two of the ship's officers talking about it (said Don), and they seemed to think that we're likely to run into some bad weather. According to them, the barometer is falling and we may be heading into a storm."

"Well, there's not a thing we can do about it," said Teddy. "Maybe if they'd hang the barometer on a stronger hook it wouldn't fall so often, and then there wouldn't be so many storms . . ."

Don aimed a blow at his friend's ribs, but the agile Teddy skipped nimbly to one side.

"I don't see anything wrong with that idea," he said, and his voice held an aggrieved note.

"You'll bring a jinx on the ship with those jokes," said Don. "I'll bet they set Jonah adrift for less."

(op. cit., p. 61)

Nevertheless Teddy worshiped his mighty chum, referring to Don variously as "the bee's knees," "the clam's overshoes," and "the eel's raincoat." Sometimes Teddy was not allowed to accompany the others, but apparently public pressure brought him back time and again. Uncles are uncles, but a boy needs a chum.

At the start of the series Don's parents and his young sister Ruth were reported to have gone down with the ill-fated schooner *Mercury*. To cheer the new orphan up, the uncles took him on an exploring trip to the Sahara Desert (*Don Sturdy on the Desert of Mystery*). It was there that he first met Teddy, who informed him that *his* father was missing too, captured by a bandit tribe. It was off to the rescue through desert heat, blinding sandstorms, and fights with savage Bedouins, and the incidental discovery of the City of Brass and the Cave of Emeralds.

Mr. Allison was saved, and word received that some of the *Mercury* survivors had been picked up by a vessel bound for Brazil.

By a stroke of luck Uncle Frank had just been assigned to go up the Amazon to capture live anacondas. Don and the professor went along, of course (this time without Teddy) and discovered Ruth in hospital. The girl told how Mr. Sturdy had been beaned by a falling spar which left him partially demented and amnesiac, like Bomba's friend Casson. He had suddenly boarded a strange vessel in a Brazilian port, his wife had rushed after him, and the two had disappeared again.

Back in Hillville, and nursing Ruth back to health, the family received a cablegram from Mom, now in Egypt. Of course Dad had vanished again in the direction of the Valley of the Kings, babbling some foolishness about Tombs of Gold. The group was on its way at once, and after a new bookful of adventures they found Mr. Sturdy and brought him back to America where his health and memory were restored.

Don had now had his apprenticeship as an explorer, and there was no keeping him down on the farm. It was off to the North Pole in an airship to hunt polar bears, adventures in Alaska in the dangerous volcanic Valley of Ten Thousand Smokes, and into the Sargasso Sea, where he and his uncles were "beset with peculiar dangers." There were head hunters in Borneo, lions and gorillas in Darkest Africa, and a tribe of strange giants in Patagonia. There were also submarine adventures in the Pacific with sharks, devil fish, and a huge prehistoric sea serpent.

In fact, there was practically nothing that had been successful in other series books that Don, in his pith helmet, didn't undergo. The series ended before he got to other planets, and he never got to the Lost Continent of Atlantis, but he did unearth a bloodthirsty ancient Mayan civilization in Central America.

On every trip he, Teddy and the uncles were beset with bizarre perils of every kind, and Stratemeyer really could think them up, especially if they were in unexplored jungles and you couldn't check up too easily. For Don and Don only "Victor Appleton" dreamed up a new chiller, bird-eating spiders! Don was trapped in a dark cave with a mass of them, each as big as a grapefruit, and wow!

> They attacked Don and his companion like so many rats, biting at face and hands and making their nips felt through their clothes. They came in myriads. Don and Uungus brushed them off, stamped on them until the floor was covered with blood and pulp, but as fast as some were dislodged others took their places. And the horrid continued rustling on floor and walls and roof showed that legions more were coming to the attack!

Pretty strong stuff that. But Don was always able to cope. Unfortunately for Don Bomba had the huge success of the Tarzan books to ride on, and Burroughs just couldn't write them fast enough. There was plenty of overflow for the Stratemeyer Syndicate and for Cupples & Leon, who had been smart enough to get Bomba before Grosset & Dunlap could cash in on him. Don Sturdy always had to take a back seat to the jungle boy.

The X Bar X Boys were a reasonably accurate facsimile of the Hardy Boys, but moved out West and riveted firmly into the saddle. They had a typical Stratemeyer surname (he had already used Sturdy and Hardy) the descriptive Manley. Roy, and Teddy Manley were brothers, and they even looked like the Hardys, with

Roy, the eldest, having dark hair and eyes, and Teddy, a year his junior, being fair and blue-eyed.

Roy and Teddy were the only heroes that ever got *younger* as the series progressed. We find them in the early books described as being seventeen and eighteen. By 1927 (*The X Bar X Boys on Big Bison Trail*) they had retrogressed to fifteen and sixteen, and there they stayed to the end.

The boys were the sons of Bradwell Manley, ranch owner and cattle breeder, who was "a large man whose appearance was like that of a grave, old-time Southern gentleman." He affected a corncob pipe and "a long drooping mustache with ends that curled nearly below the chin." Mrs. Manley was an ex-schoolteacher (English) from Denver, who was known to her husband and his cowhands as "the blonde angel of the West." There was also a saucy, adoring, pretty young sister of twelve or thirteen, Belle Ada Manley, the apple of the boys' eyes and a frequent candidate for kidnaping.

The X Bar X was "a thirty-hour train ride west of Chicago, on the Rocky Run River" which would place it somewhere in Colorado. Its main, and, in fact, only source of income, was cattle. Mr. Manley's prize shorthorns were an eternal target of rustlers, and book after book saw them herded off into hidden canyons from which Roy and Teddy would have to rescue them and bring them back again. They were aided in this by the ranch staff, a group of eccentrics out of any TV or movie Western ever written. There was Nick Looker (a Gary Cooper type), old Pop Burns, smart as a whip and the best three-card-monte player in the county, Gus, Nat, Bug-Eye (a comedy relief who drove around in his "fishmobile, a Rube Goldberg car he had built himself out of discarded parts), and of course Sing Lung the cook and Nora, a Marjorie Main-type housekeeper.

Out West in the wide open spaces, where the nearest neighbor may be many miles away, there is little opportunity to find chums. But Roy and Teddy had no need for them. Roy had Star, and Teddy had Flash, two of the finest broncs a waddy ever forked. The boy-horse relationships transcended simple palship. Once in a quagmire, as Teddy was slowly being sucked down into certain and horrible death

> "Roy—the sand! It's got us! Come! I can't—Flash—" . . .
> "Get off, Teddy!" Roy shouted. "Get off and swim!"
> "Not yet. Flash is under me. We'll come out of this together."
> Roy understood. Teddy, careless, happy-go-lucky Teddy, was staying with his horse. Roy took a deep breath, gauged the remaining distance between him and his brother, loosened the rope, and threw!
>
> (*The X Bar X Boys on Big Bison Trail, p. 131*)

Teddy's suicidal tendencies were not limited to a feeling of affinity with his horse. He would die with anyone that seemed to need dying with.

> In that instant [a landslide], the greatest moment of stress that the boys had ever experienced, Roy and Teddy looked death in the face with calm, defiant eyes.
> "We're done for!" shouted Roy in his brother's ear, riding so close to him that the two broncs seemed merged into one. "If you get out of it, Ted, look after Dad, and Mom, and—"
> "If you go, I'll go too!" shouted back Teddy. . . .
>
> (*The X Bar X Boys in Smoky Valley, p. 161*)

Not to be outdone, Roy was loth to have his brother experience even a minor flesh wound without stopping one himself.

"Just winged me," (said Teddy) cheerfully, "Only a scratch, that's all. See, it's stopped bleeding already," and Teddy showed the place where a bullet had plowed its way through the flesh. "I'll bind it up and it will be all right. Gosh! We must keep those thieves at bay . . ."

(op. cit., p. 214)

A few moments later, Roy, having daringly exposed his hand to the rustlers' crossfire

. . . held up to Teddy a finger that had a piece sliced from the end of it.

"Don't think you're the only one who got shot in the Battle of Smoky Valley," he grinned. "Reckon I'm eligible to join the Veterans' Association right now."

"Hurt much?" asked Teddy, wriggling along under cover of the rocks until he came closer to his brother.

"No, that fellow just nicked me . . ."

(Ibid.)

Roy was the dreamer of the two, and Teddy the fun-loving pragmatic one. He never could understand what Roy saw in the beauties of nature, or why he sometimes reined in Star to look at mountains or storm clouds ("black castles in the sky"). "Golly!" Teddy would say, "You see that blamed thing day after day, night after night, and still you stand and moon at it! It'll be there tomorrow! Come on, let's eat!"

Down-to-earth though Teddy may have been, he was not behind Roy when it came to love, and Stratemeyer-"Ferris" had provided the lads with a pair of high-stepping Eastern girls, friends of Belle Ada's and visitors at the neighboring 8 X 8 Ranch. The girls liked the West so much that they decided not to go back to New York, much to the satisfaction of their globe-trotting parents.

Ethel "Curly" Carew was Teddy's girl and Nell Willis
was Roy's. They were just the right age, size, and combination of moral qualities to satisfy the young Manleys.

"Well," said Teddy mournfully, after a few minutes of
silence, "I'm sorry Nell and Ethel are going home [for a
temporary visit]. We'll miss them awfully, shan't we,
Roy?"

"You bet we shall." Roy's face grew sober at the
thought. "They're the finest girls I've ever met. Good
sports, always ready for fun, and nothing slushy about
them. I hate a girl that's always wanting to pet."

(*The X Bar X Boys at Grizzly Pass, p. 22*)

Who doesn't, for Heaven's sake? The girls were always
ready to be kidnaped by rustlers and rescued too. The
relationship between the sexes, while free of petting,
was not entirely unphysical. Hugs were stolen (usually
by the girls) while getting on and off horses, and Nell
and Ethel were always teasing the boys by fondling them
to make them blush and stammer.

"Some hugger Curly is, too, Ted?"

"Didn't hug me at all," snapped Teddy, his face flushing. "I was helping her off the bronc and she almost fell,
so I caught her, that's all there was to it."

"Oh, that's how it happened! Glad to know just how it
was. But she needn't have given you a half-Nelson, it
seems to me.". . .

"Is that so?" Teddy was always quick to come back.
"Guess you needn't say anything. What were you and Nell
doing in the kitchen yesterday? When you came out your
arms were all over flour."

"Oh, she wasn't hugging me," replied Roy, trying to
speak in a casual tone and failing in the attempt. "She was

making cookies and said I bothered her; so she pushed me away with her floury hands."

Teddy grinned.

(op. cit., p. 73)

Mr. Manley let the boys manage the ranch on alternate weeks, as a kind of apprenticeship, and they did a fine job which included the maintenance of law and order, since the local sheriff (Stratemeyer noted deploringly) was a "political appointee" and was not to be depended on.

Unlike Bomba and Don Sturdy, who had a new horizon to cross every book, Roy and Teddy were stuck in the same area, no more than a day or two's ride from the ranch. There were no lost cities and no mysterious tribes there, and so the plots of the books were always the same: cattle rustlers. The boys pursued them through Thunder Canyon, Whirlpool River, Big Bison Trail, Nugget Camp, Grizzly Pass, Smoky Valley, Rustler's Gap, and other local real estate. They never killed except in absolute self defense, and most of the gunfights ended in surrender for the enemy after a great deal of harmless lead-slinging and a few flesh wounds.

Each book held a number of nature's dangers for the lads, much more to be feared than the human kind. There were landslides (one per book), forest fires, rapids, snowstorms, quicksand, timber wolves, rattlesnakes, cougars and many more, evenly distributed to keep us reading while the boys pursued cardboard badmen of the stamp of "Three Lip" Denger (an outlaw who had a scar that made him look as though he had three lips).

Villains that came from back East and had been educated were always worse than the local kind. They were more articulate, and were always trying to swindle the ranch hands out of hard-earned money.

Slowly the lawyer got to his feet. His eyes gleamed evilly. He stood for a moment, looking at the three.

"You hold the cards now," he murmured thickly. "But wait—just wait! That will case comes up in two days and when it does the only thing you'll get out of it, Nick Looker, will be the smell of dried coffee! Pack that behind the rim of your derby!" And, ramming his hat on his head, Jason Pettit stalked out into the rain.

(*The X Bar X Boys on Big Bison Trail, p. 201*)

Who but a villainous New York lawyer would speak such dialogue?

The X Bar X Boys went their way, moseying from corral to hidden canyon, until the late thirties by which time my crowd no longer needed the Stratemeyer Syndicate or its rivals. High school came and went, and we finally discovered the hard way that girls were approachable and just as curious about some things as we were. The war came and I went off to establish the persecuted of the world in freedom from fear and world peace forever after. The heroes of my youth ended up in dusty antique shops, priced considerably higher than they were when they were new. First they were secondhand, then "high camp," then rare.

A friend reading the manuscript of this book asked me if I can foresee the scene of my death some future day, with me propped up in a huge bed surrounded by the translucent figures of the boys' and girls' series heroes and heroines, like José Ferrer playing Toulouse-Lautrec in *Moulin Rouge*. I think not. We wouldn't have very much to say to one another any more, and there would be newer translucent figures ahead of them, out of later experiences that I haven't outgrown. But it was fun rereading them and getting to know them again. And there's plenty of excitement left in them even for a whole new generation of little cynics.

Anyone want to buy four hundred slightly used boys' and girls' books?